Massage Practice Planner

Where Practice Makes Profit!

Shannon Perez

SPI Publishing

Library of Congress Data 2007904821

Perez, Shannon
Massage Practice Planner
Where Practice Makes Profit / Shannon Perez
p. cm.
Includes bibliographical references and index.
ISBN 9780979780509

COLLEGES, UNIVERSITIES, QUANTITY BUYERS
Discounts on this book are available for bulk purchases. Write or call for information on our discount programs. Special books or book excepts can also be created to fit specific needs. Contact SpecialSales@MassagePracticePlanner.com

How to Contact the Author: Shannon@MassagePracticePlanner.com

I look forward to hearing from you!

Contents

Appendices

Glossary

Please Read!

Hello and thank you for taking the time to read this page! This might seem a little unusual but I would like to take a moment to welcome you to the pages of my mind.

Since we will be spending quite a bit of time together while you read, study and interact with this book I wanted to take a moment to say "Hello" and invite you to join me in forming a new community of forums, mentors, helpful advice, tips and just general chatting at the companion website to this book.

The website is www.MassagePracticePlanner.com

I will be visiting it often but even more importantly, it is my wish it becomes a forum of learning, expression and sharing.

I hope to see you there!

Again – a warm welcome and enjoy the book!

Shannon

Titles in this Series

Massage Practice Planner

Massage Marketing Planner

Massage Promotion Planner

Visit www.MassagePracticePlanner for more information, newsletters, forums, and other great offers!

Contact the author: Shannon@MassagePracticePlanner.com

Dedication

To

One Young, One Old, One Unknown, One Unspoken

One of the supreme joys in my life has been the simple pleasure of sitting between two wonderful people and just holding their hands while we talked and visited throughout the evening.

Of course, everyone believes the hands of someone they love are the most beautiful but in truth, it is hard to imagine more beautiful hands than these. I remember looking at both in wonder during those evenings as they would sit and compare notes about how each received what bruise or cut or bump throughout the week. Hard working hands; one pair so young, brown and strong...the other pair so old, so broken by the torture of WWII with clubbed fingertips where a rifle butt broke his hands and scars from grabbing a bayonet to save his life: So many scars, such broken and beautiful hands. There is the memory of a third pair of hands which I do not know but I thank you dearly for the kindness shown to me in an hour of need.

This is dedicated to The Love of my life...you know who you are
The memory of Howard Turbin
An unknown, but so very kind, stranger
The One Who Cannot be Uttered

And all of those who take the time to still hold hands
and understand the beauty, power and love contained in a touch

---

There is a riddle to be learned from the heart
It is only fulfilled when empty
Only quenched when parched
Only complete when broken
Only useful when relinquished

Shannon

Massage Practice Planner
Where Practice Makes Profit!

You will spend nearly 50 years of your life at work so shouldn't you know how to make it as enjoyable, meaningful and profitable as possible? Most Americans have a vague sense that life and work could be more rewarding – If they just knew how to make it all fit together but they aren't sure how. Instead, they work harder than ever while barely making ends meet or sacrifice the life they love in exchange for burn-out while trying to pay the bills. It doesn't have to be this way. It wasn't meant to be this way.

Society is full of practice owners who have invested time, money and effort into careers that are less than rewarding both financially and personally. Why do some practice owners struggle to make $35,000 a year while others far surpass $135,000 a year? The Massage Practice Planner explains why – and more importantly – shows you how to achieve the same results without sacrificing your personal goals and quality of life.

Many business related books resort to heavy handed marketing schemes, hard sales, shuffling clients on a massive basis and other techniques that leave the practitioner exhausted and personally unsatisfied. The author of the Massage Practice Planner believes success is only worthwhile when it reflects the full values of the practitioner. At every step of the way the Practice Planner provides real life examples along with interactive checklists and worksheets to make sure your life goals, values and ethics as a therapist are not only supported but actually enhanced through your practice. Then it provides the choices and plans of actions for you to meet your individualized profit related goals!

This positive, creative life plan allows users to define their own goals and dreams then provides real life tools, examples and information to show how and when to make those dreams come true. All from a leading expert in the fields of health and entrepreneurship – in fact, former clients include some of the largest names in the United States.

For the first time ever, you can now tap into the methods used by leading organizations and "big business" to determine how to select your perfect location, how to generate revenue even when you aren't working and many other solutions to your most perplexing problems – many you may not have even known you had!

If your business is stagnating - or you are brand new to the field - and not sure how to increase your profits while creating the life you love then the Massage Practice Planner is the solution! In this full sized book packed with specific "how to" information, worksheets, checklists, examples and more, the author helps the reader create their own future life map and then turn that individual life map into the Perfect – and Profitable – Practice!

This straight-forward planning guide for practitioners will help you:

1. Review where you are right now in terms of skills, money, health and profit
2. Create a personal and individual inventory of your life goals not just for your business but actually a "Dream List," for your life!
3. Prioritize those dreams and goals in meaningful terms
4. Put them into real life action steps with numerous examples
5. Factor in your real life resources – not some 'pie in the sky' model
6. Put the resulting action plan into motion with many options and alternatives provided to best suite your individual choices and lifestyle!

The book is designed to be used by the existing practitioner as well as the student of massage therapy. It's an excellent practice planning and problem solving guide for any stage of your practice. In fact, the book is designed to grow and change as your goals grow and change! Dozens of checklists, charts and worksheets make the planning easy and fun plus the companion website – with direct access to the author - keeps the Practice Planner current and the information growing forever.

Nominate a Therapist!

Nominate a Therapist!

Do you know someone who represents the finest that Massage Therapy has to offer? Someone who embodies the heart of the Servant Leader or has redefined the use of massage by reaching out to others?

How about someone forging ahead in the brave new world of massage? Going where no massage therapist has ever gone before!

We are looking for people who have achieved unusual success in their massage practice at any level: financial, emotional, community involvement, uniqueness and originality.

Perhaps that someone is you or your practice. Whatever the situation, we would like to hear about it. If selected, they may be featured in an upcoming book!

If your nominee is not selected it's not a negative comment. We can only choose a very select few and that segment may have already been filled. Each chosen nominee will exemplify one characteristic or attribute that is very special, inspirational and unique.

If you would like to nominate someone – or yourself (don't be bashful!), visit **www.massagepracticeplanner** and fill in the nomination form. Be sure to explain why this person deserves to be nominated, their name, business name and contact information, your name, business name and contact information and a valid return email address.

If your nominee is selected and published you will both receive a FREE copy of the upcoming book as our way of saying thanks.

Chapter 1

Why This Book?

You will spend nearly 50 years of your life working. It's a long time if you stop and think about it. The "average" person gets their first job at about age 16 and works until 65, 68, or even a proposed 72 years of age (new proposed official social security retirement age) yet research reports higher levels of stress, burn-out, dissatisfaction and longing for meaning.

Worse, research by the Americans for Secure Retirement report the average person is at greater financial risk than ever before. Not since the Great Depression have Americans saved so little [the national savings rate is now below zero – people are spending more than they make each year] while working so hard! Even so, despite working more hours than ever and to a far older age than ever – the average person has less than $10,000 in savings.

The Average Person

- The average person has less than $10,000 in savings.
- The average person spends more than they earn. In 2005 the nation's personal savings rate fell to -0.5% and has continued to decline.
- The average person does not know the rule of 72 or the concept of compound interest, passive income, equity, or even how the tax laws penalize working.
- The average person does not have a retirement plan.
- The average person is consumed with trying to make ends meet on a day to day basis – often at the expense of future opportunity.
- The average person will have to work until they die.

- The average person continues to count on Social Security benefits to fund retirement – a system that is considered "broke" by most experts and expected to run out of money before most reach retirement age.

- The average person is in denial about his/her financial future – with good reason, it's a painful subject!

- Finally, the average person spends money FIRST, then takes what's leftover and saves it because they are in a perpetual state of 'catching up'.

I don't know about you, but as recently as ten years ago I was an "average person". Actually, I was much worse than average. I had massive student loan debts acquired while pursuing a Ph.D [a degree that should stand for Perpetual horrendous Debt], a mortgage, car loan, credit card debt, doctors bills and more. In fact, all combined it was nearing $250,000.

Disaster hit. My husband – who had been the primary wage earner until then – lost his job. Not for just any reason...no, that would have been far too simple as he could simply go find another job. He went blind. Let me tell you, ADA or not, employers are not lining up to hire the blind. We had hardly any savings. No disability insurance. Nothing to fall back on. He needed a new life, training, work. This is when massage first entered my life. That was nearly 14 years ago. The field of massage holds a special place in my heart because it was one of the first areas that embraced him – with or without vision.

I wasn't finished with the Ph.D degree and my personal income to date had not even reached $30,000. It looked dismal. It was then my decision to learn and understand money and business began in earnest. I was tired of barely making ends meet and knew there had to be a better way although at that time I had no idea what it would entail.

Within a few years I managed to pay back every penny of the almost $80,000 in student loans (those buggers keep charging more and more interest!), the credit cards, the car, the miscellaneous other debts and then – even the mortgage on the house! I was thrilled, relieved and felt I had a new lease on life. In fact, I was able to invest into real estate and other investments that created even more money that I expected...with far less work.

In the meantime, I was privileged to work with many leading companies, organization and people that allowed me to grow both personally and professionally while learning more than I ever imagined about business, finances and how to literally change your life and the lives of those you love.

And when I say change lives, I truly mean it. I remember going to the library (I couldn't afford to buy books back then but was a voracious reader) and checking out books about money, finance or such that either amounted to very little – the equivalent of cutting coupons and spending less – or that assumed the reader had savings or other assets at their disposal. It used to irritate me. Heck, if I had that type of money then I wouldn't need advice!

Then there were the books that advocate using Other People's Money. Sounds good but I didn't have good credit and was not from a wealthy family. I wasn't even from a middle class family. In fact, I'm a high school drop-out with a GED....so was my husband as we were high school sweethearts. You hear a lot of people say "If I can do it than anyone can" but in my case, it's probably a bit more true than normal.

Everything in this book is something that is available to ordinary people; average people just like the ones listed above. People without much savings, people who truly want to improve their life, people who have bills and obligations, people who still want to find happiness and meaning in their work.

It's possible. If two high school dropouts facing mountains of debt, disability and zero resources can put their lives together then so can you! Join me and others on the companion website to this book: www.MassagePracticePlanner.com

How to Use this Book

Knowledge is Power

Power to change your life. Power to make choices. Power to live as you would like to live. Here is what you should know about using this book. I have tried, as much as possible, to take complex issues and bring them to life while creating tools for you to gain knowledge and information about your business. It's a LOT of information so don't expect to understand it all at once. In fact, this book is designed to grow and change as your own goals grow and change. It's a dynamic "living" document.

If you are a brand new practitioner, some of this information will make more sense after you actually begin putting it into practice but the information, activities, checklists and worksheets should save you a lot of time, money and mistakes!

If you are an established practitioner, I encourage you to do the all the exercises – even the introductory ones. It's surprising how many things you become accustomed or "immune" to seeing. You may encounter simple reasons that your business has failed to thrive or find examples of revenue that you are "leaving on the table". Of course, the more advanced topics will be of tremendous impact and are specially designed with the established practitioner in mind.

I've included basic business information specifically for massage students or those just starting out. For those of you who have been in business for awhile the first section may be a bit redundant as it covers the essentials but it also acts as a quick refresher for veteran practitioners or those exploring options of growing an existing business or changing the business structure from sole practitioner to corporation, partnership or LLC.

The book quickly delves into information that is quite literally the building block and foundation for success. For those of you who wonder, yes, I do have a Masters degree in business, specifically entrepreneurship, but most of the information comes from actual experience with real life situations, real life start-ups and real life results. Big business has used much of this information for a long time. Today, you can benefit from the same tools and trends.

I've also included information that is rarely contained anywhere else such as selecting a location, formula for pricing models, whether it makes more sense to rent or buy an office, and much more!

Finally, there is a list of resources that I hope both the new therapist and experienced practitioner will find useful. In it's entirely, this book is meant to be read, re-visited and evaluated. It is meant to grow and change as your goals grow and change.

The No Hype Zone

It's a sad truth that hype sells. There is a lot of junk out there. People make promises. Jump on fads. Promote one agenda this week and another next week. I know a lot about that – a whole lot – but the reality is only in the results. When you reach a certain level in your career you must deliver results or you will be a memory before nightfall.

I teach you the tools you need to know – and nothing else. No hype. No fads. What you learn will be as relevant today as tomorrow. Here is why...

First, any person is only as good as their reputation. You have my name and email so I really don't want to stain my reputation.

Next, you already know my personal attachment to the field of massage but that alone doesn't justify writing a book if there isn't a message.

There is a message. I've learned a lot about the methods of big business. What works. What doesn't work. How much it will really cost you in both terms of time and money. I'm from a health background myself and have two Masters degrees; one in business, one in health and of course, almost a Ph.D [ABD]. My client list includes a "who's who" roster. It's worked for others, it's worked in my own life and it can work for you as well!

Work Smarter Not Harder
Well, Sometimes Harder but Not Forever!

What is SMART????

S Sensible
M Measurable
A Achievable
R Realistic
T Time Specific

- The smart business owner understands financial freedom is only achieved through a systematic approach.

- The smart business owner understands it is necessary to define – and live - within his/her means in order to create more wealth.

- The smart business owner understands investing, equity, passive sources of income, and the concept of compound interest.

- The smart business owner has a plan for retirement, insurance and other safety nets in place.

- The smart business owner is ambitious, disciplined and knows that "get rich quick" is a fallacy.

- The smart business owner will be financially independent in 5-7 years on average.

- The smart business owner is considered an "expert in his/her field" and will eventually be able to choose how much and how often he/she works.

- Finally, the smart business owner has a GOAL. To build enough wealth in investments, assets and equity that will create a cash flow equal to, or beyond his/her current salary.

  Wouldn't you rather be a "SMART" business owner?

Even More Real Reasons

Okay, that all sounds good but it's analytical, not truly inspiring or meaningful on a personal level. Let's put it into real terms that everyone can relate to. We've already said that most people will spent nearly 50 years of their life working. Eight hours a day, plus travel to and from work, lunch hour and an ever increasingly level of work from home. For what? To barely survive retirement. Fight burn-out at the job. Struggle financially year after year?

Later in the book we will discuss how you value your time at length but let me briefly mention a few things at this point. How much money would it take you to "sell" the most precious memories of your life? The ones that truly make life worth living: Your first kiss, the birth of your first child, a special moment with a loved one. Whatever those moments and memories are, you know them best, what is a fair price for them?

Of course, there is no price on some memories for they are indeed what makes life worthwhile. Yet every day most people rush through life without spending time with the ones they love. It's worse than ever! Now that both parents work consider this startling statistic:

> ***Parents who work full-time spend just 19 minutes every day "caring for [their] own children". A further 16 minutes is spent looking after their children as a "secondary activity", like when parents do grocery shopping or cook.***

Did you catch that? Less than 20 minutes a day with their children! I've taught a college course for teachers for some 7-8 odd years and can tell you from experience with literally hundreds and hundreds of full-time school teachers that it is a major issue. Teachers report children must be taught everything – how to groom themselves, how to share, how to pick up classroom toys. The list goes on. Teachers must do it to control the classroom and because these children have simply not been taught at home. How could they? Parents are barely able to feed children, run errands and drop to bed in exhaustion!

Putting off Happiness Today in Hope of a Better Tomorrow - Will Tomorrow Be Better?

First, let me say that I am a firm believer in long term planning with a very conservative and realistic plan in place. Sometimes it is absolutely necessary to go through some pain to reach a real goal. I certain had to do so in my professional and personal life! However, that is different than what is happening to the majority of the population.

Instead of working toward a real goal that brings greater personal freedom, independence and choice, people are working hard but getting nowhere. It's like being on a treadmill. Massage Therapists are at a very real risk of this since often when they quit working the income dissolves.

The Typical Retirement

- The typical American household (40's) has a retirement account of $18,750.
- The typical pre-retiree household (age 55 and up) has a retirement account of $60,000 for the household – usually two people.
- Baby boomers between the ages of 41 and 54 have a retirement account of $30,000.
- Baby boomers have median total household retirement account of $35,000.
- Baby boomers who save in a 401k have an average 401k account balance of $80,000.
- 51 percent of workers age 55 and older have saved less than $50,000 towards savings (not including the value of a primary residence). 39 percent of workers in the same age group have saved less than $25,000 in retirement savings.
- One in five or nearly 20% of pre-retirees age 50 to 64 has less than $5,000 in retirement savings.

Now ask yourself – how many years would you be able to survive off of $50,000 or even $100,000 if you had little to no other source of income? Of course, there is the ever increasing cost of gasoline, utilities, medical care and even food to contend with. Clearly things may not be better in the future for many people! So, what can be done?

You have already taken the first step in the choice of a career in massage. Massage provides the opportunity for everything you need to increase wealth and create a life you love!

The Best Way to Increase Wealth Your Own Business!

Numerous studies have found that small business ownership remains one of the most profitable ways to acquire wealth in this nation. In fact, there are some very real limits to working for others that we will discuss later in detail but for the time being let's explore some of the benefits to owning your own business:

- Independence
- Reflects Your Own Value System
- Financially Rewarding
- Flexibility
- Equity
- Leverage of Value
- Earnings determined by You not – not arbitrarily by others
- Extension of personal life
- Many Others!

Of course with great reward also comes increased risk. However, there is risk everywhere today. I'll share my own personal "revelation" related to risk versus security. Having come from a modest family financially speaking (okay, for anyone who knows me and is reading this book that is an admittedly optimistic description), one of my biggest goals was to have a "secure" job. To me that meant a "state job". Yes, a state job was "secure", it had "benefits", you could count on it to be there and retire with a small pension.

After the typical years of working part-time in retail stores, waiting tables, bartending (for the record, the only drink people didn't complain about was the bottled beer...I was a lousy bartender), telemarketing and other less than impressive jobs to make ends meet while getting through college, a state job was my entire goal in life.

What I thought was secure at the beginning of a lifelong career didn't turn out to be so secure after all. Wages were frozen, hiring was put on hold, positions weren't replaced. Staffing shortages became critical and eventually – the entire operation was privatized. I had long since left to bigger and better things by the time that happened but those that remained were offered their jobs back at a reduction in salary. At the time the decision to leave seemed monumental. I was terrified of leaving the "security" of a state position for an untested, "dot-com" start-up that actually paid less money to start.

At the time, nobody knew much about the Internet. It wasn't the big deal it has become today. The fact was, the starting salary of the dot-com was $5,000 less than the state position, no small amount when you consider we are talking about comparing a $25,000 salary to a $30,000 state salary. However, the dot-com had flexible hours and I wanted to return to college to pursue another degree. I considered it risky. I was terrified as money was a big problem. I went for it because it allowed me to pursue a dream. A dream that seemed very far away.

What felt risky to me at the time turned out to be one of the most fortunate events of my life. Within a month my pay was increased to $30,000 so I "broke even" with the former state position plus I had benefits and even a small expense account. Within six months I was promoted with a hefty raise to $50,000 salary. It would have taken many years for that to happen with the state so I was thrilled. Within 6 more months I was again promoted to $65,000 then $85,000 then $110,000 then $150,000. But that wasn't all! There were stock options, IPO's, bonuses, expense accounts, a flexible schedule where I could often telecommute. I was working with an impressive list of people from around the world and learning more than I ever imagined.

Meanwhile, almost everyone at the state job had lost their position.

There is No Way to Escape Risk

But you can minimize it and try to increase potential. I look back at that decision with awe because I came so very close to rejecting that "risky" dot-com job. It was the beginning of a learning experience that "hooked me" on small business ownership. It began slowly as I saw how it worked from the inside out. I learned an incredible amount in the process. I was very good at my work and frequently asked to consult or speak to certain issues. It felt good to be "in demand" by even larger and more impressive companies, leading doctors and authorities in the nation, universities and even large government agencies.

Eventually however, changes take place. The Internet is now a part of life. Companies are sold, the environment changes. I was tired and overworked. Some of those small companies became well known household names and others, while less well known, made multi-millionaires out of the original owners. In case you are wondering, I left that well paying job to begin my own small business several years ago. I'm certainly not Bill Gates or even Donald Trump but at this point and time in our life, our goals are different.

One of the themes throughout this book will be on what amount of wealth you need to achieve in order to meet that need. Earlier in my life, I needed to make more money because I was heavily in debt. I had a lot of digging out to do! If that is your case then that is a valid need and is entirely "okay". To paraphrase a well known quote I've been rich, I've been poor and rich is a lot better. Well, perhaps not rich but you understand the gist! The point is, the money alone will eventually not be worth it. It all boils down to what you can do with it and how it changes your life and the lives of your loved ones.

I hope that none of you are ever faced with a major illness or disability like those we faced in our lives however, ask yourself for just one moment – what would you do?

It can be devastating emotionally, financially, physically and even spiritually. That is the next step this book will focus on....creating a permanent income for you and your family even without working. In addition to having mortgage paid off, one of the most meaningful options provided by all of the above was to know that we had a permanent income even when we aren't working. It's not huge but it is enough to pay the bills and lack for nothing even if tragedy should strike twice and we experience another major disability or other event.

What would that mean to you and your loved ones? What price can you put on choices or the ability to survive a crisis in your life? What price can you put on spending more than 19 minutes a day with your children while still providing for the financial needs of your household?

That is what this book is about. Giving you the tools, resources and even support via the companion website to truly change your life and the lives of those you love!

Yes, risk is everywhere but as a small business owner you are one of those who have the opportunity to impact risk and reward through your direct action and choices rather than at the hands of others! Don't fear risk – respect it and then learn to minimize it while embracing the potential! This book will show you how.

Finally, understand that there is no "magic scheme" to make you rich instantly. You need a SYSTEMATIC method to build a Perfect Practice and create the life you love. Understand that becoming successful is not easy, it requires patience, self-discipline and hard work, but it is entirely possible.

One final note before we begin; it is my sincere hope that this book motivates, encourages and supports your dreams. I would love to hear from you if it does! Even more so, share the knowledge with others. Consider becoming a mentor, writing an article or even a book. If nothing else, just drop me a line and let me know it made a difference. I can be reached at Shannon@MassagePracticePlanner.com

TIPS

Talk Massage instead of symptoms and gossip

Make a list of your ten best responding patients and focus on their success. Ask for testimonials!

Book all new patients as close to the time they call to make an appointment as possible

Chapter 2

The Nature of the Work

Massage therapy is an ancient and noble practice; in fact, the medical benefits of "friction" were first documented by the Greek physician Hippocrates around 400 BC. In many respects, the business of massage remained relatively stable throughout most of its history but today, the business of massage therapy is rapidly changing. There is perhaps greater interest than ever related to massage but that interest brings "mixed" results. Increased demand has resulted in a flood of new massage schools, practitioners and even massage franchises; expanding both the opportunity and creating new challenges for the practitioner.

Massage therapists can specialize in over 80 different types of massage, called modalities. Swedish massage, deep tissue massage, reflexology, acupressure, sports massage, and neuromuscular massage are just a few of the many approaches to massage therapy. Most massage therapists specialize in several modalities, which require different techniques. A massage can be as long as two hours or as short as five or ten minutes. Usually, the type of massage therapists give depends on the client's needs and the client's physical condition. For example, they use special techniques for elderly clients that they would not use for athletes, and they would use approaches for clients with injuries that would not be appropriate for clients seeking relaxation. There are also some forms of massage that are given solely to one type of client, for example prenatal massage and infant massage.

Because the work is so individualized, a comprehensive patient intake is generally performed especially for medically related therapy. This gives therapists a chance to discuss which techniques are to be used and which could be harmful. Because massage therapists tend to specialize in only a few areas of massage, customers will often be referred or seek a therapist with a certain type of massage in mind. Based on the person's goals, ailments, medical history, and stress- or pain-related problem areas, a massage therapist will conclude whether a massage is advisable, what type of massage or other modality is to be performed or if a referral is to be made to another healthcare provider. Medically advisable massage is often supervised by a physician or other healthcare provider and conforms to the prescribed plan of treatment outlined by the referring physician or provider.

Why People Use Massage Therapy

In the 2002 a large national survey on Americans use of massage found people used massage because:

- They believed that massage combined with conventional medicine would help a medical problem: 60 percent
- They thought massage would be interesting to try: 44 percent
- They believed that conventional medical treatments would not help: 34 percent
- Massage was suggested by a conventional medical professional: 33 percent
- They thought that conventional medicine was too expensive: 13 percent

According to recent reviews, people use massage for a wide variety of health-related intents: for example, to relieve pain (often from musculoskeletal conditions, but from other conditions as well); rehabilitate sports injuries; reduce stress; increase relaxation; address feelings of anxiety and depression; and aid general wellness.

License, Certification & Training

Licenses or certifications for massage therapists include:

- LMT Licensed Massage Therapist
- LMP Licensed Massage Practitioner
- CMT Certified Massage Therapist
- NCTMB Has met the credentialing requirements (including passing an exam) of the National Certification Board for Therapeutic Massage and Bodywork, for practicing therapeutic massage and bodywork
- NCTM Has met the credentialing requirements (including passing an exam) of the National Certification Board for Therapeutic Massage and Bodywork, for practicing therapeutic massage

There are about 1,300 massage therapy schools, college programs, and training programs in the United States. The course of study typically covers subjects such as anatomy and physiology (structure and function of the body); kinesiology (motion and body mechanics); therapeutic evaluation; massage techniques; first aid; business, ethical, and legal issues; and hands-on practice of techniques. These educational programs vary in many respects, such as length, quality, and whether they are accredited. Many require 500 hours of training, which is the same number of hours that many states require for certification. Some therapists also pursue specialty or advanced training.

At the end of 2004, 33 states and the District of Columbia had passed laws regulating massage therapy--for example, requiring that massage therapists graduate from an approved school or training program and pass the national certification exam in their field in order to practice. Cities and counties may have laws that apply as well. Professional organizations of massage therapists have not agreed upon the standards for recognizing that a massage therapist is properly and adequately trained.

Working Conditions

Massage therapists work in an array of settings both private and public: private offices, studios, hospitals, nursing homes, fitness centers, sports medicine facilities, airports, and shopping malls, just for example. Some massage therapists also travel to clients' homes or offices to provide a massage. It is common for full-time massage therapists to divide their time among several different settings, depending on the clients and locations scheduled. One of the benefits of a career as a MT is the ability to choose the condition, location, population and setting that suites your personal preference!

Self Care

Massage is physically demanding so therapists can succumb to injury if the proper technique is not used. Repetitive motion problems and fatigue from standing for extended periods of time are the most commonly cited problems but burn-out, exposure to illness and a wide range of other issues may prove problematic at some time during the career of most therapists. This risk can be limited through the use of proper hygiene, good technique, systematic spacing between sessions, exercise, and in many cases by the therapists themselves receiving a massage on a regular basis.

Since the majority of massage therapists are sole practitioners or independent contractors, sick time or injury often results in unpaid leave or a disruption of finances. A serious injury or illness can be a severe financial blow. This is a common complaint among therapists but it doesn't need to be! Later in the book information on reducing this risk while increasing your income will be outlined in detail!

Status - Where & How Are Therapist Working?

According to government data, about two-thirds of therapists are self-employed and of those, the majority owned their own business with the rest working as independent contractors. Others found employment in salons and spas; the offices of physicians and chiropractors; fitness and recreational sports centers; and hotels. Despite the independent nature of massage therapy, only about half of all massage therapists report having liability insurance, either through a professional association membership or through other insurance carriers. For legal and professional purposes, liability insurance is strongly suggested. For those practitioners who always carry liability insurance, be sure to explain the professionalism and benefits of this to your clients so they know what to expect when comparing or referring massage therapy to their friends. Health insurance coverage also remains a problem for many practitioners.

Because of the physical nature of the work, administrative duties and time needed in between sessions, massage therapists typically perform massages less than 40 hours per week. These are "billable" hours and most therapists find there is a limit to their earnings beyond these billable hours. One of the major themes of the Massage Practice Planner is to demonstrate how to move beyond this limitation in order to maximize your potential earnings.

Roughly three-quarters of massage therapists work part-time, although it should be noted that many massage therapists who work 15 to 30 hours per week consider themselves full-time due to the nature of the work. According to the AMTA, most massage therapists consider 27 hours of massage to be full-time work

Independent Contractors

A popular status among many massage therapists is that of an Independent Contractor. It is also a very popular method to "outsource" some of your overload capacity for your own practice especially if you are growing past your ability to handle the full load but not quit ready to hire an employee.

Many therapists that work with other professionals, athletic clubs, or other affiliations may also be classified as Independent Contractors. This basically means you are in business for yourself and will receive a 1099-Misc form at the end of the year. We will discuss more specifics later but for now, you should realize this is a form of self employment even if you work out of someone else's office or location. You are responsible for your own taxes and most of your own expenses.

There are many reasons to hire or work as an independent contractor rather than an employee: Employers are not monetarily or legally responsible for paying state, federal or local taxes, making FICA payments or providing unemployment insurance benefits, Workers' compensation or disability benefits. Likewise, therapists may prefer to be classified as independent contractors because of increased tax deductions, and the control the therapists have over payment of estimated taxes, flexibility of schedule and so forth.

However this can be a complex area and the government uses very specific criteria to determine whether a worker is deemed an employee or an independent contractor. The rule of "substance over form" applies which means certain rules must be followed or someone may be considered an employee rather than independent contractor despite the contract!

There are a host of regulatory bodies governing the classification of a worker including the Internal Revenue Service (IRS), the local labor department, state unemployment and Workers' Compensation insurance agencies, state tax departments and the National Labor Relations Board. The criteria used to determine the classification of a worker is different for each agency. It is in your best interest to research this carefully, and minimize your risk and exposure as much as possible by consulting with a legal advisor; an audit by any regulatory body can result in substantial penalties and assessments if it is determined that someone has been misclassified!

Independent Contractor - IRS Quick Question Checklist

According to The Independent Contractor Report, IRS uses these and other criteria to determine status as an Independent Contractor. Answer the following "Yes" or "No" for each and be sure to discuss with legal counsel.

1. Instructions: Are employees required to comply with another persons instructions about when, how and where they must work?
Yes ______ No ______

2. Training: Is there formal training or direct and detailed oversight of the actual job performance? Are there specific meetings and other training events – outside of those individually required for personal licensing or certification - mandated for continued employment?
Yes ______ No ______

3. Integration: Are workers merged or independent of business operations? Is there evidence to demonstrate independent direction and control of their own marketing, administrative and other documentation?
Yes ______ No ______

4. Scheduling: Are workers able to set their own schedules? Work for other entities? Secure their own clients? Outsource or make independent referrals?
Yes ______ No ______

5. Payment: Do workers collect their own payments and pay for their own expenses, training, continuing education and business license?
Yes ______ No ______

Not Sure If You Are Self Employed?

You are considered self-employed and subject to self-employment tax laws if you answer Yes to any of the following on this short checklist:

Yes______ No ______ Own your own business
Yes______ No ______ Have a profit motivation for your business activity
Yes______ No ______ Are a sole proprietor
Yes______ No ______ Are an independent contractor
Yes______ No ______ Have a net profit of $400.00 or more during the year

Quick Tips for Hiring IC's

- Make sure the therapist you are hiring is operating a business entity: whether a sole proprietor, a DBA (doing business as), a PC (professional corporation), a PLLP (professional limited liability partnership), a LLC (a limited liability company), a PLLC (professional limited liability company) or in states that allow it, an Inc. (C corp.) Remember, even a sole proprietor should have a local business license etc...

- Pay the therapist in the business's name - not their personal name.

- Make sure the therapist has their own business cards, stationery, etc. or some mechanism to hold out to the public as a service provider (i.e., ads in yellow pages, Web sites etc.).

- Non - Exclusive: The therapist should NOT perform services exclusively for you but rather should be able to provide services to others and solicit their own clients.

- Invoice: Have the therapist submit a bill to you for services rendered.

- Limit your role as far as scheduling, training, supervision and control.

Job Outlook & Earnings

Employment for massage therapists is expected to increase faster than average through 2014 as more people learn about the benefits of massage therapy. In States that regulate massage therapy, therapists who complete formal training programs and pass the national certification exam are likely to have very good job opportunities.

A massage therapist in a major metropolitan area typically charges $60 to $100 an hour, and $50 to $75 elsewhere. According to the Bureau of Labor Statistics, the median hourly earnings of massage therapists, including gratuities earned, were $15.36 in May 2004. These earnings have increased in many areas while remaining relatively stable in others depending upon the local economy. The middle 50 percent earned between $9.78 and $23.82. The lowest 10 percent earned less than $7.16, and the highest 10 percent earned more than $32.21. Generally, massage therapists earn 15 to 20 percent of their income as gratuities.

A Note About Self Employment. Be cautious when interpreting the earnings listed above. Remember, a large percentage of therapists are self employed and as such, may have fewer employer sponsored benefits including paid leave, retirement benefits, insurance and they are subject to self employment taxes of 15.3% of net earnings. This is higher for self employed people than normal employees because the job or employer usually pays ½ of this amount and the employee the other ½. Self employed people are responsible for both portions.

This figure is comprised of two components— a 12.4% old age, survivors and disability insurance (OASDI) tax and a 2.9% component for hospital insurance (Medicare). The 12.4% OASDI portion is paid on net income (revenues less expenses) up to a set amount similar to social security. The 2.9% Medicare tax is paid on all net income. If you receive any wage income on which Social Security or Railroad Retirement taxes were paid then the self-employment tax income maximum is reduced by the amount of wages received. If self-employment income is below $400 no self-employment tax is due.

Areas to Watch for Future Growth

Workplace: As workplaces try to distinguish themselves as employee-friendly, providing professional in-office, seated massages for employees is becoming a popular on-the-job benefit. Massage Therapists interested in worksite health can expect continued interest and growth for this segment during the next 5-10 years.

Alternative Health: The field of alternative medicine and holistic healing translates into opportunities for those skilled in massage therapy. Practitioners well versed in alternative health modalities can provide supplemental or primary services either alone or in conjunction with other alternative health practitioners.

Traditional Health & Medical: Healthcare providers and medical insurance companies are beginning to recognize massage therapy as a legitimate treatment and preventative measure for several types of injuries and illnesses. The health care industry is using massage therapy more often as a supplement to conventional medical techniques for ailments such as muscle problems, some sicknesses and diseases, and stress-related health problems. Massage therapy's growing acceptance as a medical tool, particularly by the medical provider and insurance industries, will greatly increase employment opportunities. However, it should be noted that changes in insurance reimbursement, paperwork, liability and general "attitude' are often cited barriers to entry for this area.

Nursing Homes & Other Special Populations: Older citizens in nursing homes or assisted living homes find benefit from massage as do a wide range of other special populations. There is a wide range of response from administration so therapists interested in pursuing this track should have experience and/or spend time developing relationships and expertise in the population of interest.

Consulting: Demand for massage therapists as consultants is relatively new but should continue to grow for those therapists who have highly specialized skills, an entrepreneurial flair and excellent communications skills.

Here is a powerful message everyone should commit to memory

Recognize the Truth that You Only Need a Limited Amount of Wealth to Be Happy

TIP

Place a Mirror Near the Phone
What you see is what you are relating to the customer.

Keeping a mirror next to your phone lets you see what your customers hear. A warm smile can be heard over the phone.

Chapter 3

Business Basics

Since the majority of Massage Therapists have their own business or will eventually form their own business this is an area that can initially appear deceptively simple. Simple that is, until you actually begin the process then you are confronted with what seem like endless details!

Whether you are a student contemplating your options upon graduation or a veteran therapist wishing to expand your practice to a new level, this section provides a basic overview required. It is by no means comprehensive but it should provide a firm foundation to get you started in the right direction. For those practitioners who are currently sole practitioners, Independent Contractors or even partners, this will also provide information for you to consider whether or not you are ready to form an LLC, S or C Corporation or other type of entity.

Business Structure

When beginning a business, you must decide what form of business entity to establish. Your form of business determines which tax forms you have to file, types of deductions you can take, forms of insurance required and even how you will pay yourself.

The most common forms of business are the sole proprietorship, partnership, corporation, and S corporation. A Limited Liability Company (LLC) is a relatively new business structure allowed by state statute. Legal and tax considerations enter into selecting a business structure.

Sole Proprietor

A sole proprietor is someone who owns an unincorporated business by himself or herself. However, if you are the sole member of a domestic limited liability company (LLC), you are not a sole proprietor if you elect to treat the LLC as a corporation.

Partnership

A partnership is the relationship existing between two or more persons who join to carry on a trade or business. Each person contributes money, property, labor, or skill, and expects to share in the profits and losses of the business.

A partnership must file an annual information return to report the income, deductions, gains, losses etc., from its operations, but it does not pay income tax. Instead, it "passes through" any profits or losses to its partners. Each partner includes his or her share of the partnership's income or loss on his or her tax return.

Corporation

In forming a corporation, prospective shareholders exchange money, property, or both, for the corporation's capital stock. A corporation generally takes the same deductions as a sole proprietorship to figure its taxable income. A corporation can also take special deductions.

The profit of a corporation is taxed to the corporation when earned, and then is taxed to the shareholders when distributed as dividends. This is commonly referred to as "double taxation". Shareholders cannot deduct any loss of the corporation.

S Corporation

An eligible domestic corporation can avoid double taxation (once to the shareholders and again to the corporation) by electing to be treated as an S corporation. Generally, an S corporation is exempt from federal income tax other than tax on certain capital gains and passive income. On their tax returns, the S corporation's shareholders include their share of the corporation's separately stated items of income, deduction, loss, and credit, and their share of non-separately stated income or loss.

Limited Liability Company (LLC)

Many times you will hear these incorrectly referred to as Limited Liability Corporations but in fact, these are not corporations at all but rather a distinct business type. A Limited Liability Company (LLC) is a relatively new business structure allowed by state statute. LLCs are popular because, similar to a corporation, owners have limited personal liability for the debts and actions of the LLC. Other features of LLCs are more like a partnership, providing management flexibility and the benefit of pass-through taxation.

Owners of an LLC are called members. Since most states do not restrict ownership, members may include individuals, corporations, other LLCs and foreign entities. There is no maximum number of members. Most states also permit "single member" LLCs, those having only one owner.

Taxpayer Identification Numbers (TIN)

A Taxpayer Identification Number (TIN) is an identification number used by the Internal Revenue Service (IRS) in the administration of tax laws. It is issued either by the Social Security Administration (SSA) or by the IRS. A Social Security number (SSN) is issued by the SSA whereas all other TINs are issued by the IRS.

Common Types of Taxpayer Identification Numbers

- Social Security Number "SSN"
- Employer Identification Number "EIN"
- Individual Taxpayer Identification Number "ITIN"

Do You Need One?

A TIN must be supplied when filing your individual or business tax returns, statements, and other tax related documents. If you operate as a Sole Practitioner or Independent Contractor then you will typically use your Social Security Number (SSN) for filing tax related documents. However, if you are a corporation, S Corporation or other entity then you will need an Employer Identification Number (EIN).

How to Obtain a TIN

- **SSN**

  You will need to complete Form SS-5, Application for a Social Security Card if you do not have one. You also must submit evidence of your identity, age, and U.S. citizenship or lawful alien status. For more information contact the Social Security office by calling 1-800-772-1213 or visiting your local Social Security office. These services are free.

- **Employer ID Numbers (EINs)**

  An Employer Identification Number (EIN) is also known as a Federal Tax Identification Number, and is used to identify a business entity. Generally, businesses need an EIN. You may apply for an EIN in various ways. Before applying, check with your state to make sure you need a state number or charter.

How to Apply for an Employer ID Numbers (EIN)

- **Toll-Free Telephone Service**

  Taxpayers can obtain an EIN immediately by calling the Business & Specialty Tax Line (800-829-4933). The hours of operation are 7:00 a.m. - 10:00 p.m. local time, Monday through Friday. An assistant will take the information, assign the EIN and provide the number to you over the telephone.

- **Fax**

  Taxpayers can request the appropriate form (SS-4 application) and then Fax it to their state FAX. If it is determined that the entity needs a new EIN, one will be assigned using the appropriate procedures for the entity type. If you supply a return fax a fax will be sent back with the EIN within four (4) business days.

- **Mail**

  The processing timeframe for an EIN application received by mail is four weeks so double check Form SS-4 contains all of the required information.

How Long Will it Take to Get an EIN Number?

You should apply for an EIN early enough to have your number when you need to file a return or make a deposit. You can get an EIN quickly by calling the Toll-Free phone number (800)829-4933. If you prefer, you can fax a completed Form SS-4 to the service center for your state, and they will respond with a return fax in about one week. If you do not include a return fax number, it will take about two weeks. If you apply by mail, send your completed Form SS-4 (PDF) at least four to five weeks before you need your EIN to file a return or make a deposit.

If you don't have your EIN by the time a return is due, write "Applied for" and the date you applied in the space shown for the number. Do not use your social security number.

Do You Need an EIN - Checklist

You will need an EIN if you answer "Yes" to any of the following questions.

Additionally, if you provide health insurance for your employees, you may need a National Standard Employer Identifier (NSEI) for your electronic health transactions.

Yes No Do you have employees?
Yes No Do you operate your business as a corporation or a partnership?
Yes No Do you file an Employment or Excise tax returns?
Yes No Do you withhold taxes on income paid to a non-resident alien?
Yes No Do you have a Keogh plan?

How to Name Your Business

There is more to naming your business than just coming up with something that sounds good that you happen to like. Thought must be given to state and local requirements and making sure you don't infringe upon the rights of someone else's business name.

Legal Requirements and Implications

Picking a name for your business requires more than just creativity and a working knowledge of your target market. First you need to decide which business structure you will use, since each structure has its own peculiarities. For example, many states require a sole proprietor to use their own name for the business name unless they formally file another name as a trade name, or fictitious name.

Similarly, you need to determine whether your trade name will be the same as the full legal name of your business. Of equal importance is finding out whether your name or a very similar name is being used by another business, and if so, what rights they may or may not have to use the name in the area where you do business. Keep in mind that some businesses only file trademarks within their locality, so it's possible that the same name can be used elsewhere.

Search And Registration

Trade names can be registered through state Secretary of State offices, and for wider marketplace protection, through the U.S. Patent and Trademark Office (USPTO Trademark Search). Businesses should first use the USPTO's online system to search all state and federal trademark registers to see if their proposed name is being used.

Domain Names

For many businesses that operate on the Web, trade names are synonymous with domain names, such as Amazon.com and Monster.com. Domain names obtained through numerous online businesses, most of which allow you to conduct a name search prior to purchase to make sure your chosen name isn't taken. My personal favorite is www.1and1.com which allows you to register a domain name for approximately $6 per year and includes a basic website and email for free!

Business Licenses and Permits

State Requirements

While business licensing requirements vary from state to state, some of the more common types are listed below. See the resources in the back of this book for a state by state listing of where to apply online!

Business Licenses

A state business license is the main document required for tax purposes and conducting other basic business functions. Many states have established small business assistance agencies to help small businesses comply with state requirements. A comprehensive state by state list is available in the back of this book.

Occupations and Professions

State licenses are frequently required for occupations as varied as building contractors, physicians, appraisers, accountants, barbers, real estate agents, auctioneers, private investigators, private security guards, funeral directors, bill collectors, and cosmetologists. In most states, you must be licensed or certified in order to open a Massage establishment. Check with your state to determine the exact requirements.

Tax Registration

If the state in which you operate has a state income tax, you will need to register and obtain an employer identification number from your state Department of Revenue or Treasury Department. If you plan to offer retail sales you will need to obtain a sales tax license.

Trade Name Registration

If your business will only be operated in your local community, registering your company name with the state may be sufficient.

Employer Registrations

If you have any employees, you will probably be required to make unemployment insurance contributions. For more information, contact your state Department of Revenue or Department of Labor. If you will be using an Independent Contractor or forming a partnership then those are not typically considered employees but be certain that you understand how to properly establish the relationship and boundaries for both your benefit and theirs. A complete state-by-state contact list is included in the back of this book!

Insurance

Buying business insurance is among the best ways to prepare for the unexpected. Without proper protection, misfortunes such as the death of a partner a lawsuit, or a natural disaster could spell the end of a thriving operation

Ranging from indispensable worker's compensation insurance to the relatively obscure executive kidnapping coverage, insurance is available for nearly any business risk. Considering the multitude of available options, business owners must carefully weigh whether the cost of certain premiums will justify the coverage for a given risk.

Here are some of the most common and pertinent forms of business insurance you will want to explore.

General Liability

Many business owners buy general liability or umbrella liability insurance to cover legal hassles due to claims of negligence. These help protect against payments as the result of bodily injury or property damage, medical expenses, the cost of defending lawsuits, and settlement bonds or judgments required during an appeal procedure.

An “umbrella” policy is usually quite affordable and can typically be purchased from the same agent that sells your homeowners or auto policy.

Home-Based Business Insurance

Contrary to popular belief, homeowners' insurance policies do not generally cover home-based business losses. Commonly needed insurance areas for home-based businesses include business property such as business equipment and supplies, computers and other items used for conducting business; professional liability, personal and advertising injury, loss of business data, crime and theft, and disability.

Workers Compensation

Required in every state except Texas, worker's compensation insurance pays for employees' medical expenses and missed wages if injured while working. The amount of insurance employers must carry, rate of payment, and what types of employees must be carried varies depending on the state . In most cases, business owners, independent contractors, domestic employees in private homes, farm workers, and unpaid volunteers are exempt. A complete list of state-by-state contact is included in the back of this book!

Criminal Insurance

No matter how tight security is in your workplace, theft and malicious damage are always possibilities. While the dangers associated with hacking, vandalism, and general theft are obvious, employee embezzlement is more common than most business owners think. Criminal insurance and employee bonds can provide protection against losses in most criminal areas.

Business Interruption Insurance

Some businesses may wish to acquire insurance that covers losses during natural disasters, fires, and other catastrophes that may cause the operation to shut down for a significant amount of time. This can be a meaningful investment for many massage practice owners since a natural disaster can dramatically impact their earnings.

Malpractice Insurance

Some licensed professionals need protection against payments as the result of bodily injury or property damage, medical expenses, the cost of defending lawsuits, investigations and settlements, and bonds or judgments required during an appeal procedure.

Specific Massage Industry Insurance Sources

You can also purchase insurance from several organizations that deal directly with massage. Many people mistakenly believe they can only purchase from these associations which is not always the case so be sure to compare. However, in many cases these may offer a better value depending upon your situation.

- American Massage Council
  (800) 500-3930

- American Massage Therapy Association (AMTA)
  (847) 864-0123

- Associated Bodywork and Massage Professionals (ABMP)
  (800) 458-2267

- International Massage Association
  (540) 351-0800

Chapter 4

Money Matters 101

This is a big topic so the focus of this section is on acquainting the reader with some of the budget, accounting and tax concerns required in the practice planning stage. For example, the decision to follow a "calendar year" versus "fiscal year" has many implications and is not easy to change once you adopt one form over another. These are to introduce you to the topic and allow you to follow-up with professional advice from CPA, lawyers etc as to how it will be suite your individual needs for the type of business structure you decide upon and the state where you will conduct business.

Calendar Year vs. Fiscal Year

A year is a year, right? Yes and no. Different types of businesses may use different types of "tax years" when it comes to calculating their taxable income.

A tax year is an annual accounting period for keeping records and reporting income and expenses. A calendar year runs from January 1 through December 31. Generally, anyone can adopt a calendar year for his or her tax returns. Whether you choose a calendar year or a fiscal year, you must use it on your first tax return and for all subsequent tax returns unless you get IRS approval to change your tax year.

Basic Accounting Concepts

If you decide to keep your own books, or even if you hire an accountant, you should know a few things about accounting methods. An accounting method is simply a set of rules used to determine when and how you report income and expenses. You choose your method of accounting when you file your first tax return. The two most commonly used accounting methods are the cash method and accrual method.

Cash Method

This is the accounting method used by individuals and many small businesses. Due to its simplicity, it may be appropriate for your practice. Determining gross income with the cash method is merely a matter of adding up the cash, checks, and fair market value of property and services you receive during the year. Using this method, your income for the year includes all checks you receive, regardless of when you cash the checks or withdraw the money. You cannot avoid paying tax by not depositing checks or credit card charge slips.

Using the cash method, your business expenses are usually deducted in the year you pay them. For example, let's assume you order some office supplies from a mail order catalog in November 2006 and they arrive in December. You send a check to pay for them in January 2007. Under the cash method, that business expense deduction should be claimed on your 2007 tax return because that is the year you paid for the supplies.

Accrual Method

This method of accounting is more precise than the cash method. Its main purpose is to match income and expenses in the correct year. Under the accrual method, income is reported in the year in which all events that fix your right to receive it have occurred. You can determine the amount with reasonable accuracy even if you received the income in a different year. For example, the accrual method calls for you to report income for the year when you perform a service for a customer. It doesn't matter that your customer doesn't pay you until the following year.

Similarly, you generally deduct your business expenses in the year you become liable for them, regardless of when you actually paid them. Let's look at the office supply example again. Under the accrual method, you can deduct the business expenses for supplies on your 2006 tax return, the year you ordered the supplies and they were delivered. You sent a check to pay them in January 2007. You can deduct the expenses in 2006 because that is when you became liable for the expense.

Once you decide which accounting method is the right one for your business, you must follow it consistently. Generally you cannot change your method of accounting unless you get special permission from the IRS to change.

Hiring Family Members

One of the advantages of operating your own business is hiring family members. However, the employment tax requirements for family employees may vary from those that apply to other employees.

A spouse or other family member is considered an employee if there is an employer/employee type of relationship. This happens when one spouse substantially controls the business in terms of management decisions and the second spouse is under the direction and control of the first spouse. If such a relationship exists, then the second spouse is an employee subject to income tax and FICA (social security and Medicare) withholding. If you are trying to control costs then workers compensation and other costs associated with having an employee may be an area to keep an eye on in the beginning.

However, if the second spouse has an equal say in the affairs of the business, provides substantially equal services to the business, and contributes capital to the business, then a partnership type of relationship exists.

If spouses carry on a business together and share in the profits and losses, they may be partners in a partnership whether or not they have a formal partnership agreement.

Form 1099-MISC Miscellaneous Income

Many small business owners decide against having employees due to the cost, paperwork and other factors. Instead, many use Independent Contractors – which are actually small business owners or sole practitioners. When you use the services of an Independent Contractor or other related, you need to send them a Form 1099-Misc for their tax reporting purposes. It also establishes your business deductions.

When to Use a Form 1099-Misc

Use this form to report certain payments you make in your business. For example:

- Payments of $10 or more for royalties, interest, or dividends;
- Payments of $600 or more for rents, prizes, and awards for services rendered
- Payments of $600 or more to workers who were not your employees.

Keep your employment tax information organized and in a safe place. Not only will you be able to take full advantage of all your deductions for payroll taxes, you'll also be able to avoid costly penalties and interest for late payments or errors on returns.

Outsourcing Payroll

Many small business or practice owners with employees decide to outsource payroll and related tax duties to third party payroll service providers. This helps employers meet filing deadlines and deposit requirements and streamline business operations. Some of the services provided include administering payroll and employment taxes on behalf of the employer. The service provider also reports, collects, and deposits employment taxes with state and federal authorities.

This can be a very effective way to deal with paperwork and time required however, you should keep in mind that you are always responsible for the deposit and payment of federal tax liabilities. If the third-party fails to make the federal tax payments, the IRS may assess penalties and interest on your account. The employer is liable for all taxes, penalties, and interest due and may also be held personally liable for certain unpaid federal taxes. So, it's always important that you understand what the requirements are and keep track of what is taking place.

Setting Up Your Records

Keeping your business records in a filing system is just as important as any other aspect of your business. So, what's the best way to keep good records? It doesn't have to be complicated. Use any recordkeeping system suited to your business that clearly and accurately shows your income and expenses.

Your tax records must support all the income, tax deductions, and credits you show on your tax return. Carefully track all of your income and where it comes from. It's important to separate your business and personal receipts and your taxable and nontaxable income.

Be careful if you transfer personal funds into your business account or vice versa. You are essentially making a "loan" to the business. Keep complete records of that transaction so that you don't include the money in your taxable business income by mistake.

Expenses

Record your expenses when you pay or incur them, depending on your method of accounting. It's easy to forget about some of last year's expenses when you're filling out your tax return. Overlooking deductible expenses can cost you.

Assets

Your business assets are the property and equipment you own and use for your business. Keep a complete and detailed record of your assets, showing when you acquired them, how much you paid for them and how you use the assets in your business. This detailed record will allow you to depreciate your assets properly and report the correct gain or loss when you dispose of them.

Self-Employment Earnings

If you are self-employed, you must pay self-employment tax. This tax provides for your Social Security benefits when you retire or are disabled. The amount of benefits you receive depends on how much you earn and contribute to the Social Security system.

Car Expenses

It's important to get into the habit of recording your business mileage at the time you actually use your car. Try keeping a logbook in the glove compartment and jotting down the mileage at the beginning and end of each business-related trip. Record parking fees and tolls, and save your insurance and repair receipts.

Payroll Taxes

If you have employees, you must keep all records dealing with federal employment taxes for at least four years after the tax is due or paid, whichever is later. Make sure your records include your employer identification number, the confirmation number or tax record from any electronic payments, copies of the tax returns you filed, and the dates and amounts of all the employment tax deposits you have made.

Keep track of your employees' Social Security and Medicare (FICA) taxes and income tax withholding in the same way, by recording the date and amount of each paycheck and the date and amount of the taxes you withheld.

You must also keep a record of the federal unemployment (FUTA) tax you paid. Record the total amount you paid for each employee and the amount you paid into the state unemployment fund.

Travel and Entertainment

Keep all business-related travel and entertainment receipts. Indicate the exact business reason for these expenses.

Paying Taxes

Death and taxes. Benjamin Franklin said they are the only two things in life that are certain but you don't have to let your tax responsibilities drive you or your business to an early grave.

One problem many new business owners may run into is not budgeting enough money to set aside for taxes. You may find yourself short on cash when it comes time to file so it's important to understand some of the basics about taxes.

Don't wait until the time to file has come and gone. Gather your records and file all your tax forms by their due dates—even if you can't pay a cent. Of course, to keep down the interest and penalties, try to pay as much as you can. If you receive a notice from the IRS, respond right away. Don't ignore it; it won't go away.

If the next deadline rolls around and you still can't pay, go ahead and file on time. At least you'll avoid the failure-to-file penalty. Along with your return, attach an Installment Agreement Request (Form 9465). You can propose your own monthly payment date and amount using this form. If circumstances make it unlikely that you could pay the full tax even on an installment plan, ask for a copy of Publication 594, The IRS Collection Process. This publication lists alternative methods for resolving your account.

The failure-to-pay penalty may be reduced from .5% to .25% per month during the period in which an individual installment agreement is in effect. However, you must have filed on time. If you file and cannot pay, apply for an extension but file!

Social Security

For most employees, social security and Medicare taxes are deducted from every paycheck, helping to provide retirement income and Medicare coverage. If you are self-employed, you pay for your coverage through the self-employment tax that you compute and pay when you file your federal income tax each year.

Generally, if you carry on a trade or business as a sole proprietor, an independent contractor, a member of a partnership that carries on a trade or business, or are otherwise in business for yourself, then you are self-employed. Part-time work can qualify as self-employment even if its work you do in addition to a regular full-time job.

Many self-employed people will have to make quarterly estimated tax payments. Remember, your self-employment tax will increase the total federal tax you owe. Be sure to take this into account when you determine how much estimated tax to pay each quarter. When you file your tax return, fill out Schedule SE, where you report your self-employment income and calculate the self-employment tax owed.

Self-Employment Tax

Self-employment tax (SE tax) is a social security and Medicare tax for individuals who work for themselves. It is similar to the social security and Medicare taxes withheld from a paycheck when you work for someone else but since you work for yourself there are different requirements. These can be a bit confusing if you are not familiar with them so be sure to ask your accountant for advice.

You will need to calculate SE taxes by using Schedule SE (Form 1040). Social security and Medicare taxes of most wage earners are figured by their employers. Also you can deduct half of your SE tax in figuring your adjusted gross income. Wage earners cannot deduct social security and Medicare taxes.

Self Employment Tax Rate

The self-employment tax rate is 15.3%. The rate consists of two parts: 12.4% for social security (old-age, survivors, and disability insurance) and 2.9% for Medicare (hospital insurance). Normally when you work for someone else, your employer pays a portion and you pay a portion. As a self employed Sole Proprietor or Independent Contractor you will be responsible for the entire tax.

This tax is in addition to your income taxes so plan accordingly! Many people are surprised to learn how much they owe in taxes if they have not planned ahead! It is also very important to understand so you can calculate your cost, expenses and hourly rates.

Maximum Earnings Subject to Self Employment Taxes

Only the first $94,200 of your combined wages, tips, and net earnings are currently subject to the 12.4% social security part of SE tax. After that point you are not currently required to pay more. However, this is subject to change at any time. All your combined wages, tips, and net earnings are subject to the 2.9% Medicare part of the SE tax or social security tax.

How to Pay Self-Employment Taxes

To pay your portion of Self Employment taxes you will need a social security number (SSN) or an individual taxpayer identification number (ITIN).

Estimated Taxes

Federal income tax is a pay-as-you-go tax which means you must pay the tax as you earn or receive income during the year. For example, when you work for someone else, taxes are typically deducted from each paycheck. Now that you work for yourself it is your responsibility. You generally have to make estimated tax payments if you expect to owe tax, including SE tax, of $1,000 or more when you file your return. There are two ways to pay as you go: withholding and estimated taxes. If you are a self-employed individual and do not have income tax withheld, you must make estimated tax payments.

Business Expenses

Business expenses are the cost of conducting business. These expenses are usually deductible if the business is operated to make a profit and can greatly benefit the small business owner by offsetting many of the out of pocket expenses required to perform business.

Unlike working for someone else, most small business owners have more expenses to pay: everything from rent to communications, supplies to marketing. It is beyond the scope of this book to delve into this area in great detail but there are many excellent books directed to the small business owner on the most up to date tax laws and deductions. It's also a very good idea to consult with a competent tax advisor or CPA to determine what is most advisable for your specific business type and situation.

Examples of Typical Deductions

To be deductible, a business expense must be both ordinary and necessary. An ordinary expense is one that is common and accepted in your trade or business. A necessary expense is one that is helpful and appropriate for your trade or business. An expense does not have to be indispensable to be considered necessary.

It is important to separate business expenses from the following expenses:

- The expenses used to figure the cost of goods sold,
- Capital Expenses, and
- Personal Expenses.

Cost of Goods Sold

If your business purchases products to resale – for example you decide to add a line of natural health products to your waiting area available for resale - you generally must value inventory at the beginning and end of each tax year to determine the cost of goods sold. Some of your expenses may be included in figuring the cost of goods sold. Cost of goods sold is deducted from your gross receipts to figure your gross profit for the year. If you include an expense in the cost of goods sold, you cannot deduct it again as a business expense.

The following are types of expenses that go into figuring the cost of goods sold:

- The cost of the actual product - including shipping
- Storage
- Direct labor costs
- Overhead

Capital Expenses

You must capitalize, rather than deduct, some costs. These costs are a part of your investment in your business and are called capital expenses. Capital expenses are considered assets in your business. There are, in general, three types of costs you capitalize:

- Business start-up cost (See the note below)
- Business assets
- Improvements

Note: You can elect to deduct or amortize certain business start-up costs. Check with your CPA to find out specifics for your situation.

Personal versus Business Expenses

Generally, you cannot deduct personal, living, or family expenses. However, if you have an expense for something that is used partly for business and partly for personal purposes, divide the total cost between the business and personal parts. You can deduct the business part.

For example, let's say you take out a loan and use 70% of it to get your business started and the other 30% for family needs. You may be able to deduct 70% of the interest as a business expense. The remaining 30% is personal interest and is not deductible.

Business Use of Your Home

If you use part of your home for business, you may be able to deduct expenses for the business use of your home. These expenses may include mortgage interest, insurance, utilities, repairs, and depreciation. However, be sure to consult with a tax advisor before doing so as it may not save you much in the long run. Some of that will be recaptured when you sell the home and could present a big surprise years later!

Business Use of Your Car

If you use your car in your business, you can deduct car expenses. If you use your car for both business and personal purposes, you must divide your expenses based on actual mileage.

Car Expenses

To take a business deduction for the use of your car, you must determine whether the use was business or personal.

If the answer is personal, no deduction is allowed. Personal use includes commuting or driving from your home to your regular place of work.

A deduction may be allowed if you have multiple jobs or businesses. Driving from your home to "business one" is commuting, but driving from "business one" directly to "business two" is deductible. Also, you are usually allowed to deduct transportation costs for going from your home to temporary workplace regardless of the distance.

Deductible car expenses can include the cost of

- Traveling from one workplace to another
- Making business trips to visit customers
- Attend business meetings away from your regular workplace
- Going to temporary workplaces.

To claim the deduction, keep a written travel log with complete and accurate mileage records for each business use of your car. If you are unable to produce a clear and accurate business mileage record, the IRS may disallow the deduction.

There are two methods for claiming business car expenses: actual expenses or the standard mileage rate.

Actual Expenses

You can add your entire car operating expenses for the year, including gas, oil, tires, repairs, license fees, lease payments, registration fees, garage rental, insurance, and depreciation. Deduct the percentage of the total that was for business, based on your mileage records of business and personal travel. Deductions for business parking and tolls do not have to be divided.

Standard Mileage Rate

Beginning January 1, 2007, the standard mileage rates are:

- 48.5 cents per mile for business miles driven;
- 20 cents per mile driven for medical or moving purposes; and
- 14 cents per mile driven in service of charitable organizations.

Travel Expenses

Travel expenses are your "ordinary and necessary" expenses while you are traveling away from home on business. You are required to show that your trip away from home was primarily for business.

Keep all receipts and whatever other documents you can gather at the time of the trip to prove where you went, why you went there, how long you stayed and how much you spent. If your travel includes some business and some personal aspects, be sure to keep clear records showing exactly how much is related to business.

Keep the following:

- Lodging receipts: These should show where you were, how long you were there, and charges. Also keep records for cleaning and laundry, telephone charges, tips, and other charges not shown separately.

- Transportation receipts: These include airplane, train or bus ticket stubs, travel agency receipts, rental car or taxi receipts, etc., all showing the amounts, dates and destinations involved.

- Meal receipts: Generally, you must keep a log of your meal expenses and save receipts for amounts of $75 or more. If you do not want to keep track of the actual costs of your meals, you may qualify to use the standard meal allowance. In 2006, the rates ranged from $39 to $64 a day depending on where and when you were traveling in the United States.

Whether you use the standard meal allowance or actual expenses, you generally can only claim a deduction for 50 percent of the un-reimbursed cost of your meals while you are traveling.

Other Types of Business Expenses

Employee Pay - You can generally deduct the pay you give employees for the services they perform for your business.

Retirement Plans - Retirement plans are savings plans that offer you tax advantages to set aside money for your own, and your employees', retirement.

Rent Expense - Rent is any amount you pay for the use of property you do not own. In general, you can deduct rent as an expense only if the rent is for property you use in your trade or business. If you have or will receive equity in or title to the property, the rent is not deductible.

Interest - Business interest expense is an amount charged for the use of money you borrowed for business activities.

Taxes - You can deduct various federal, state, local, and foreign taxes directly attributable to your trade or business as business expenses.

Insurance - Generally, you can deduct the ordinary and necessary cost of insurance as a business expense, if it is for your trade, business, or profession.

TIP

75% of First Time Callers will Not Leave a Message or Call Back if they Get Voice Mail or an Answering Machine

Chapter 5

Personal Considerations

Not everyone is meant to own their own business. It takes a lot of work. Although it can be very rewarding it can also be risky. Whether you are interested in working as a sole practitioner, partner or set up a small corporation with or without employee's it is important to first count the cost and commitment required.

Success: What Do You Want and Why?

It has been said that "Nothing Succeeds Like Success." But what is this concept we call Success? If we consult the dictionary it will provide the etymology of this much used word, and in general terms the meaning will be "the accomplishment of a purpose." But just as the goals for every individuals' life differ, so does the meaning of success to each individual. It doesn't mean the same thing to all people.

The artist's idea of success is very different from that of the business person and the scientist differs from both, as does the politician. We read of successful gamblers, doctors, lawyers and police but find high rates of incarceration, suicide and alcoholism. No true measure of success was ever won or ever can be won that sets at defiance the laws of God and man.

To win, so that we ourselves and the world is content, happy and a better place for our having lived, we must begin by defining this elusive concept of success. Without an idea of the final goal there can be no determination of whether the journey is worthwhile or not much less when it's time to change direction, redefine goals or simply celebrate reaching your goals!

Establish Your Personal Goals Worksheet

List things you do today that you were unable to do five years ago:

1. ______________________________
2. ______________________________
3. ______________________________
4. ______________________________
5. ______________________________

List those things you could have done but did not do five years ago:

6. ______________________________
7. ______________________________
8. ______________________________
9. ______________________________
10. ______________________________

List those things you would like to do in five years that you are not doing today:

11. ______________________________
12. ______________________________
13. ______________________________
14. ______________________________
15. ______________________________

List Why you are not doing them today:

16. ______________________________
17. ______________________________
18. ______________________________
19. ______________________________
20. ______________________________

List those things you would like to be able to do in five years but cannot do today:

21. ______________________________
22. ______________________________
23. ______________________________
24. ______________________________
25. ______________________________

List why you are not doing them today:

26. ____________________
27. ____________________
28. ____________________
29. ____________________
30. ____________________

Explain how your business practice will facilitate these goals:

31. ____________________
32. ____________________
33. ____________________
34. ____________________
35. ____________________

Explain how you will know and understand when you reach your goals:

36. ____________________
37. ____________________
38. ____________________
39. ____________________
40. ____________________

List those things you are unwilling to compromise in order to reach those goals:

41. ____________________
42. ____________________
43. ____________________
44. ____________________
45. ____________________

List those things in your life, character or personality that you hope will change due to reaching those goals. How will it make you, your family and community better?

46. ____________________
47. ____________________
48. ____________________
49. ____________________
50. ____________________

What You Need to Survive

The first place to begin is by calculating your needs. This will be used repeatedly throughout this planner but even more importantly, it forms the foundation of everything else that comes after.

Small business ownership of any type can be profitable, exciting and rewarding however, it can also be full of pitfalls if you are not making enough to pay your personal bills. Sit down and complete the following personal budget worksheet and be honest with what you need to survive. Later we can focus on increasing that profit potential to generate the lifestyle and/or type of earnings that formulate your goal but for now, the focus is on the essentials of life.

Personal Budget Worksheet

Anticipated Income:___________________________

Median annual starting salary:_________
Gross Monthly income:_________

Estimated Tax Rate: ___________ Use a minimum tax rate between 15% and 25%. Use the higher if you are to be self employed or an Independent Contractor).

Monthly net income after taxes ___________

Personal Expenses
_____ Housing
_____ Transportation
_____ Food
_____ Utilities
_____ Phone
_____ Cable
_____ Clothing
_____ Entertainment & Recreation
_____ Student Loan
_____ Savings
_____ Miscellaneous
_____ Total Expenses

_____ Difference between Income and Expenses

Personal Readiness Worksheet

The next section will focus on your individual level of readiness. While starting a business is one of those areas of life that few people report ever finding a "perfect" time, there are a few realities that will certainly make the outcome much less likely. Be honest with yourself including how much each of these situations are likely to change either for the good or bad during the next 1 to 3 years. Use this worksheet again when contemplating expanding or growing your business to the next level. For example, if you are a sole practitioner and thinking of forming a corporation or hiring employees.

Are you able and willing to commit time, money and additional work to make the business grow? What limitations are you facing?

____

____

____

____

____

Are you willing and able to personally fund – or guarantee the funds – required to start and grow the business? Remember, even if you form a corporation, until your business is well established and able to generate several years of tax returns, earnings and build its own credit record, you will usually be required to personally guarantee all funds for the business.

____

____

____

____

____

Do you posses the needed knowledge and expertise to run the business? Not just for massage but for the administrative, marketing and other requirements needed to run the day to day operations of the business? List any limits you have or gaps in knowledge that you need to address.

____

____

____

____

____

Will you work independently, hire employees or independent contractors? Do you understand the legal and financial pro's and con's for each option?

Do you enjoy the business side of massage therapy or running a massage practice or do you just like to focus on performing the massage itself?

Are you able to tolerate, or do you enjoy, a higher level of risk with the potential for higher levels of profit or do you prefer a steady and more predictable situation?

Do you have vision and zeal to inspire others – and yourself – especially when things go wrong or do you have a tendency to get flustered or give up?

Are you willing to initially make significant trade-off's and invest more time and money today for greater potential returns later?

Are you able to handle confrontation and risk (unreliable clients, inability to achieve time or budget estimates, under estimating the magnitude of a problem, personality problems among employees or hired help)?

Are you willing and able to remain in the current location for long enough to make it worthwhile to build a business of your own?

Are you able continually learn, enjoy a challenge and have a drive to achieve? Where will you continue to obtain knowledge and information related to your business?

Are you self motivated? How do you handle discouragement, rejection & risk?

Leadership – A Disclaimer

A lot has been written about leadership and a lot could be written here that will not be. That is because of a very strong personal philosophy so let me get the disclaimer out of the way.

The topic of leadership is one of those areas which I believe to be filled with nonsense – or worse – harmful advice and opinions. What most often passes under the guise of leadership is much more about making money, exerting control, usurping power, dominating those without a voice or pure outright manipulation.

I believe there is only one type of true leadership; that of the servant leader. No, it's not a popular idea although some of the greatest leaders in history have dedicated their lives to this concept. It requires dedication and discipline of self rather than others. It's not always the most profitable although it inspires dedication and loyalty while making the world a better, kinder place.

My hope is that anyone who is reading this will contemplate on the calling of the servant leader in your own capacity of leadership.

How Do You Rank as a Leader? - Worksheet

For each of the following attributes, honestly rank your ability as either strong, average or weak. Any weak areas should be addressed via training or practice.

Problem solving	Strong	Average	Weak
Communication	Strong	Average	Weak
Interpersonal Relationships	Strong	Average	Weak
Planning	Strong	Average	Weak
Decision Making	Strong	Average	Weak
Conflict Management	Strong	Average	Weak
People Management	Strong	Average	Weak
Scheduling and Organization	Strong	Average	Weak
Negotiating	Strong	Average	Weak
Vision and Influence	Strong	Average	Weak
Teamwork	Strong	Average	Weak
Helping & Coaching/Mentoring	Strong	Average	Weak

**Could This Be YOU
Or Your Next Manager?**

**Leadership Secrets of Hitler and
other Tyrannical Maniacs
Aka…
How to Be a Leader
Not a Tyrant!**

WANTED: Leader

[NOTE-Below is Taken from Actual Leadership Position Discussion]

Must be analytical and skilled in problem-solving and decision making, must have both vision and organizational awareness. Must have the energy, determination, frustration tolerance, and tough-mindedness to bring the two into conformance, resolve problems, and mediate conflicts. Must be skilled communicator able to articulate the organization's goals and objectives and send clear signals about what must be done.

Passion - Must demonstrate passion for a cause that is larger then yourself and ability to rally others to join in making that dream a reality.

Vision – Must be able to give direction to, and breathe life into, a passionate dream. Will answer the question, what is versus what *can* be?

Creativity - Must be able to think outside the box and not afraid to try new solutions.

Intellectual Drive and Knowledge - Must be a perpetual student willing to read, learn, and get ideas from others.

Confidence - Communicate confidence that your vision is correct

Communicator – Must be able to speak, write effectively and encourage others to follow.

Introduction to Leadership

A recent study by two Gallup organization researchers, Marcus Buckingham and Curt Coffman, concluded managers are the single most significant influence of the morale of employees. Simply stated, happy employees are more productive and stable. If the single most important factor of employee satisfaction is the relationship with their immediate supervisor, then what leadership characteristics are deemed most important?

When asked to define "leadership", most people respond with a list of attributes related to motivation, inspiration, ability to communicate and more; but taken alone these same attributes can be harnessed to produce a tyrannical manipulator rather than a stellar leader as in the Hitler example of a job applicant response. How does a business owner differentiate between a true leader versus a manipulative nightmare? One differentiator centers around the concept of Servant Leader.

What is a Servant Leader?

According to Robert Greenleaf, the "father" of servant leadership; "Servant-Leadership is a practical philosophy which supports people who choose to serve first, and then lead as a way of expanding service to individuals and institutions. Servant-leaders may or may not hold formal leadership positions. Servant-leadership encourages collaboration, trust, foresight, listening, and the ethical use of power and empowerment."

One of the critical differentiators between a servant leader and others is a "calling" or willingness to serve. Servant leaders have a desire to make a difference in the lives of others and will often cite examples of their responsibility to humanity or those they work with rather than vice versa. Servant leaders define leadership as a mandate for service rather than a position of authority. It is the orientation difference between "What do I give?" versus "What do I get?".

Based upon the works of Robert Greenleaf, the "father" of the Servant Leader movement; Barbuto and Wheeler developed the following checklist describing the attributes of the servant leader.

Servant Leader Checklist

1. Do people believe you are willing to sacrifice your own self-interest for the good of the group?
2. Do people believe you want to hear their ideas and will value them?
3. Do people believe you will understand what is happening in their lives and how it affects them?
4. Do people come to you when something traumatic has happened in their lives?
5. Do others believe you have a strong awareness for what is going on?
6. Do others follow your requests because they want to as opposed to because they "have to"?
7. Do others communicate their ideas and vision for the organization when you are around?
8. Do others have confidence in your ability to anticipate the future and it's consequences?
9. Do others believe you are preparing the organization to make a positive difference in the world?
10. Do people believe you are committed to helping them develop?
11. Do people feel a strong sense of community in the organization you lead?

In Their Own Words Comparisons Between Servant Leaders and Tyrants

We can do no great things - only small things with great love." - Mother Theresa

The [Nazi party] should not become a constable of public opinion, but must dominate it. It must not become a servant of the masses, but their master!
- Adolf Hitler

"Any alliance whose purpose is not the intention to wage war is senseless and useless" - Adolf Hitler, "Mein Kampf"

"How fortunate for leaders that men do not think." - Adolf Hitler

"To be a leader means to be able to move masses" - Adolf Hitler

"Whatever goal, man has reached is due to his originality plus his brutality" - Adolf Hitler

"We will not capitulate - no, never! We may be destroyed, but if we are, we shall drag a world with us - a world in flames." - Adolf Hitler

The broad masses of a population are more amenable to the appeal of rhetoric than to any other force." - Adolph Hitler

"The mass, whether it be a crowd or an army, is vile"~ Benito Mussolini
A lie told often enough becomes the truth. Vladimir Ilyich Lenin

I must follow the people. Am I not their leader?~ Benjamin Disraeli

Coercion cannot but result in chaos in the end. One who uses coercion is guilty of deliberate violence. Coercion is inhuman. The more efficient a force is the more silent and the more subtle it is. Be the change you want to see in the world. --Mahatma Gandhi

Above all, leadership is a position of servanthood. Max Deere

People are supposed to serve. Life is a mission, not a career. Stephen R. Covey, The Leader of the Future

Ultimately the choice we make is between service and self-interest. Peter Block, Stewardship, Choosing Service over Self-Interest

Everyone who exalts himself will be humbled, and he who humbles himself will be exalted. JESUS, Luke 14:11

Those who don't know how to weep with their whole heart, don't know how to laugh either. -Golda Meir.

The leader of genius must have the ability to make different opponents appear as if they belonged to one category."
- Adolph Hitler

Individual Knowledge Gaps

By now you may feel a bit overwhelmed especially if you are considering your very first business. Don't worry! Everyone has felt that way at one time or another. It's simply a learning experience that becomes easier as you actually do it. The important part is to understand what to expect, know yourself including your strengths and areas in need of improvement and then determine the best ways to fill in the gaps of information and knowledge you still need to acquire.

And speaking of knowledge gaps, everyone has them but like the old cliché' goes; you don't always know what you don't know. The important thing is to identify what you don't know and then figure out how to obtain that information.

Our next step is to begin doing just that.

The following criteria are considered universally important to any small business owner so answer each honestly. For each item rank you level of experience and knowledge from 1 to 5 with 1 = None and 5 = Very Experienced/Knowledgeable.

Any areas below a three require immediate attention. Items ranked at three should be reviewed and put into practice while those ranked four or above indicate a readiness and valuable personal asset at your disposal to grow your business.

Don't worry if you have low rankings. By the time you finish reading this book you will have a great deal more information! It's more important for you to properly identify your weak areas in advance of making costly mistakes.

Individual Knowledge Gap Assessment Worksheet

Market Research: finding and interpreting your local market and competitors.
1 2 3 4 5

Market Planning: planning sales, advertising and promotions.
1 2 3 4 5

Product Pricing: determining pricing methods, break-even analysis and positioning
1 2 3 4 5

Customer Service: determining customer needs and motivations, phone and personal communications, problem solving.
1 2 3 4 5

Operations management: managing schedules, setting up office procedures etc…
1 2 3 4 5

Cost analysis and control: calculating actual cost of doing business, controlling costs and increasing profitability.
1 2 3 4 5

Basic accounting and book-keeping: preparing profit and low statements, paying taxes and other money related measures for a business.
1 2 3 4 5

Small business legal concerns: selecting name of business, how the structure of a business impacts profit and earnings, hiring help, hiring employees.
1 2 3 4 5

Taxes: understanding federal and state reporting requirements as related to your business structure and type.
1 2 3 4 5

Real Estate: understanding rental and lease agreements, zoning and use permits and the purchase or sale of real estate.
1 2 3 4 5

Taking the Plunge

Some people make decisions based on intuition, others on analysis and still others on pure whim. For the massage therapist it is often a combination of all of these combined with a passion for working with people in an environment and setting they enjoy. In fact, before creating the Perfect Practice, it's important to make sure the new enterprise is a good fit with three critical business factors: personal values, individual goals and available resources. We will revisit each of these throughout this planning guide so I encourage you to take the time to work through each of these exercises and activities.

Values are those things you consider important in life. Examples of business might be to work with a specific medical need or serve a specific population. Perhaps it is to develop long-term client relationships and become an integral source of support in your local community. Values are as individualized as the person who owns them. It's important to know and understand your values and then determine if your business reflects them.

Goals are what you want to achieve with your new business. Goals should be stated in specific, measurable and achievable terms. For example: We/I want to earn an extra $35,000 a year from my massage business within the next two years by working an average of 25 billable hours per week.

Resources include personal resources (skills and abilities), financial resources and other resources such as land, inventory and equipment. Although we don't like to speak of it in these terms, people also can be valuable resources. Finding a mentor is a wonderful method to bounce ideas, get feedback, obtain advice. Being a mentor is equally compelling as it forces you to get creative, truly understand and contemplate on your methods, learn how to effectively communicate these ideas and even stretches your own comprehension in the process. Consider volunteering or finding a mentor at the MassagePracticePlanner.com website!

In the next step we will consider how you go about the actual decision-making process. It is indeed an actual process and by using this method, you can later compare and contrast when it is time to make a change or grow. You will literally be able to use it to standardize evaluation criteria and compare "apples to apples"

The Decision-Making Framework Worksheet

Define Your Problem

What are you trying to accomplish? Be specific! Is it to increase income? Gain greater independence? Reduce your workload? Create a more self fulfilling environment? Start a brand new business? Get clients right after graduation? Whatever it is, define your problem as precisely as possible.

____

____

____

____

____

Explore Your Options

Think about all the different ways your business could change. Is the alternative you're considering the best one to solve the problem you've identified? List the Pro's and Con's associated with each option.

Pro's

____

____

____

____

____

Con's

____

____

____

____

____

Review your Alternatives

Review your options. How will each option impact your existing operation? Consider how well the option solves your problem or achieves long-term business goals. Is there another way to look at business goals?

What are your options?

____

____

____

____

____

Select the Best Alternative

A decision-making checklist is a particularly useful took when you need to choose between two or more alternatives. Below are two different methods that help you to rate and rank what is important to you. For example, Sal wants his accomplish the following things:
1. Increase the family living income so his wife can stay at home with their first child.
2. Use his natural talent and inclination to work with people in pain
3. Provide an atmosphere that he enjoys
4. Increase his long term passive income
5. Not expose the growing family to high level of long term risk
6. Spent time with his wife and growing family

Sal is trying to decide between starting his own practice on the outskirts of town that is just a few minutes from home or taking a position with a Chiropractic office in town. The Chiropractic office would not allow Sal and his wife to visit or have lunch during the day and although he would still be working with people in pain, Sal really has a special enjoyment for a variety of pain relief settings including those outside of just Chiropractic care.

Sal and his wife have put their criteria into a chart like the one below to rank their decision on a scale between 1 and 10 with 1 = low and 10 = high agreement. They decided each criteria was of equal weighting to their decision.

	Personal Practice	Chiropractic Office
Increase family living income	5	6
Utilize personal skills	8	6
Good return from time involvement	5	8
Utilize resources	8	3
Increase time together	8	3
Reduce risk	3	8
Total	37	34

This decision-making framework helped Sal and his wife objectively look at their decision making process from a different perspective. But, what happens if some things matter more to you than others? In the above example, all of these criteria were given equal weight or importance. Of course, that is rarely the case in real life because some things are more important than others at different times during our life.

What happens if you are not even sure what is most important? Here is a quick way to evaluate and prioritize your needs and goals. First, make a list of ALL the criteria to be used...everything that you would like to have in a perfect practice. It doesn't need to be in order...just write it all down.

1. ______________________________
2. ______________________________
3. ______________________________
4. ______________________________
5. ______________________________
6. ______________________________
7. ______________________________
8. ______________________________
9. ______________________________
10. ______________________________

Great! Now, if you had to choose between #1 and #2 which would you choose? 1 or 2 [circle your answer]. Between #3 and #4? #5 or #6? And so forth. Once you are done choose between each of your prior selections until you have reached a priority list.

Chapter 6

Take Action

There comes a time when you have to make the decision to take the plunge or not. If your research, ratings and analysis have helped you clearly see how the business might look and run after your decision is implemented, the image of your new business can energize your entire team. It is at this stage you should begin putting together more formal descriptions and plans of action that will provide a foundation for internal communication. If you've done the market research and financial analysis, you are able to proceed with confidence.

To put your decision to proceed into action there are several activities you need to do. Develop an implementation plan, including a development timetable, pricing and schedules, marketing plan, management or business structure and a financial plan.

Evaluate

You need a process to monitor the effectiveness of your decision. For example, Sal and his wife need to identify the impact the decision to open his own practice will have on their family living income, their time together and themselves due to the risk they've taken on.

Accept Responsibility

You and your business team must be prepared to accept the consequences of your decision. If the business works out, celebrate your success. If the business doesn't work out, analyze why and learn from your mistakes.

If you decide not to proceed with your business idea, don't be discouraged. It's better to find out that your business idea has some weaknesses before you invest a lot of time, energy and money.

Be Realistic!

At times, assumptions you make in calculating business activities could be wrong due to changes or events outside of your control. Changes happen at critical times – sometimes for the good and sometimes for the bad so it's always wise to "expect" the unexpected! Even the best plans require 'tweaking' or refining in response the the changing economy, local business structure and individual situation. As you grown your business you will have better information about your specific location, clients, skills and abilities!

Prepare a Business Development Time Line

Once you have made the decision to move forward there are a lot of steps you will need to take in order to make your business a reality.

You will need to select a name, establish what type of legal structure you will operate the company under such as Sole Proprietor, S Corporation, C Corporation, LLC or other forms.

Confirm local, state and nationwide certifications, licensure requirements, zoning restrictions, permits, business licenses, insurance and much more. There are a multitude of books available on establishing a business structure and setting up these requirements. If you are new or just establishing your practice, then by all means, select several of the more well known ones and read up on them carefully. However, that is not the intention of this book.

If you are considering incorporating your business either as a C- corporation, S-Corporation or other related then two books that I found to be valuable, easy to read resources that outline both the good and bad for each decision include:

Inc. Yourself: How to Profit by Setting up Your Own Corporation (Inc Yourself) by Judith H. McQuown ISBN-13: 978-1564147417

Nolo's Legal Guides to Incorporating, LLC's or other by Anthony Mancuso

Both of the above resources are excellent overviews of what is involved and whether or not the decision is the right one for you at this stage of your practice. Particularly for established practitioners, this may be the next stage of your growth but it is not a decision to be made lightly.

Your Business Timeline Checklist

Use this as a starting point to create your own timeline. Be sure to establish dates based upon your personal goals. Example dates are provided but easily changed to match your individual situation.

Set up a file for yourself to keep forms, copies of submissions, important contact information and duplicates of important information for your own use. As you complete each item on the list be sure to mark it off the list.

_____ **MONTHS PRIOR TO START-UP**

_____ Choose a business based on your skills and interests.

_____ Choose business name, verify right to use name, register the name.

_____ Determine time required to obtain business permits: ask about fee's.

_____ Research the feasibility of forming different business types, your market etc

_____ Identify helpful business related membership organizations (e.g. Chamber of Commerce, Builders Association, etc.) in your local area.

_____ Visit with –or select if you don't have a relationship – professional advice such as attorneys, bankers, CPA's, consultants, competition.

_____ Check out community amenities (real estate, schools, etc.) that may prove helpful.

_____ Subscribe to local papers, magazines or other information.

_____ Decide on business location

_____ Obtain licenses (city, county, state, industry)

_____ Prepare preliminary business plan and budget.

_____ Interview bankers

_____ Determine when phone book is printed

_____ Months

_____ Complete business plan including marketing plan.

_____ Decide on form of business organization (sole proprietor, corporation, LLC, etc.) and file papers.

_____ Select Board of Directors for corporation.

_____ Prepare advertisements

_____ Prepare final budget and review with banker. Order business systems: receivables check disbursements, payroll system.

_____Order sign for office

1-2 MONTHS PRIOR TO START-UP

_____ Check utility requirements.

_____ Prepare leasehold improvement plan for any changes you will need to make

_____ Determine office layout and design

_____ Review leases and contracts with attorney and advisors

_____ Open business bank accounts

. _____ Order business cards

0-4 MONTHS PRIOR TO START-UP

_____ Make sure business filings and license applications are complete and confirmed!

_____ Arrange for insurance (business and health).

_____ Arrange for telephone service installation.

______ Open business checking accounts

______ Sign up for credit card systems at local bank.

______ Arrange for business announcement ads in local papers.

______ Order announcements for office opening

______ Arrange to give talks to community groups.

______ Obtain Federal Employment ID number

______ Apply for state ID number.

______ Find out about workers' compensation if you will have employees.

______ Apply for seller's permit if you will sell merchandise

______ Contact state for tax forms and employer's requirements

______ Obtain payroll withholding booklets from tax authorities

______ Review tax requirements with your accountant

______ Arrange for janitorial service, waste removal, laundry service, grass mowing.

______ Order supplies: appointment cards, business cards, stationery, deposit stamp for checks, telephone message pads.

______ Determine business hours

______ Determine pricing schedule.

______ Order print materials (price lists, brochures, receipt forms, etc.).

______ Purchase office equipment and furniture, computers, software etc

______ Start setting up office.

______ Schedule utilities to be turned on

_____ Establish petty cash fund.

_____ Prepare press release and begin advertisement.

_____ Mail announcement

_____ Plan an open house.

_____ Call everyone you know and let them know you are in business.

Business Plans

A business plan helps you formalize the thinking and planning process. Writing a plan helps you systematically think through the steps involved in your business development. By completing a business plan you better understand the markets, costs and competitive factors that influence the future of your business. A well thought out plan gives you increased confidence and better prepares you to obtain necessary financing and resources. Think of a business plan as a working document, one that changes, expands and shifts with the times.

There are times when a formal business plan is a requirement. If you need a loan from a financial institution, you'll likely be asked for a business plan. Depending on your situation and your business idea, you may not need to include all the information, but the questions are all worth considering. The following represent the essential information contained in most business plans:

Your Business Plan Outline Checklist

Executive Summary

Include a few sentences on each of the following:

- Business goals
- Critical success factors
- Services
- The market and industry
- Staff skills
- Financial position and performance (current and projected)

The Business

- What are the business goals?
- What are your past achievements and strengths?
- What are your past problems and current weaknesses?

Services

- What is the planned productivity output and sales mix for your practice?
- For each product or service, what is the cost and profit?
- Who are your clients?
- How up to date are your skills, products or services?
- Areas of specialization, differentiations or other notable information?

Market Analysis

- What is your target market?
- Who are your competitors and what is their market size, market share, competitive strengths and weaknesses, and prospects?
- Who are your customers and what are their product/service preferences and reasons for purchasing?
- What are your sales and profits by market segment?
- What is your current and projected market share?

Marketing Strategy

- What customer groups will your business target?
- To generate sales, what product or service attributes will you emphasize?
- What location advantage and disadvantages do you have?
- What distribution channels will your business use?

Potential Risk and Pitfalls

- What, if any, critical risk does your business face and how can you minimize the potential risk?
- What problems may hinder or prevent implementation of your business plan?

Financial

- How much do you need to make personally?
- What does the business need to generate to “break even”?
- How will you price your services?
- Is it better to rent or buy your office?
- How much can you generate from item sales?
- What is the potential earnings for practice?

15 Steps to Business Success:

1. Choose the areas of specialization and environment you love.
2. Create a perception of high quality and superb service.
3. Start small and grow naturally but methodically.
4. Make decisions based on good records, analysis and good business.
5. Give your customers what they want.
6. Establish a loyal customer base.
7. Provide more than service. Provide an experience.
8. Get the community involved.
9. Stay informed.
10. Never stop learning.
11. Never stop growing.
12. Plan for the future.
13. Set goals for your business.
14. Establish a plan of action to achieve your goals.
15. Give back.

George Bernard Shaw said, "Two percent of the people think, two percent think they think, and everyone else would rather die."

Start Up Financial Checklist:

Assets

Current Assets

Cash & Equivalents

Accounts Receivable

Inventory

Security Deposits

Other Current Assets

Total Current Assets

Fixed Assets

Property, Plant & Equipment

Computer Equipment

Equipment/Machinery

Furniture & Fixtures

Vehicles

Leasehold Improvements

Building

Land

Less: Accumulated Depreciation (Do not enter a negative number)

Other Non-current Assets

Total Non-current Assets

Total Assets

Liabilities

Current Liabilities

Accounts Payable

Line of Credit

Other Current Liabilities

Total Current Liabilities

Long-term Liabilities

Loans

Real Estate Loans

Other Non-current Liabilities

Total Long-term Liabilities

Total Liabilities

Start-up Expenditures

Security Deposits

Rent (last month's)
Telephone Deposit
Utilities Deposit
Other Deposits

Total Security Deposits

Start-up Expenses

Accounting Fees
Activation Fee
Corporate Fees & Taxes
Federal Tax ID
Fictitious Name Costs
Insurance
Legal & Consulting Fees
Meals & Entertainment
Office Supplies
Payroll Expenses (training/setup)
  Salaries & Wages
  Payroll Taxes
  Benefits
Pre-opening advertising
Printing (cards, stationery, brochures)
Sales Tax Permit
Other Start-up Expenses

Total Start-up Expenses

Other Costs

Opening Inventory

Capital Expenditures

Computer Equipment
Equipment/Machinery
Furniture & Fixtures

Vehicles
Leasehold Improvements
Buildings
Land
Total Start-up Capital Expenditures

Total Start-up Expenditures

Operating Expenses:

Operating Expenses
- Advertising
- Bank Charges
- Dues & Subscriptions
- Insurance
- Licenses & Fees
- Marketing & Promotion
- Meals & Entertainment
- Miscellaneous
- Office Expense (postage)
- Office Supplies
- Outside Services
- Payroll Expenses
  - Salaries & Wages
  - Payroll Taxes
  - Benefits
- Professional Fees
- Property Taxes
- Rent
- Repairs & Maintenance
- Shipping & Delivery
- Telephone
- Training & Development
- Travel
- Utilities
- Vehicle
- Other
- Other

TIP

Use the New Business License data for your county and state to find New Business Referral leads for your practice!

Excellent sources include new real estate brokers and sales persons, new beauty salons and spas, new health clubs, new dry cleaners and many others!

For more great information, tips and ideas like these sign up for Massage Marketing Planner

Chapter 7

Show Me the Money or Crazy Profit Potential

Before going further let's take a little time to explore the potential of Massage as a Business. Is it profitable? Can it be more profitable? Is there a difference between working as a Massage Therapist and being a small business owner of a Massage Practice? Yes, at last potentially, to all of the above. To provide a quick glance of the profit and pitfalls, hypothetical situations drawn from deliberately simply scenarios will be used.

Let's begin by creating the Perfect Profit Storm to show the "upper limit" of what type of revenue could be generated from a Massage Practice. I'd like to do this for several reasons...first, to set the stage for what is possible!

That's important – notice, I did NOT say what is Probable but rather what is Possible. What is probable is that which happens most often. What is possible does not happen often but it DOES Happen!! What is possible may not even be what is most desirable since it may require more sacrifice, risk or other life style changes than what you want to make however, those are choices that You can actually Make once you know and understand the full potential! This is such an important point that I want you to really read through this while examining your own expectations.

But before we begin it's important to set the stage. First, Your actual potential could be much higher or lower than another persons due to your location, assets, personal characteristics like determination and motivation and a host of other reasons. It's important to understand that many things we would usually consider obstacles are rarely obstacles. For example, people will often cite a lack of money as a major obstacle. Now to be sure, it's certainly a challenge but many people have started a business with very little to nearly no money whatsoever. In fact, some think it is an asset in the long run because it teaches you how to be conservative with your money and make good business and financial decisions. So let's begin by evaluating your individual earning expectations.

Your Earnings Expectations Worksheet

Take a few minutes for self examination and contemplation of the following questions:

Lowest Hourly Wage Ever Earned: ______________________________

Doing what job or project? ______________________________

Was it enjoyable? Why or Why Not?

____

____

____

Highest Hourly Wage Ever Earned: ______________________________

Doing what job or project? ______________________________

Was it enjoyable? Why or Why Not?

____

____

____

What is your idea of a "Good" income?
Hourly: _________ or Annually: ________

What is your idea of an "Acceptable" income?
Hourly: _________ or Annually: ________

How close or far is your current or best income from the acceptable or good income?

____

____

____

Rigid Thinking Versus Right Thinking

Mind Games

Ahhh, mind games. Head trips. Self defeating attitudes. If we are honest with ourselves then sooner or later most of us come to realize we have engaged in this type of negative, restrictive thinking.

I'll use personal experience as an example on this one. I enjoy running/jogging but it wasn't always that way. In fact, for most of my life I have been noticeably clumsy and anything but athletic. Worse, because I was blessed with an active metabolism when younger, I remained naturally thin which only worked to hide the fact that I was a "couch potato" of the highest order!

This trend continued until a few years ago when I decided to begin walking each day and then eventually jogging. Now, I'd like to tell you it came easily but nothing was further from the truth. In fact, my husband commented I sounded like a "heard of buffalo" coming around the bend! I was so lead footed people would stop and ask if I needed help ("No, I'm doing great!" just didn't seem to reassure them) and so slow that I was routinely passed by an elderly retired gentleman who jogged at about the same time of day, children, pregnant women and even people walking!

Still, I kept with it and eventually hit my "one mile" goal. At that stage my "ambition" was to reach the 5k marker or just over 3 miles. Mentally, reaching that first mile was the absolute hardest for me though. Yes, one entire mile without stopping. It took me six months of going to the park each and every day to reach that goal. Now, it's true that I had to build up to it and had a host of other valid "reasons' but it was also due in part to a lifelong negative self talk that I was "not a runner", I was "not athletic". In fact, I "hated running".

Then one day, very shortly after running the first mile, the weather was just right and I felt strong, happy and content. I realized I loved – not just liked but literally loved running! Perhaps I wasn't the fastest and maybe I wasn't even the most graceful athlete to ever live but all of a sudden I understood that I had the heart of a runner. I longed for it. I missed it. I was proud of it. I would sacrifice other pleasures to run better. Indeed, I had become a runner.

I made one other change about that time. Every time I came close to reaching my pre-determined destination or goal for the day, I found myself struggling. Of course, this type of self fulfilling prophecy will never do so I decided to tell myself "one more lap" every time I began to think of quitting. I rapidly reached three miles without stopping – far ahead of my personal schedule and then ten miles and so forth.

By that point I knew my mind was either my best friend or worst enemy. The knowledge alone can go a long way toward identifying and defeating these types of mind games or defeatist thinking and so my research about exceptional runners began in earnest.

The knowledge and understanding of those who face – and overcome – tremendous challenges and obstacles demonstrates with irrefutable facts, the true Potential that I personally possess. I came across a senior citizen with a heart transplant who was running marathons, people who had amputations, those with debilitating chronic diseases and so much more. They were a tremendous inspiration and what is more – they provided the Proof that it Could be Done.

If They Could Do It then I Could Do It

That is the Power of the Possible

If Anyone Can Do It then Why Not YOU?

It sets our expectations not on ourselves or our prior history or expectations but rather on that which is possible.

The Possible and the Probable

Don't confuse what is possible with what is probable. What is possible requires preparation but also a multitude of other factors which may or may not be completely under your control at any given time. However, it does show you the potential and allows you to strive toward that goal, take advantage of situations that may arise and make conscientious decisions about the destination and desirability of your plan of action.

Does it Matter?

Not all outcomes are equally desirable. Sometimes what is desirable today may not be so tomorrow. People change. Circumstances change. Goals change. The ability to dictate your own life in accordance with those changes is a special freedom.

In my own life I have gone through several stages. I worked my way through college and like many people at that stage of life, found it challenging to secure a flexible schedule that paid the bills. I remember standing in front of a job bulletin board thinking I'd be happy to make $10 an hour (without benefits and part-time) if I could just work it into my class schedule. A couple years later I was actually thrilled to finally break the $30,000 level – with benefits- which had seemed rather elusive at the time.

I bring this up for a reason. During that same period I remember speaking with someone who had previously earned a six-figure income and wondering why they would give it up to make ¼ of their former salary. Even more revealing, I remember wondering why they seemed so down to earth having made "so much money". A six-figure income wasn't on my scope during those days...not even near it!

As I continued toward my first Masters degree and then Ph.D, my student loans steadily increased as did my other bills until I was forced to "figure out" money. My goal became to fix my personal financial situation and increase my earnings. I still didn't have any real figures in mind but I knew I wanted to be out of debt and the faster the better. I worked – a Lot, took zero vacations and landed in a position that allowed me to grow personally and professionally as fast as I was able and desired. I soon realized how little a six-figure income really can be but even more importantly, I realized why it's not always desirable.

I was working non-stop. I had been promoted into a toxic environment that was aggressive, non supportive of family life or individual goals. I was barely able to maintain a personal life and no longer worked in the areas that I found rewarding. I had discovered I enjoyed the business side of my work tremendously and decided to return to pursue a Masters in Business degree along with the return of some of those things I enjoyed most such as teaching, writing and consulting while pursuing hobbies and other projects. I was simply ready for a new stage of life and fortunately, was able to make that transition.

In much the same way, your goals may have a financial focus today or maybe you are seeking to spend more time with your family. You may be preparing for retirement in a few years or wanting to provide for a college fund. Whatever your needs, desire and goals they are worth the time and effort to understand, put to voice and work toward.

Lessons Learned from Others

We've already mentioned how our minds and personal expectations can influence our perception of what is possible but because that trend is so strong, I'd like to draw your attention to a few facts from other fields and disciplines in much the same way that my personal horizons were expanded from the research and study of others.

Let's begin by examining salary data for other professions that tend to work in a practice situation.

Chiropractors: The U.S. Bureau of Labor Statistics estimates the Median annual earnings of salaried chiropractors to be $69,910. The middle 50 percent earned between $46,710 to $118,280 a year which is a wide range but still represents the middle range. Some chiropractors make less and some make much more. What is the difference between a Chiropractor that earns $40,000 a year versus one that earn $240,000 a year?

Lawyers: In May 2004, the median annual earnings of all lawyers were $94,930. The middle half of the occupation earned between $64,620 and $143,620. Again, that is a large variation and some lawyers make much less while others can earn in excess of a million dollars per year. What is the difference between a lawyer that earns $50,000 annually versus one that earns $500,000 annually?

Veterinarians: Median annual earnings of veterinarians were $66,590 in May 2004. The middle 50 percent earned between $51,420 and $88,060. The lowest 10 percent earned less than $39,020, and the highest 10 percent earned more than $118,430 with some far in excess of that amount. What is the difference between a Vet who earns $40,000 a year versus one who earns a $140,000 per year?

So, What is Possible?

Of course there isn't one answer nor is there actually a limit to the potential of a massage practice. Yes, an individual massage therapist may have very real limits based upon their time, energy and availability but a massage practice can earn income for the owner even when they are not performing any sessions. This is the very real long term benefit to be derived from a properly planned practice. In fact, the practice may continue to generate revenue for the owner long after they sell the business depending upon the specifics. Keep in mind, this is a "Perfect Profit Storm" and therefore everything is "optimized" however, still within the realm of potential.

Not necessarily probable but certainly possible and in fact, these numbers are of a similar order – appropriately scaled for massage – as generated by successful practice owners in various related areas. Remember, this activity is to show you what is Possible and break the mental habit of poverty, settling for less, and other mind games we play with ourselves. For the sake of simplicity, let's just go through a Perfect Profit Storm scenario.

Perfect Profit Storm

In this situation I'll use Joy and Lucky as our theoretical practice owners. They are a husband and wife team who act as a partnership for business purposes. Joy and Lucky began like most practitioners by working as Independent Contractors for others when first leaving school. After a short period of time it was obvious that each enjoyed medical massage so with that in mind, they began to search for a location to build their own practice.

Joy and Lucky searched for over a year until they found the perfect location in a growing but relatively stable area near a well known anchor store and with several complimentary business providers nearby. It's an older home that can be converted to the needed office space and sits directly across the street from a major shopping plaza and adjacent to a bank. Since Joy and Lucky are well established in their hometown and plan to remain in the area permanently, they decided to purchase the location and remodel the business. This option took a much larger amount of up-front cash but it assures their mortgage payments remain fixed while building equity in the real estate. Due to their location and the decision to offer a host of amenities to both clients and other therapists, they calculate $100,000 to cover all business expenses including the mortgage, taxes, insurance, utilities and all other business related needs. They use several part-time receptionists obtained via an employment agency and have laundry, cleaning and yard maintenance services which add an additional $65,000 annually for a combined total of $165,000. They opt to purchase equipment including computers, treatment tables, reception area furniture and so forth at a discount by shopping at eBay, used furniture, Craigslist and local classified advertisements. They shop carefully and pay cash for everything.

Keep in mind, unlike an individual who needs down time, vacation time, time for administrative and other items, rooms and machines don't. They can be used and generating an income as long as there is someone to make use of them!

Joy and Lucky have enough space for a reception area, three treatment rooms, one storage area and either one large or two small self service areas. It is fully furnished with all amenities provided. Joy and Lucky decide to rent rooms by availability which means rooms rotate constantly based upon availability throughout the day. By doing this, they are able to maximize the amount of contact hours and keep rates lower for other therapists. They are also able to rent to numerous therapists based upon blocks of time while still maintaining plenty of availability for their own use. Room rentals are available from 6 AM to 10 PM daily for the entire seven days per week or 16 hrs per day x 7 days per week or roughly 112 hours per week x 50 weeks for a total of 5600 hours annually. Occupancy is roughly 75% due to holidays and roughly 10 minutes between each session for a total of 4,200 annual hours for each room x three available rooms for a grand total of 12,600 minus their own billable hours of roughly 1,000 hours each (2,000 total) leaving just over 12,000 hours annually that is rented to other therapists.

Because some hours are more "in demand" than others, and because Joy and Lucky provide all equipment, yellow page advertising, monthly promotions and more, they charge a variable rate by the desired time with hourly averages ranging from a low of $10 per hour to $20 per hour with an average of $15 per hour. At 12,000 session hours annually x $15 average the room rate rental generates $180,000 annually while providing a very real benefit to other therapists who only pay for what they actually need and use. Since the average therapist provides approximately 15 to 20 sessions per week their cost is only $150 to $350 per week which includes all utilities, yellow pages, laundry and more. However, therapists are all Independent Contractors and responsible for actually marketing and building their own client list, keeping their own books and so forth.

Total generated from room rental rates: $180,000 annually with a 25% vacancy rate and two weeks downtime per room minus their own use of rooms.

Joy and Lucky also still perform approximately 1,000 sessions each (20 per week x 50 weeks annually) throughout the year at an average of $60 per session for a combined total of $120,000.

Joy and Lucky invested in "self service" massage, roller massage and hydro-massage beds for their clients to stop in throughout the week. These can be scheduled in short 15 minute increments and correspond to the weekly grocery shopping or other errands in close proximity. These are also available free to members of the wellness plan but paid self service items are used at approximately 10 hours per week per item for a total of 30 hours per week (30 hours paid per week x 60 minutes in an hour = 1,800 minutes) at an average cost of .50 cents per minute or $900 per week x an average of 50 weeks annually or $45,000.

Joy and Lucky carefully selected merchandising that is on display in the reception area and throughout the treatment rooms. In fact, everything including the ergonomic chairs in the reception area, the music in each area, lotions, art, calendars and everything else is a "Try Before You Buy" item and available for sale or order at the front desk. No hard pressure or sales tactics are ever used. Instead, a simple information card or description is provided with encouragement for people to interact with the items. If they like the item, they can purchase it when checking out (or order it for large items such as the chairs). They also provide a wellness club membership and other service related sales in this amount. Because Joy and Lucky were very selective and took time to build a unique set of merchandising offers, and because the traffic generated by so many therapists and near constant use of rooms; the merchandising ads roughly 15% to their gross revenue each year or nearly $50,000.

Joy and Lucky are active in many groups across town and actively pursue corporate wellness contracts with the use of chair massage. They keep a half dozen additional tables and chairs in the storage room and offer practitioners a chance to earn additional income by splitting the fee's of providing services to the corporate wellness clients. Because each corporate wellness entity is individually negotiated, Joy and Lucky assure the practitioner will receive no less then $25 to $35 per hour while they retain the remainder. It's a win-win situation as many new practitioners appreciate the additional income potential and it provides a wonderful way for them to meet potential new clients in order to grow their own client list. Joy and Lucky continue to benefit since they derive a steady income, increased visibility for the practice and goodwill among the community without performing any additional sessions in person. This is an area they would like to continue to expand but it generates approximately $1,000 a month or $12,000 annually.

Let's tally this up and see where Joy and Lucky stand for the year.

Room Rental Rates:	$180,000
Personal Session Incomes:	$120,000
Self Service Sessions:	$45,000
Merchandising Sales:	$50,000
Corporate:	$12,000
Total:	$407,000
Minus Expenses:	- $165,000
Total After Expenses:	$242,000

Notice, even if Joy and Lucky both stop working they still would generate over $120,000 annually After paying all of their expenses! In fact, without the two of them working, there would be more room rates so they would actually generate more than $120,000 because they would be able to rent the space they normally require for their own sessions.

However, it doesn't stop there! Joy and Lucky are building equity in both the business and the actual real estate. Once the building is paid in full, their expenses will actually go down further increasing their earnings even without working. Even after retirement, Joy and Lucky could continue to own and operate this business with very little time required yet retain a significant income well into their old age. In fact, the business represents a very real asset to their heirs even after they pass away!

But even if they decided to sell the business, then they would still have options. They could sell the business with or without the real estate. If they sold just the business, they can then literally turn around and rent or lease the real estate including the building and land it sets on to the new buyers and allow them to remain in the same location while Joy and Lucky collect rent on just the building itself providing a nice steady income during retirement.

They could sell the entire business including the real estate either as a package or individually. In general, real estate is known to keep pace with inflation and over a 20 or 30 year period of time you can usually count on it to at least double if not triple – even by conservative estimates. Even if they paid a relatively modest $100,000 and it turned into $250,000 after 20 years they easily cleared another $10,000 annually just calculating the real estate. The business itself is also a very real asset capable of being sold for substantially more. Now, in addition to earning over $240,000 annually the business real estate generated additional earnings and the business itself generated additional earnings.

What's more, much of these earnings are taxed lower than that of earned income. Earned income or your personal income tax is often one of the highest forms of taxation whereas capital gains taxes are often taxed at a lower rate. For instance, capital gains tax on real estate may be as low as 15%.

As you can see, the difference between practice owners of all types; from massage therapists to attorneys, chiropractors to podiatrists, is influenced by many factors. This is just a sample of the type of format that doctors, attorneys, veterinarians and many other practice owners use to generate literally millions of dollars annually!

There are many more specifics including advanced topics for those who are seriously interested in learning more but this provides an example of the outline and type of potential available. Massage practice owners can duplicate these same types of options to dramatically increase their potential earnings even without doing more work!

Notice, Joy and Lucky are not out there trying to perform 40 sessions a week. In fact, once their business is built and matured, they can literally stop working entirely while continuing to derive well over a six-figure income each and every year! If they need more help they can afford to hire someone without dramatically hurting their bottom line because the source of their earnings is spread across several areas.

Joy and Lucky also have room to grow and expand either through increasing current service offers such as the corporate program or through expansion to another location. Downturns in one area are "buffered" by income from another area and even other clients since their clients include massage customers, other therapists and corporate clients.

Also notice, Joy and Lucky could charge more – substantially more because they currently provide an exceptional 'win-win' to both clients and other therapists. However, should they choose to do so, the model would easily support price increases.

Joy and Lucky took lessons from big business and many other types of practice owners who literally generate million dollar a year practices! As we have already seen, there is a huge discrepancy between the earnings of many types of professionals. This is by no means a complete description of the advanced methods, business arrangements and other possibilities but it should give you an expanded view of the profit potential that can – and is – generated by a properly planned practice!

Your Practice Profit Checklist

Yes No Is Your Practice Operating as a Job Replacement?
Yes No Does Your Practice Provide "passive revenue" even if you don't work?
Yes No Is Your Income derived from 3 or more sources?
Yes No Is Your Practice building equity?
Yes No Is Your Practice dependent upon more than one type of client?

TIPS

Never turn away a new patient who wants to see you that same day!

Develop a written plan for emergency new patients

Always give someone at least two or more business cards – Never give just one! Make it easy for people to share it with others or put a backup card in other places

Chapter 8

Thoughts on Location

What is this elusive concept of location? Does it ***Really*** matter? The answer is a resounding YES! Location does matter and in fact, it may be one of the most important aspects of what makes – or breaks – your business. Consider the following quotes and musings regarding the importance of location...

> ***"Whenever I arrive on a real location, I have to move around and work out what the best angles are going to be. When I was moving around with the lens, I discovered things that the naked eye would not have."***
> ***Pedro Almodovar***

> ***"People use location as a language in films....It's more of an emotional beat than it is a physical beat."***
> ***Lucy Liu***

> ***"The thing is, when I am on location I first look to see what the location offers me...."***
> ***Robert Muller***

> ***"Location is the key to most businesses, and the entrepreneurs typically build their reputation at a particular spot."***
> ***Phyllis Schlafly***

Yes indeed, location matters. It matters in life. It matters in business. It matters in art. It matters to your clients and it should matter – very much – to every practitioner! In the following pages you will learn how to select the perfect location for your practice or how to find under served populations to expand your practice. I hope you enjoy it!

The Journey Starts At Their Front Door - Not Yours!

Repeat these words again because they are very important. The Journey Starts at Their Front Door – Not Yours! Yet few practitioners in any field understand how to properly select a location for their practice. Big business understands the importance of location selection and has used this information to create thriving business locations for decades by using sophisticated analysis and database information. Fortunately, by combining general "know how" with a few tools, you can pick a perfect location for your practice!

Location is one of the most important decisions you will make when it comes to creating a successful massage practice: a mediocre or even less than impressive businesses may thrive due to a great location whereas many talented practitioners have struggled year after year due to a bad location.

I'll give you a real life example from a different type of practice provider: optometrists. In the town where I live there is a small optometrist office that has done well over the years but has never grown or expanded. The service is impeccable but the location is out of the way, in an area of town that is declining and the building itself is set off a distance from the road so it's difficult to see even when driving right by. Now, it's important to understand, the town in question is one of the fastest growing cities in the entire nation so there is ample opportunity for growth! On the other hand, there is another optometrist in the same town who is actually quite inferior in terms of training, client relationships and even service – yet his practice has expanded to several nearby cities with multiple locations in each. Is it any wonder that big business spends tens of thousands - sometimes hundreds of thousands - of dollars annually in order to select the very best location?

The good news is you can select a great location for your practice if you are willing to do a little research and work. Even if you already have an established practice, you may find a great source of new clients by identifying and then providing service to an unmet population or example why you have struggled in generating or growing your business!

Density, Proximity & Saturation Analysis

The first rule of thumb is to make sure there are enough clients to support a massage practice in your area. This is commonly referred to as “Density”. A massage practice only thrives when it is able to attract enough clients to sustain the business – not just in the short term when it first opens its doors – but long term year after year. Closely related to this is the level of Saturation in the area. How many competing therapist are located in the same general area? This means your practice must be located where there are plenty of people…without an over-abundance of other practitioners. But, how many people is “plenty”?

Common wisdom for most service related industries says you need approximately 5,000 to 10,000 households for ***each*** massage practice to support a thriving business. The majority of your clients will live within 3-5 miles with a second tier located 5 – 10 miles from your office. Few clients will travel more than 15 miles for a routine office visit so for optimum results, measure the number of households no farther than 10 miles from your office. The closer and more convenient your office is then the easier it is for them to schedule a massage. So, you want a minimum of 5,000 to 10,000 households within a 10 mile distance of your office location.

Remember, not everyone is interested, able or willing to take advantages of your services at the same time or with equal frequency.

If there are already established massage practitioners or other multiple practitioner practices, then you need to divide your findings by the total number of practitioners in the area.

Location and Modality or Special Service Types

If you offer – or are thinking of offering – a highly specialized service or modality then you will need to know what percentage of the population use that service in order to determine whether or not it will be popular. Let’s take Reiki as an example. Research indicates far less than .01% of the US Population use this service. If you are in a predominately Hindu area or one with a strong following then this may be an excellent niche area for you to consider however, the vast majority of practitioners will find the request for Reiki to be relatively limited.

Furthermore, given the religious, lifestyle and system beliefs associated with Reiki and other forms of energy work it may be that it inadvertently hurts your practice as much as it helps since well over 80% of the population consider themselves of the

Christian denomination. Furthermore, many physicians feel threatened or ill at ease when making referrals to controversial modalities.

This type of training and work should be carefully considered prior to making the investment of time, money and commitment required. It may be a personal decision and one that fits you as a practitioner very well, just remain cognizant of the potential Business and financial impact it may have on your practice!

Likewise, if you are in some locations throughout the nation this may be at tremendous asset so it's important to analyze your locale conditions and market!

On the other hand, some specializations are in very high demand! For instance, medical massage and sports related massage are typically highly sought after in most locations but even those can experience significant location variation. For instance, in some areas known for retirement living; sports massage may be less popular than most other areas of the nation.

Saturation

If you are an established practitioner who is experiencing a down-turn in your business then you should analyze your location carefully. With the rapid growth of massage therapy in recent years, some areas have hit a Saturation point where established business owners are unable to continue to grow at a steady rate and new business owners have greater difficulty "breaking into" the area.

Once an area hits its saturation point, where there are enough - or more than enough -practitioners to serve all 5,000 to 10,000 household segments, then continued growth will become strained as practitioners must now compete either against one another or for the relatively fewer new residents moving into the area.

There are several ways to determine the number of households in your area but two quick and easy sources are the local Chamber of Commerce or the Census Bureau data [www.census.gov].

Express Example

Let's use my friend K as an example. K lives in AnyTown USA with a population of 150,000. Due to the specific demographics of the area, there are approximately 65,000 households. Notice, the number of households is NOT the same as the total population! Some households will have only one adult with children, others will have two or more adults with children and finally others will consist of only adults. According to the data, K's area should support somewhere between 6 to 13 therapists. K finds there are only two other licensed practitioners in her immediate area. That's good news!

Affordability & Selecting Your Profile Client

Now that you have established there are enough households in your target area to support a practice, you must determine if they are able to regularly and routinely afford your service! The key to this is "regularly and routinely" because those are the clients that will provide your "bread and butter".

If you were to conduct a survey of how many people "want" a massage then it would be pretty safe to assume it would be a high percentage...just remember how excited people were when you were practicing your technique during massage school...but that can be sporadic. To build your practice requires a steady solid foundation of clients that routinely use your service. Not a huge number but a solid foundation nonetheless. The more you are able to build this foundation, the more firm and profitable your practice will become.

Remember, although the majority of your target population may "want" or desire a massage, not everyone will be "able" to afford a regular or routine massage due to financial, time constraints or a host of other factors. Although there are exceptions to every rule, households struggling to pay for basic necessities like rent, groceries and school clothes may still use the services of a skilled massage therapist but typically for very special occasions [Mother's Day, gift, etc...] or via insurance reimbursement. On the other end of the spectrum are those households with substantial excess income who can essentially afford what they want when they want it. These may be superb clients but may not reflect the "typical" client depending upon your location. The success of your practice will revolve around those 5,000 to 10,000 households able and willing to afford your service on a regular basis.

The "magic range" roughly translates to a minimum household income of approximately $75,000 to $150,000 annually. Typically these are the clients who are most able to afford the repeated services of a massage practitioner on a weekly to monthly basis. So, now you need to review how many of the 5,000 to 10,000 total households in your local area have household incomes of at least $75,000. This is the first step in establishing your "profile" client. A "profile" client is one that conceptually represents the foundation client who will help build your practice. The range for a foundation is highly individualized depending upon the therapist but for this step you should decide what your absolute base monthly income should be and then translate that into the number of regular repeat clients you will need.

Nearly all types of marketing and site selection utilize household income data so it is available in many formats – from highly detailed analysis that cost thousands of dollars to very basic data you can access for free. One of the easiest formats is to search by zip code. This is a general but useful method since your practice will typically be located in only one or two zip codes. Simply type in the zip code and the information will tell you how many households are in the area and then how many households fall within specific income ranges. Again, many local Chamber of Commerce chapters provide this information or you can access it online via a Free database search at the US Census Bureau "Zip Code Statistics" page: http://www.census.gov/epcd/www/zipstats.html

Express Example

Let's once again use my friend K as an example. K has decided she needs a base monthly income of $4,000: $1,500 to cover her basic expenses and $2,500 to pay her absolute minimum living expenses. K charges $60 per hour so she will need a base foundation of roughly 67 one hour massage sessions per month. K finds that out of the 65,000 households in her area there are approximately 9,300 that have an annual household income of at least $75,000. Since 67 sessions represents less than 1% of the total target households, K can realistically hope to attain her base income goal.

Piggy-Back & Anchor Yourself!

Many successful names in business have used the concept of piggy-backing on an "anchor" store to launch their own start-up. An "anchor" is a frequently utilized store or business that serves as a destination point in an area. For example, most grocery stores serve as "anchor stores" in a plaza setting. All of the surrounding business locations benefit from the association through repeated name recognition, high levels of exposure and convenience...in short, Visibility!

Increased visibility afforded by an anchor store can be a tremendous asset when selecting a great practice location. Remember, people need to see your business name at least three times before remembering it and nine times before becoming a client! Marketing and advertising is expensive so by selecting a less visible location that saves you a little on rent, it may cost you hundreds more in advertising and marketing each month! Instead, select a highly visible anchor location whenever possible. It can increase your odds of success since your business becomes familiar and memorable to potential clients as they go about their daily driving or other activities.

If it is not cost effective or possible to secure a location adjacent to an anchor location due to zoning, availability or other factors; search for locations in the direct path and within a short distance from the anchor location. Remember, most anchor locations serve thousands of potential clients on a routine basis which results in consistent exposure combined with supreme convenience! Other potential anchor locations would include physician offices or hospitals for therapists who specialize in clinical related concerns or gyms and sporting related establishments for those who perform sports related massage.

Express Example

K drives by the local grocery plaza but finds all available space is taken. Even if the space was available, it would cost more than she is able to afford. K likes the idea that nearly all of the target households in her zip code shop at that specific grocery store each week and realizes the increased visibility translates into a lot of free advertising but is unable to secure a location in the plaza. K finds three other potential locations in the nearby area: an older home converted into a business location one street behind the plaza, another potential location two blocks over on the main

highway leading to the plaza and finally, a third possible location at a major intersection near the plaza. K intends to research all three.

Accessibility

Accessibility encompasses a wide range of items ranging from a safe, secure environment to adequate parking and lighting. It also includes less obvious features such as traffic patterns. For example, a busy intersection may initially appear to be a desirable location due to high exposure, but depending upon the flow of traffic it may be all but impossible for the driver to enter the parking lot from an opposite direction. Likewise, if turn lanes are not available, mid-street locations can be problematic. Other important access considerations include site specific factors such as the requirement to climb steps or quickly find convenient and Free parking.

Test potential locations by driving, parking and walking to the establishment from ALL possible directions. Pay attention to how long you must wait to pull into the parking lot from any given direction, make sure your signage will be visible from all directions, measure the distance a client be forced to walk once parked and pay special attention to any particularly undesirable elements you may encounter. It often helps to bring a friend with you or ask several trusted people to drive by and give you honest feedback on their first impression.

Compliment versus Compete

Be very careful when selecting your location that you will be surrounded by complimentary - but not competing – service providers or institutions! This is a common problem among practice owners of all types and involves a misunderstanding of a phenomena usually encountered by large business owners.

Now, here is the problem. If your town is like mine then there are usually a few areas that seem to attract certain types of business. For instance, one main road has most of the car dealerships, another has restaurant after restaurant and still another has the majority of massage practice locations in town. You can literally look in the phone book and see one establishment after another up and down that specific road!

So what's the problem you may wonder? After all, it's common to see one fast food restaurant on each corner or one gas station facing another one. Indeed, that is true but let's see why it doesn't work for massage or most practice related entities.

To begin with, everyone eats and most people who are driving will eventually need gasoline or maybe even buy a new car. Essentially, Everyone who passes by is a potential client. Then it is a matter of preference or convenience. In the example of a gas station they know that most people will turn in to get gas at the station located on the same side of the street they are driving on unless the station across the street had a deep discount which is rarely the case. Gasoline is typically within a few cents of each other so it's primarily a factor of convenience which station one turns into to fill up the tank.

Then there is preference. If you happen to really like a specific brand or model of car then everyone has received the same visibility but you are still likely to purchase the car of interest from them. Now it's a matter of "stealing you" away from another dealership by showing you comparable cars that may catch your eye. In this case, all of the dealers benefit by being located in a nearby location since anyone might attract the attention from another.

Massage doesn't work that way. It's not a convenience purchase like gasoline and the skill, individual factors and other requirements create a much more personalized experience than car shopping.

Now, let's define exactly what is meant by complimentary and competing.

Complimentary services or institutions are those that are enhanced by your practice or that enhance your practice. Often you will serve the same types of clients – or even the exact same clients – but those clients are not forced to choose between your service and the other service. Instead, they are likely to use your service AND the other service. For example, if your specialization was Equine massage then it would be most advisable to be located near horse farms, large animal veterinarian practices or surgical units, farm supply stores and so forth.

On the other hand, a competing service or industry is one where clients or potential clients choose your practice OR the other practice or service. Examples of competing services or practices would include other massage therapists or even schools of massage that provide deep discounts.

To Good to Be True – The Danger of Perfection!

So what happens if you find what appears to be the most perfect location possible? Let's fabricate a "perfect storm" for the perfect location. We'll call our therapist Gerry. Gerry has a special interest in working with the elderly. She lives in a moderate sized town experiencing rapid growth over the past few years. Until recently, there were few services for the elderly or senior population but due to the major real estate development for retiree's, an entire market has now emerged.

There is a strip mall associated with the area grocery store and surrounded by a podiatrist, chiropractor, golf course and community athletic clubs, a small branch of a local hospital and much more. In short, Gerry is now surrounded by the population of her dreams AND literally dozens of complimentary service providers, organizations and institutions! What's more, there are exactly zero other massage practitioners or other competing service providers.

For Gerry, the sky is the limit – but, as with all good things it will come to and end. Gerry's lease expires in 2 years and with such high demand, she has heard from others that rates are rapidly escalating. Worse, she's heard rumors through the grapevine that both Chiropractors as well as several others are considering hiring MT's to have on staff since demand and internal referrals could sustain several therapists for those practitioners. Finally, several therapists have head of Gerry's success and are in the process of securing space in the area.

Eventually, these situations tend to swing completely the other direction and become oversaturated before finally resolving somewhere toward the middle. It is a painful correction and often results in hardship to all involved for quite some time in the future. While these locations can be wonderful foundations to establish and grow your business it is vital to realize the early success will eventually be minimized if not severely impacted. Those who plan accordingly may be able to ride out the correction. Those who fail to plan may find themselves in the worst of all possible situations: high cost combined with a saturated market.

Site Selection Worksheet

Part I - Compliment or Compete

(List any and all services, practitioners or other sources of competition)

Compete: Clients Choose My Practice OR the following

1. ______
2. ______
3. ______
4. ______
5. ______
6. ______
7. ______
8. ______
9. ______

Compliment: Clients Choose My Practice AND the following

1. ______
2. ______
3. ______
4. ______
5. ______
6. ______
7. ______
8. ______
9. ______

Calculate Your Score:

Give yourself one point for each Compete listing.

Give yourself one point for each Compliment listing.

Subtract the Compete score from the Compliment Score.

If your total score equals:

<0 This is a potentially detrimental location. While it's not impossible to build a practice in a detrimental location, you will face challenges that others won't simply due to the location. If you are in practice and have been struggling or stagnating, then this may be partially to blame.

0 You are either at a neutral level or considering a location that is far removed from anything and anyone else. Either way, you need high ranking scores in other areas to consider selecting this location as it would otherwise be a potentially detrimental location.

1-3 This is a typical but not exciting score. You are like many practitioners across the nation. A change or downturn from any one of these complimentary services or institutions could hurt your business disproportionately since you are more heavily dependent upon fewer sources.

4-6 This is a strong score. It provides a solid foundation for complimentary services, referrals and diversification of professional relationships. Loss of one would be unlikely to severely injure your business (assuming you have taken advantage of all available sources rather than concentrating on only one). If other items check out properly then this location may be a serious contender for future consideration. Remember, always have several locations to choose from and Never fall in love with any location!

7+ You have either fallen in love (in that case get help and do it over again!) or you have hit a potential jack-pot WITH a potentially large future problem! The area may be very new and experiencing widespread growth, redevelopment or other related issues in which case, your advantage may be short lived. Ultra hot zones tend to increase in price faster than other areas since demand is greater. Your initial client advantage may quickly dwindle as others move into this hot new area. Eventually it's possible that saturation takes place and what was formerly the perfect location becomes a perfect nightmare! Caution is advisable!

Part II - Site Selection Comparison

Answer Yes or No for each site under consideration.

Yes No Is the location zoned for a massage practice?

Yes No Is the facility large enough for your business including treatment room(s), office or reception area and storage?

Yes No Does the building require repairs or demonstrate health hazards?

Yes No Are the terms of the lease and/or rent favorable?

Yes No Are Maintenance & Repairs provided by the landlord?

Yes No Is the location convenient to where you live?

Yes No Do your customers live within 10 miles from the location?

Yes No Is the population density of the area sufficient?

Yes No Has the area reached stabilization or saturation level yet?

Yes No Has the area experienced more than 10% growth in past 3 years?

Yes No Have 10% + of surrounding business died in past three years?

Yes No Is there a school or other reduced service provider within 10 miles?

Yes No Is the population density sufficient for your niche modality needs?

Yes No Is the facility consistent with the image projected by your practice?

Yes No Is the facility located in a safe neighborhood?

Yes No Is there an "anchor" business that will attract customers?

Yes No Are there competitors located close to the facility?

Yes No Is the facility readily accessible to your clients?

Yes No Are there complimentary services located nearby?

Yes No Will the facility accommodate growth or will you be able to find an acceptable new location within a 2-3 mile radius?

Calculate Your Score for Part II

Give yourself one point for each "Yes" above.

Subtract 1 point for each "No" on items 5, 6, 9, 10, 11, 12, 14, 16, 17, 18, 19, 20

Subtract 5 points for each "No" on items 1, 2, 3, 4, 7, 8, 13, 15

Calculate Your Total Score

Now, combined the scores of Part I with Part II to derive your Total Score. The higher the Total Score the better for each property under consideration. If all of your scores tend to be low, then continue to search for a more desirable location. Always compare at least three locations and never fall in love with a specific location. Remain objective to the greatest degree possible.

Chapter 9

"You Never Get a Second Chance to Make a First Impression"

The Office Environment

First Impressions Matter

Yes, we all remember the old saying but it's important to evaluate and then re-evaluate the first impression you make on your clients. This can be difficult to do but it's important for both new and established business owners.

To begin, pretend you are a customer (if possible ask trusted friends and family to do this too) or ask someone who is unfamiliar with your location to do this for you and provide honest feedback.

Start at the Beginning

For most people this will be the front door of their office so there are some special instances you need to take into consideration. First, if you are building a new practice location then Remain Critical! Don't fall in love but rather try to notice everything. If you have been in business for awhile then chances are you have grown familiar with the surroundings and may not notice the small imperfections or deterioration that easily creep up. Unfortunately, others will notice!

Take a few minutes to really focus on the surrounding environment. Is it clean? Are there any unpleasant sights or sounds? Are visitors required to walk beside a trash container or other unpleasant obstacle on the sidewalk leading to the door of your office? Is the door handle clean and easy to use? Is the door itself easy to navigate or does it slam shut creating a loud bang or other disturbance? Do you have something to Welcome the client and invite them to come in? Take time to view the entrance just like you would for the first time.

Now, continue through the door to counter or first greeting area. Take the path your clients follow when they walk in. Again, it's important to put yourself in their shoes to see what they see. Is the carpet worn? Are there attractive visual displays? Is everything clean and tidy? Do you encounter any obstacles or impediments? Is there something to greet each client with a warm welcome and then hold their attention should there be any type of interruption or short wait?

Continue the path your clients take as they proceed through the office to the actual treatment room and table. Notice the sights, sounds, smells and textures surrounding you through the journey. Is each pleasant and inviting? Does anything elicit a small hesitation or pause? If so, what and why? Be sure to make special mention of any deficiencies or negative aspects you encounter.

It's a good idea to ask family and friends to do this unexpectedly for you every few months just to remain fresh and viable. In fact, first time visitors can also provide excellent feedback related to their first impressions. Select a small sample of first time visitors each month, typically from 1-3 should be fine, and request an honest appraisal of their first impressions on a postcard sized form. Pay very special attention to anything negative they point out because it's very likely that others have also noticed.

Environment Rating Checklist

For each of the following assign a rating between 1 – 10. Anything below 5 requires immediate attention. The goal is to have ranking that remain in the 7-10 range.

1 = Poor and 10 = to Excellent

Office Appearance

_____ Top of picture frames, mirrors, shelves, light fixtures, ceiling fans etc… especially if you are not tall. Your clients may be taller and can often see the tops of items that you may miss!

_____ Office and bathroom fragrance. Does your office and bathrooms have a pleasant – but neutral – odor! Remember, some clients have allergies and sensitivities to fragrance or other odors. Also, smell may elicit very strong emotional reactions. Any fragrance – no matter how much you and most others enjoy it – may have a negative connotation for a client due to specific memories or associations. Keep odors and fragrances neutral but pleasant.

_____ Clean floors. Do you Vacuum and/or mop at least every other day (under the tables and chairs)

_____ Clean the bathroom. This is an area which must remain immaculate at all times. When in the bathroom wipe down the toilet seat, sink and mirror (1x day)

_____ Have live plants and keep them alive and green, remove dead leaves

_____ Remove waste from waste baskets within the view of patients daily.

_____ Remove fingerprints and dust from front door and windows.

_____ Clutter removed. Everything is situated in its own place.

A quick note. This is a tough one! You need to be objective and realistic which is hard to do. As humans we have a tendency to either overlook our own faults OR focus to strongly on our own faults. It is probably advisable to ask others to do this for you and explain that you are asking for honest feedback. Then do what it takes to correct any deficiencies without becoming offended.

All service workers that deal with the public must maintain the highest degree of personal cleanliness and appearance. Think for a moment: have you ever gone to a restaurant where the waiter or waitress had a really bad cold? Spoiled your appetite didn't it?!

Personal Appearance List Checklist

_____ Clean, comfortable yet professional attire.

_____ Complete lack of body odor and /or halitosis.

_____ Personal fragrance. Many clients have allergies or find certain fragrances, perfumes or colognes to be a strong emotional stimuli…positive or negative. If you happen to be wearing a cologne that a divorcee associates with an ex spouse then chances are you have just created a negative association. Likewise, if you wear a perfume that someone associates with an intimate moment then it could lead to an embarrassing moment. Keep odors and fragrances neutral.

_____ Healthy, enthusiastic, light stepping! It's contagious. Your clients will pick up on it immediately!

_____ Shoes. Pay special attention to them as it may be an item your clients see more than usual. Many people are very "cued in" to shoes and feet!

_____ Manicured, clean hands. This goes without saying but a MT should pay extra special attention to their hands.

Interaction Intersections

Make it Personal
Create Interaction and Involvement

At each natural resting point make sure there is an "Interaction Intersection" that invites your client to draw closer and creates an opportunity for them to interact with the environment. It's not merely enough that clients are not displeased. Instead, a successful practice invites a client to smell, touch, taste, sit, read, listen, write, experience and so forth...in short, interact with the environment. The deliberate inclusion of stimuli that will "speak" to each client will not only make them feel important and relaxed but create a sense of identity and 'ownership" that this is a place they belong.

Yes, people primarily come for a massage and nothing will take the place of providing the very best massage experience possible but stop and think for just a moment about another common service...dining out. Yes, restaurants are also a service industry and as such, they understand the environment or atmosphere has a lot to do with their success. Indeed, if the food is bad then atmosphere alone won't compensate but all things equal, an excellent atmosphere and environment shapes the experience to a much larger degree.

Take for instance my own favorite restaurant. It's a moderate sized family owned restaurant with a superb menu selection (although my personal favorite item isn't on the menu...but more on that later!). I enjoy the music, friendly waiter who knows my selections, original art work and more. Likewise, another favorite is a local 'hang out" with swimming, singing and a fun casual atmosphere. Nothing matches but there is plenty to do including reading all of the fun signs painted everywhere in this rustic restaurant! What are your favorite restaurants? What role does environment and atmosphere play in your overall feeling about the establishment?

Now, how does that translate into a massage practice? Very simple: every natural pause should have an "Interaction Intersection" for your client! Take a step outside your office door. The door is typically the first pause for most clients as they must stop, grab the door handle and then step inside. Is there a clearly denoted sign that invites or welcomes them inside? If not – get one! Make it warm and personalized to reflect your business and the environment they can expect inside.

Once you have stepped inside – Stop! Stand still and notice where your eyes naturally drift. If you have a reception desk then it's probably toward that direction. If not, it may be toward a sitting area with table etc...whatever direction, stop and notice what you see. Is it a fresh vase of flowers that invite you to stop and smell the roses or a big pile of unfinished files? What sounds and smells greet you? At the moment you enter and then pause - your senses should all feel a sense of relief and approval.

Move throughout your office and pause at each natural location where a client would normally stop or slow down. Make sure each contains something of beauty, interest or engagement. At No time – Never EVER – should a client be left standing at a counter, table or other area without anything to touch, feel, smell or contemplate. If you are taking a call at the reception desk and a client is standing at the desk waiting – what is there to engage them in interacting with their environment? As the client moves down the hallway toward the treatment room and their eyes naturally focus on the end of the hallway, what do they see? Is there a "dead end" or is there a welcoming object that invites them to move forward? Clients feel more engaged and take ownership with that which they interact with. Create an environment that makes them feel important and which elicits a response – both physical and emotional – in them as they move through your office.

Interaction Intersections Checklist

Use this as a starting place for creating inviting, engaging and interesting client interaction. Each location represents typical stop or pause points for the client. Place a check mark beside the Type of Interaction available at each Intersection in your office – blank spaces are available to customize your needs. If you are a new practitioner or just establishing your office, fill in an item for each location.

Try to use a variety throughout the office and keep it balanced! For example, if you find all of your stimuli are in the visual area, then it's time to "tune in" to your kinetic, auditory and mental clients!!!

Location	**Touch**	**Smell**	**Visual**	**Auditory**	**Mental**
Front Door	______	______	______	______	______
Reception Desk	______	______	______	______	______
Reception Seating	______	______	______	______	______
Hallway	______	______	______	______	______
Bathroom	______	______	______	______	______
Treatment Room	______	______	______	______	______
Doors – Inner	______	______	______	______	______
Table	______	______	______	______	______
Mirror	______	______	______	______	______
Linens	______	______	______	______	______
Other	______	______	______	______	______
________________	______	______	______	______	______
________________	______	______	______	______	______
________________	______	______	______	______	______
________________	______	______	______	______	______
________________	______	______	______	______	______
________________	______	______	______	______	______

Chapter 10

Communication Process & Design

Everyone understands some services are required to conduct the normal day to day business function but do not generate an actual income – for example, ordering office supplies is a critical function when you run out of office supplies and can create inefficiencies or even lost business...but it does not create profit on it's own.

Understanding your cost and profit nodes is the next critical step in determining what areas to concentrate on and which to minimize or avoid. It is also imperative in determining your short and long term strategic analysis with particular attention to reducing costs or improving productivity for borderline situations.

For example, perhaps you have a home visit client that relocated so it now requires extensive travel for the visit which formerly only took 15 minutes. Does it make sense to continue or not? Can you realize further efficiency in time, money or energy by automating certain duties – for example, reordering office supplies to be delivered on a set schedule rather than shopping in person? Does the increased billable hours, travel and other outweigh the additional cost or not? These and many other similar situations require careful planning and period review.

Remember, Establish Process Designs that are **SMART:**

S Sensible
M Measurable
A Achievable
R Realistic
T Time Specific

This includes projected revenues, gross and net profits, productivity per person and/or venue, contracts, life time value of clients, lifecycle of clients, and MORE!!!

Weekly Goals

Write them down and then Share your goals with others! Most people don't even list their weekly goals fewer actually voice them to anyone. Here and now determine in your own mind to put an end to that!

First, you work hard in the treatment of your clients whether their goal is stress reduction or pain relief. You are partners in their care with them. Consider how you feel when a client shares with you their accomplishment brought about through their dedication but also in part –through your help. Now consider why you don't allow others to share in the success of reaching your professional goals?

I'm not talking about becoming unprofessional but rather a heightened level of professionalism that clearly demonstrates a commitment to service, quality, integrity, and yes – even growth and profit! Your clients understand your need to make a living and you will often be surprised how often people are more than happy to help reach a goal when they understand that it is important to you!

This point involves selecting several goals to be accomplished each week by yourself and individual members of your team. At the beginning of the week they are assigned and at the end of the week they are reviewed. It often turns into a little friendly competition between staff members and this is good for team building and actually getting things done! More importantly, by taking just a few minutes to clarify and put into writing your goals, feelings, needs and desires research indicates you are not only more likely to accomplish them but also the mere act of sharing these with others forms a greater commitment to your own success and that of your practice.

Balance

Not "Me" but "We"

Not greed but rather creed

Massage Practice Planner Weekly Goal Worksheet

Feel free to modify this to better suit your needs. Then, print it out and allow others to share in the success of your business!

Date: From ____________ To ______________

Inspiration, Quote or Motto for the week:

____

____

____

Desired Short-term Goals/ Outcome:

____

____

____

Desired Long term Goals/ Outcome:

____

____

____

I Want to change the following this week:

____

____

____

I Need to change the following this week:

____

____

____

These changes are important because:

Why this area is hard for me to change:

What I must do to allow the change:

Other reasons for wanting this change:

At the end of the week, evaluate your progress and make a few notes about what went right, what went wrong, unexpected events and any lessons learned.

Raise - Then Standardize - Expectations

This point calls for a review of how you go about preparing what we will call your "Menu Items". Menu items are those things that people come to know and expect from you without having to think about it. Take an example from the popularity of fast food restaurants. Why are fast food restaurants so popular even when the food isn't that tasty (not to mention unhealthy)? Because people are tired, hungry and don't want to work hard. They also don't want surprises. When you go to a fast food restaurant you know what to expect. If you order a cola then it will taste like a cola – not fruit punch. To make it even easier on tired weary consumers, fast food restaurants combine the menu down to just a few numbers that include the most popular meal combinations. Now, don't get me wrong, I'm not a fast food fan so that is where the comparison should end! But the point remains; make it easy on your clients to understand what to expect and how to ask for it! Don't make them work at it. They are there to relax and unwind.

Now it is time to evaluate your "menu". Hopefully you are not offering the fast food menu of services but rather a delightful array and variety. Again, take an example from gourmet restaurants...they describe every detail so your mouth is watering just reading the menu! Do you have a written "recipe" for each service on your menu? Is there a process of constructing the item that is followed each time the item is ordered by a guest? Prepare beautifully descriptive "service menu's" that highlight why your service is unique and what each client can expect. Combine some of the complimentary and more popular "menu items' together into packages that can be easily ordered. Spend time on the description and set the standard of what they should expect – not just from you but any service provider!

Here is a small tip: Establish a high standard and take time to explain, educate and describe what you offer. When You set the standard then even if a client goes to another provider, the client will naturally compare the service to what you provide! In their mind, why go to someone else when they can go to the best?

Standardized menus also help control cost, create consistency and help in inventory and scheduling. Customers appreciate getting the same quality each time they come to you. In the words of Samuel Alexander, "*Expectations and memories are more than mere images founded on previous experience*". Take time to create both. Your clients will thank you!

Winners and Losers

Remove the bottom 10% of your menu and other items that are not generating consistent interest. Remember, always revitalize. Eliminate the bottom 10% each year and replace it with something new, exciting and in demand.

This accomplishes several things; first, it offers your clients something new. Existing clients may add a new service or increase the frequency of their visits. You may also attract new clients who were searching for that particular service. Finally, it keeps you fresh and invigorated while eliminating a non-productive portion of your business. Some things never go out of style – pain relief for example. Those are the cornerstones of a good business and will represent the core foundation of your skill set. However, there are other complimentary services that may tend toward the "faddish" side of things or which become obsolete due to technology progress or other reasons while other services rise to take their place due to innovation.

Take a close look at your service menu and products each week to determine which items are the winners and which ones are the losers. Then compare month over month growth or loss against year over year growth or loss. Some things may be seasonal – for example, gift certifications are likely to be more popular around Mothers Day or other special occasions. If they are consistent then you will need to compare the growth or loss on an annual basis rather than simply month to month.

Let's assume you offer paraffin baths. By evaluating the monthly growth or decline in demand for paraffin baths you determine it has resulted in a steady decline with only sporadic requests month after month and year after year. Beginning in January of 2006 until March of 2007 you found the following:

January	2	January	1
February	7	February	4
March	5	March	3
April	3		
May	2		
June	0		
July	0		
Aug	0		
September	0		
October	1		
November	2		
December	2		

Let's interpret this data. First we see that from Jan to Feb there is an increase but then a steady decline each month. However, we could chalk this up to a seasonal variation. When we compare January against January there is an overall downward trend in use compared to the same month a year ago. Of course, the final decision would be whether this was instrumental to your service for a special segment of the population or simply just not "in demand". If not a critical component, then it may be time to eliminate the paraffin bath and find something more of your clients desire.

What happens if you have two equally non-performing menu items? This can happen however, I do NOT recommend eliminating more than the bottom 10% of your service menu at any given time. People enjoy fresh and innovative but in general, they do NOT enjoy major changes! Too much change too soon may not go over well with your clients. Change must be introduced slowly and methodically. It's also difficult for the therapist to become expert on more than one item at a time. Never compromise quality!

So, let's use another example. In this case hydrotherapy versus chromotherapy. Let's assume both generate exactly the same number of request per month which for the purpose of this example will be four or roughly one per week. Neither is a huge profit center but they are both part of your current list of service offered. It's time to get rid of one and replace it with something new. Which one do you eliminate? Here is where the long term trend makes a dramatic difference. Is one falling while the other is rising? If so, eliminate the one that is falling but by all means, keep the one that is growing or rising even if right now they are both equal!!!

That is an important tip to keep in mind – Never eliminate a growing trend even if it's small! Only eliminate declining or falling trends! Use your historical growth and decline information both on a monthly and annual basis to determine the trends then eliminate the bottom 10% each year. Replace it with growing new and innovative services then showcase your winners and growing trends.

Clear, Comprehensive & Cohesive Communication

"Can You Hear Me Now?"

"Have it Your Way"

"It's everywhere you want to be"

"The quicker picker-upper"

Recognize any of the above? Of course you do! Each of these slogans are powerful statements that uniquely identify the primary benefit of their company while propelling their respective companies to success. Once again, take a lesson from the "big boys"; it's important for a growing business to build upon the word of mouth that was the foundation for their early success and identify then strategize around your Unique Selling Proposition [USP]. A Unique Selling Proposition is essentially that which differentiates Your business from the competition.

Alert! Don't be a 'Me too" company!

"Me too" companies rarely survive. Today more than ever competition is tough and only getting tougher. Trying to thrive without distinguishing yourself results in a price war. You will eventually find there is only one method remaining to compete with...price. That is a BAD place to be because it will eventually become a race to the bottom and one that a small business owner can rarely win simply due to economies of scale. It's simply impossible to work more than a set number of hours or purchase in enough bulk when you are a small practice trying to compete with large corporations who demand [and receive] huge incentives due to the tremendous volume of their purchasing power. Unless you have a significant cost advantage, this becomes a downward spiral of lost revenue.

The solution

Have a clearly defined Unique Selling Proposition (USP). BUT not just any USP will do; it MUST be something the client actually values! This of course, begs the question...what does the client actually want? Many small business owners are surprised at what motivates their clients and few have taken the time to analyze their clients nor determine their Purchasing Drivers. Even within a target client company, different people have different perceived and real needs. You must understand both the industry trends as well as analyze the "performance" and other "gaps" in the environment then take all of that into consideration for the actual client.

This will eventually result in three primary findings:

1. Expected - Elements that if not met or missing will result in the loss of a client but having them will not increase clients. Cleanliness is an example. People Expect cleanliness so the fact that your establishment is clean will not flood your business with new clients but if your business isn't clean for some reason then it's highly likely to result in a lost client.

2. Anticipated – These are services or items that are highly desired. If you provide this and people know about it then it will result in increased clients, increased number of visits or both. An example of this might be the current interest in Chromatherapy which is highly valued by many but relatively rare.

3. Neutral - Does not increase or decrease sale but is part of doing business. The client intake is an example. There are certain expected elements of it but it's typically considered a rather tedious and somewhat time consuming element of doing business. Instead, if you were able to create an intake that people actually enjoyed then it would be highly unlikely to generate more clients even though it still enhanced their overall experience. Likewise, if you failed to have an enjoyable intake form and instead, used the tried and trusty boring intake forms then it also wouldn't result in the loss of a client (at least until the point and time when the new and nifty intake became expected at which point it has changed categories).

Once you have selected your USP, integrate it into all of your communication efforts to establish your company as the primary provider. Whenever possible, be sure to educate your customers on what to expect from others—set the standard so that your clients or potential clients use your company as that which they compare all others!

Create Your Own USP Worksheet

Acquire Competitive Intelligence

Business takes place in a highly competitive, volatile environment, so it is important to understand the competition and then determine what you do differently in your practice. Questions like these can help:

- Who are your five nearest direct competitors?
- Who are your indirect competitors?
- Is their business growing, steady, or declining?
- What can you learn from their operations or advertising?
- What are their strengths and weaknesses?
- How does their product or service differ from yours?

Tip: Start a file on each of your competitors; include advertising, promotional materials, and pricing strategies. Review these files periodically, determining how often they advertise, sponsor promotions, and offer sales. Study the copy used in the advertising and promotional materials and their sales strategies.

What to Address in Your Competitor Analysis

- Names of competitors: List all of your current competitors and research any that might enter the market during the next year.

- Summary of each competitor's products: This should include location, quality, advertising, staff, distribution methods, promotional strategies, customer service, etc.

- Competitors' strengths and weaknesses: List their strengths and weaknesses from the customer's viewpoint. State how you will capitalize on their weaknesses and meet the challenges represented by their strengths.

- Competitors' strategies and objectives: This information might be easily obtained by getting a copy of their annual report. It might take the analysis of many information sources to understand competitors' strategies and objectives.

Ideas for Gathering Competitive Information

Internet: The Internet is a powerful tool for finding information.

Personal visits: If possible, visit your competitors' locations. Observe how employees interact with customers. What do their premises look like? How are their products displayed and priced?

Talk to customers: Learn what your customers and prospects are saying about your competitors. Listen – don't offer opinions and NEVER say anything negative about a competitor.

Competitors' ads: Analyze competitors' ads to learn about their target audience, market position, product features, benefits, prices, etc.

Written sources: Use general business publications, marketing and advertising publications, local newspapers and business journals, industry and trade association publications, industry research and surveys, and computer databases (available at many public libraries).

Once you understand the local environment you are better able to create a meaningful differentiation between you and other providers in the area. Remember, it must be something that matters to the client. As mentioned previously, most people get a massage for the following reasons:

- 60% massage combined with conventional medicine for a medical problem
- 44% massage would be interesting to try
- 34% believed that conventional medical treatments would not
- 33% suggested by a conventional medical professional
- 13% thought conventional medicine was too expensive

As we can clearly see, Medical related massage is what the majority of people desire!

Create Your Own USP

1. List those things that motivate clients to get a massage.
   Use both explicit and hidden criteria.
2. Rank yourself and your competitors by these criteria;
3. Determine where you rank well and craft a USP using those strengths.
4. Use this USP throughout your business. It should be reflected in your mission statement, goals, client communication and throughout your office.

Criterion	You	Competitor 1	Competitor 2	Competitor 3
Stress Relief				
Pain				

USP Statement

First Visit Confirmation Call

The foundation for any relationship is established during the first few encounters so it's important that you, as the therapist, recognize and establish the boundaries for your practice. One of the most frustrating problems that massage therapists or indeed, anyone who works with the public encounters is "No Shows" or missed appointments.

Of course, legitimate emergencies arise and that should be taken into consideration, but missed appointments are a tremendous drain on energy, wasted time, missed revenue and outright disregard and respect for another. It is also a rampant problem among nearly all service providers.

Even the most modest estimates of one missed appointment per month still represent hundreds of dollars. Unfortunately, many practitioners experience far more than one per month especially among new clients.

The First Visit Conformation Call has been implemented across a wide variety of service settings for the simple reason that it "helps". Notice, I did not say it solves the problem, it won't, but it does help minimize the problem. Research has demonstrated a confirmation call for all new clients increases the likelihood of keeping the appointment by 30%.

Modern day society places a premium on concern so when you take the extra time to call the new client prior to the first visit it sends a strong message. First, it lets them know you are prepared and ready to work with them. People like to be remembered. It also lets them know it matters to you and should matter to them. People are less likely to bother with a cancellation or last minute urgency if they think nobody will notice. You have also established an expectation that communicates the fact that you notice. Finally, it establishes a standard of treatment that they can expect even before experiencing the massage itself.

Confirmation Call Checklist

1. Collect new patient information in advance. Be prepared! Have the patients name, home and work phone number and referral source available while you make the call.
2. Nothing is worse than writing down a phone number but forgetting the clients name. At the bare minimum have the clients full name and contact information as well as the scheduled time of their appointment and your full daily schedule.
3. If you aren't sure how to pronounce their name, be straightforward about it...simply say something such as "I'm sorry but could you confirm the proper pronunciation of your name". Always use Mr., Ms., Mrs, and the last name for the first phone call.
4. If the client is a referral be sure to acknowledge this fact.
5. Confirm appointments with all new clients the day prior to the scheduled appointment. Make sure they have the time correct, know how to get to your office and have a good idea of what to expect once they arrive.
6. If the client is in pain and you have an earlier appointment, offer it to them! Again, be sure to have your schedule available to make changes during the call itself.
7. If the client plans to cancel then ask why. Offer to reschedule if it's a scheduling conflict or address other concerns they may have. Immediately update your schedule to reflect all changes.
8. Don't just leave a voice message but actually call back to speak to the person. Use this time to confirm the time, location etc but also clarify or respond to any specific questions or concerns they may have.
9. Pre-send intake or other first visit forms. It never hurts to ask and many clients prefer the ability to fill out forms in advance of the actual office visit. Have intake and other forms available to fax, email or access via your webpage. Remind clients of the availability of these forms.
10. Make confirmation calls in the afternoon or early evenings when possible. This is usually the best time to reach someone at home.
11. Be friendly and responsive. You may be tired and just hoping to go home but remember, this is the clients first impression with you. Make it count! Give them your complete attention.
12. Communicate compassion, caring and concern.

First Visit Follow-Up Call

Is it important?

Yes! Some therapists have been doing this for years...if you are one of these then give yourself a big "kudos" of congratulations...but many therapists neglect this all important step. Research across a variety of other practice professionals has found this to be an important step in bonding with the client, providing an enhanced level of service and assuring things are going well. It has also been found to increase client levels of satisfaction as it is perceived as caring, concerned and committed.

Who Uses a First Visit Follow-up?

All types of professionals. My veterinarian routinely calls to make sure there hasn't been any side effects of a vaccination, chiropractors frequently call to make sure the patient understands the effect of spinal manipulation and most health or medical providers realize this is an important consideration.

Massage therapists – whether specializing in medical, sports, relaxation or any other type of modality – should incorporate the First Visit Follow-Up call as a routine part of their service but particularly those who deal with clients who are in pain or are referred as part of a medical related service.

Objectives of the Call

Calling a new client allows the therapist an opportunity to make sure the patient is responding appropriately to treatment. Let's examine the situation of a chiropractic referral: after a chiropractic adjustment 5% of clients report feeling worse, 50% report no change and 45% report feeling better. Let's assume you have a new client that was a chiropractic referral...are they aware of the fact that they may feel worse or no change simply due to the manipulation itself or do they erroneously expect the massage to "make it all better"?

Take the time to remind the new client they may feel a range of response, inquire if they experience any problems and show you care.

Making the Call

The first visit follow-up call should be made at a convenient time by the close of business each day or sometime during the next day. If the client isn't available, simply leave a message stating the reason for your call and your return phone number should they have any questions or concerns.

Establish this as a typical routine in your practice whether you feel like making the call or not. New clients may have questions, concerns or even confusion regarding how they should feel, their level of pain relief, stress reduction or even emotional triggers related to the massage. The follow-up phone call is the responsibility of the therapist to reach out and address these concerns while allowing the client support, education or follow through.

Always affirm the clients response. If they report improvement then wonderful but be prepared when clients report no change or even a negative response to a session.

Don't take it personally! If the client reports anything that could be a medical emergency or worsening then be sure to provide appropriate referral and or the suggestion to seek medical attention as appropriate. If the client simply reports a less than positive experience then listen carefully and affirm that you understand what they are saying. Remember, new clients may sometimes have unrealistic expectations.

For example, returning to the chiropractic referral situation, a client may expect the massage therapist to 'make it all better' without realizing the chiropractic adjustments and manipulations can sometimes bring out discomfort in and of themselves while the massage works to keep the muscles from the level of discomfort they would typically feel after an adjustment, they still may not have relief – but rather a reduction from what would otherwise be much worse stiffness or pain.

Likewise, emotional or other response mechanisms may surprise the client who is unfamiliar with massage and could perceive this as a generalized anxiety, discomfort or other feeling. Always listen, affirm and then educate the client on appropriate actions. Never argue or try to change their mind!

Remember, the new client is assessing not just the quality of the session and the skill level of the therapist but also the relationship! Routinely schedule and adhere to a follow-up call. It establishes a caring, concerned and educated professionalism in the minds of new clients.

Inactive Re Calls

Sometimes clients just stop coming even though nothing is really wrong and they could still benefit from massage. Often this is due to a mistaken perception that they should just "learn to live with" the problem. Let's use back pain as an example. There are between 80 and 100 million people who experience significant back pain each and every year! Of those, 40% will eventually suffer from chronic back pain.

Now here is where a strange fact of human behavior comes into play: people have a tendency to deny a problem until it become serious. It makes little sense when you take the time to objectively approach the subject but nonetheless, denial is a very real problem for many people. Even people who have successfully used and benefited from massage and who understand the importance of taking preventative action will often delay scheduling an appointment!

Why? Why would someone use an effective method of treatment with positive results yet not return to it? Again, denial. Research has shown people will put it off or ignore a problem until they can't. They may be in pain but think they can just "toughen up" and it will go away. Instead, what usually happens is a disaster – they can no longer function and are forced to seek help. In the situation of back pain, over 90% only seek help once they are in severe pain and once more damage has been done.

We've used back pain as an example but there are numerous conditions where the same fundamental "reasoning" is at work; from a host of chronic conditions to stress and emotional concerns. Society itself is not well versed in promoting prevention and early intervention – yes, there is the recognition of the need for and cost effectiveness of both but in reality, most of modern medicine and the societal constraints tend to recognize crisis above prevention or early intervention.

Instead, by validating the clients understanding of prevention and/or early intervention you are in effect, giving them "permission" to acknowledge the pain whether it is physical or emotional. People still feel guilty about taking the time they need to meet their own needs so this is no small concern. Never underestimate the need for validation.

The Inactive Re-Call is quite simple. Simply give your clients a courtesy call if they haven't scheduled an appointment with you in the past 90 days. This will not include every client but it should include any client who suffers from a chronic condition or who regularly uses massage to reduce stress.

The call should be simple and direct. Tell them up front that you were thinking of them, know they suffer with xyz condition and just wanted to check on them to see how they are doing. If they report feeling great then congratulate them and inform them of any specials you may have running at the time or any other news you may have to share from your practice. If they report feeling a little under the weather then ask them if they would like to schedule an appointment.

Frequently you may encounter people who will minimize the seriousness of the problem at that point. Again, you want to validate their pain and remind them of the importance of taking time to care for their own needs before it becomes a critical situation but do not push them. Offer your services and act from compassion and concern – not "sales".

Casual Calls: Reach Out and Touch – Everyone!

As a massage therapist you understand the importance of touch in the lives of your clients but all too often, the emotional touch is also missing from their lives. Setting a high expectation and then exceeding it, goes beyond the location, beyond the environment and even beyond the massage...if you are able to truly touch each client on an emotional level then you have created a complete experience for your client. One they will likely remember far after the massage has diminished.

Just a few tips to keep in mind – seek ways to make more memories on your own!

1. Call them when they seem down.
2. Send a small note card to just "say hello".
3. Celebrate with them during a happy occasion like the birth of a child, marriage, retirement, promotion or other life event by sending a card or special acknowledgement.
4. Remember their birthdays! Sadly, many people in this society are not near family or loved ones and may not even get a card from anyone else!
5. Learn and use their full names or nicknames as well as the names of family or other important people and/or events in their lives. Again, it's tragic but true that people suffer from lack of being "known" in their day to day lives. Yes, it can be difficult to learn their name but just think back to your own response when someone unexpectedly knew your name!
6. ALWAYS smile at them when they enter and make sure the last thing they hear when exiting your office is something positive and caring attached to their name!

Chapter 11

Time is too slow for those who wait, too swift for those who fear, too long for those who grieve, too short for those who rejoice, but for those who love, time is eternity.

Henry Van Dyke

Every moment is a golden one for him who has the vision to recognize it as such.

Henry Miller

Time

It has been said time is the only real commodity on earth. It's precious. It's truly limited. We all must eventually die and therefore will never experience everything the world or life has to offer. We must pick and choose. When you have very little money then you sell your time for a price.

What are those moments worth? Of course, attempting to place a value on time is utterly absurd. What price would you require to trade your first kiss of true love for time spent flipping burgers at a local restaurant during your youth? How much would a new mother charge in exchange for watching her child take its first steps? Think back over your life and try to come up with a price for those memories that mean the most to you. They are priceless! What would be a "fair and equitable" rate to charge in exchange?

How Do You Value Your Time?

Quickly we realize that time is priceless when put into those terms and it is for this reason above all else that you should enjoy your life's work. Yes, we sell our time and thereby our life day after day. Later, when we have more money then it becomes economical and wiser to pay others to use their limited allocation of time here on earth to do those things for us that don't bring enjoyment. It may be that their expertise allows them to do it better or faster than ourselves or it may mean that our income has increased to the point that it makes better financial sense to pay others to take care of mundane tasks. Either way, we are placing a value on time.

What Are You Worth?

In a similar manner we place a value on risk, labor and other criteria which are often disproportionate to the actual value derived. Many years ago when we were first married, my husband worked at a factory building trusses for houses. Minimum wage was $3.35 an hour back then and he made slightly above that amount at $4.85 an hour or roughly $39 per 8 hour day of work. There was a malfunction that resulted in his thumb being caught in a machine and nearly severed. Fortunately, the tendons were spared and after surgery, rehabilitation and much pain most feeling was restored. However, there was a point when partial amputation was considered. Of course, if you have read this book then you also know my husband later lost his vision so his hands are of tremendous importance to him!

Certainly the $39 he earned for that day seemed so small in comparison – in fact, his entire years salary would not have compensated for the lifetime loss of a thumb should that have been the case. Yet insurance standards assign value to loss of limb, vision, fingers, toes, thumbs, arms, legs and even life itself all the time based upon the productivity or average profit you – or that portion of you that was harmed or lost – are able to generate.

It is a far from perfect system and one that places the productivity of the individual above the life and experience of the individual. Worker's compensation, lawsuits and accidental death and dismemberment (AD&D) policies pay based upon the "monetary worth" of your body parts, depending on what profession you are in. So for example, if a famous guitar player lost a thumb, the part would be "worth" far more than my husbands thumb.

Typically, in the event you lose a body part on the job, worker's compensation will cover the cost of your injury. Each part of your body is assigned a set number of weeks for compensation purposes. The general equation they use when determining the worth of your body part is by taking a percentage of your weekly salary and multiplying it by the number of weeks assigned to the lost part.

Clearly this does not reflect the value any reasonable person would place on either their time or body function yet productivity measures are the primary means of measuring time. For that reason it will also be the unit used here since it is a discussion of business and productivity. However, on a personal note, I like to use it for another even more important reason: to remind others to respect and properly value your own life by loving what you do and never selling yourself short. Use the business as an extension of your life and create the lifestyle with the type of meaning that brings you more than mere money.

Finally, treat your time as though you were already making the money you would like to make. Always ask yourself "What is the best use of my time right now?".

Calculating Productive Time

Assumption		8 hr day, 244 work days annually				Extra Time Value Annually		
Salary	Month	Wk	Day	Hour	Min	15m	1hr mo	1 hr yr
20k	$1,667	$385	$82	$10.25	0.17	$625	$208	$2,500
25k	$2,083	$481	$102	$12.81	0.21	$781	$260	$3,125
30k	$2,500	$577	$123	$15.37	0.26	$938	$313	$3,750
35k	$2,917	$673	$143	$17.93	0.30	$1.094	$365	$4,375
40k	$3,333	$769	$164	$20.49	0.34	$1,250	$417	$5,000
45k	$3,750	$865	$184	$23.05	0.38	$1,406	$469	$5,625
50k	$4,167	$962	$205	$25.61	0.43	$1,563	$521	$6,250
60k	$5,000	$1,154	$246	$30.74	0.51	$1,875	$625	$7,500
75k	$6,250	$1,442	$307	$28.42	0.64	$2,344	$781	$9,375
100k	$8,333	$1,923	$410	51.23	0.85	$3,125	$1,042	$12,500

Express Example

Natalie has been in practice for several years and has a strong client base however, she would like to maximize her profitability without dramatically increasing her workload. Natalie's business expenses run approximately $35,000 and her annual salary has been roughly $40,000 for a total of $75,000.

Natalie has identified several productivity problems in the daily workflow of her business but to keep it realistic, she has decided to begin slowly. Natalie finds she has a tendency to take a longer than average lunch especially if she doesn't have a client scheduled. Instead of prolonging her lunch time, Natalie decides to make it productive time by taking care of administrative duties until the next client arrives. She determines this would save her at least 30 minutes per day.

Using the table above, Natalie calculates that at a $75,000 level, 15 minutes per day over a one year period equates to $2,344. She multiplies that by 2 since she will be saving a minimum of 30 minutes per day. $2,344 x 2 = $4,688 annually.

Now notice, Natalie's fixed cost for business didn't increase whatsoever! The entire $4,688 becomes part of Natalie's personal income assuming she continues to fill her productive and billable hours.

Time Limits and Earning Constraints

Sooner or later ever small business owner reaches a point where they cannot increase prices, work more hours, or dramatically improve productivity. Worse, when they stop working so does their income. That is what a job is all about right? Well, yes. But it's not what a business is all about.

Take a look at most large business entities and you will quickly notice that the CEO is not doing each and every task personally. They delegate responsibility. The bigger the entity the more delegation and specialization takes place.

Let's examine how this plays out in "real life". Using Natalie from the example above, we find that if Natalie misses a day of work her lost earning potential = $307. On top of that, her cost of rent, utilities and other items didn't diminish so she's actually in even worse condition.

On the other end of the spectrum, what would happen to the daily earnings if the CEO of Sony didn't show up to work that day? It would not really impact the business in any meaningful way whatsoever.

Establishing the Work Week When Less is More and More is Less

When to Work More (or Less!)

Many massage therapists work either part-time or as independent contractors but at some time or another, the question often arises whether or not to take a second job, expand or change positions. It's essential to understand the "costs" as well as benefits before making the decision.

In addition to the additional labor and time, there are other expenses including travel, increased tax bracket, insurance and other issues to be considered before deciding if it's a good decision. Bigger is not always better – sometimes it's just more tiring!

Express Example

Ted has been in business for several years and has a solid income. Last year he made $55,000 but he's thinking of expanding his business by taking a 2nd office on the other side of town in a rapidly growing area which has been underserved according to his location data. He will rent out a small location at first in order to build clients in that area. Ted comes to the conclusion he can realistically expect to grow his new location business to earn an additional $20,000 next year, making his total annual income an anticipated $75,000. By doing so, Ted will push himself into the next tax bracket in addition to the self employment taxes and

other expenses. Ted realizes that over 40% of each new dollar generated will go toward taxes [between the higher tax bracket and self employment taxes] and that is before calculating in the additional time and energy required. Ted comes to the conclusion that the effort is disproportionate to the return and decides instead, to focus his energy on increasing his proportion of weekly and monthly clients rather than open a new office at this point.

Express Example Two

Julie is a single mother who has been working as an independent contractor. Last year her annual income was $22,000. As an Independent Contractor she is responsible for self employment taxes of over 15% in addition to her tax rate of 15%. Julie does not have benefits and has worried about the problem of healthcare coverage especially with a young child. However, her schedule allowed her the flexibility to pick up her son from school and avoid the cost of day care. Julie has the opportunity to become an employee with full benefits but the additional hours would require Julie to put her son in day care after school. Day care would cost roughly $500 per month however her income would increase to $27,000 annually with healthcare and other benefits including 2% toward retirement. Julie would remain in the same tax bracket and her self employment taxes would be reduced in half. Julie realizes this would more than compensate for the cost of daycare and decides to take the offer.

When to Work More or Less - Worksheet

The accompanying worksheet helps you focus on whether taking a second job or expanding your current workload will be worthwhile. By using the worksheet you will have an estimate of the net gain or loss to be expected. Use this whenever you are contemplating whether or not it makes sense to expand or take on additional work.

Anticipated Gross pay from second job: $__________

The value of employer's contribution [if any] to:

- Retirement plan: __________
- Health & disability insurance (self, family): __________
- Life insurance: __________
- Gifts, bonuses, etc.: __________
- Savings on dependent insurance coverage: __________
- Other monetary benefits (tips, meals, etc.): __________

(A) Total gross income from second wage-earner: $__________

Expenses (not tax deductible):

Additional tax on family income (federal, state, local):

- When both parties are employed: __________
- Subtract taxes paid when one party employed: __________
- Equals additional taxes paid: __________
- Additional Social Security Tax paid: __________

Extra cost of convenience food for home consumption: __________
Extra cost of meals eaten away from home: __________
Extra expense for general-wear clothing, including maintenance: __________
Extra personal care expenses: __________
Transportation to and from work, including parking: __________
Employee clubs, gifts, flowers, etc.: __________
Work-related parties and special meals: __________
Extra expense of hired help including day care if applicable while you are away:

- Household help: __________
- Child and dependent care costs minus any tax credits: __________
- House repairs & maintenance you will no longer do: __________

(B) Total Expenses (not tax deductible): $__________

Expenses (tax deductible)

Specialized work clothing & maintenance: $__________
Transportation on the job, not reimbursed: __________
Dues to union, professional, and business organizations: __________
Tools, licenses, and supplies for the job: __________
Professional & business meetings, conferences, etc.: __________
Educational expense of maintaining and increasing skills: __________
Professional and business publications:__________
Other specific expenses of producing income: __________
Contributions to an IRA (from second job): __________

TOTAL
$__________

After tax computation
100% less tax rate on second earners income times total expenses if itemize
Deductions * (e.g. 100% – 15% = 85% x expenses) : _________%
(C) Total Expenses (tax deductible) (multiply total by percent) $__________
Net economic gain from second wage-earner's employment
(D) Total gross income (A) $__________
(E) Total expenses related to income production (B + C) __________
(F) Net economic gain from second job (D – E) $__________
Subjective value (loss or gain) in family activities

(G) Value of family activities, one partner employed $__________
(H) Value of family activities, both partners employed $__________
(I) Possible value loss/gain in family activities (G – H) $__________
Net value gain from second wage-earner's employment

(J) Net income from second wage-earner's job (F) $__________
(K) Possible value loss in family activities (I) __________
Net family gain or loss from second wage-earner's employment (J – K) $__________

* Married: income less than $6,450 = 0%, $6,450 to $47,499 = 15%
Single: income less than $2,650 = 0%, $2,650 to $27,129 = 15%, $27,300 to $58,499 = 28%.
Don't forget self employment taxes of 15% if applicable in addition to the higher tax bracket if your earnings increase enough to require it.

Job Replacement vs. Business

It's here that we need to make a somewhat arbitrary distinction between a "job" and a "business". While it is true that many people own their own business, that business may still function as a "job replacement". They get paid for their time and effort. Sick or vacation time as well as insurance is actually calculated as part of the overall average but essentially, when they stop working then the income stops. That is true whether they work for someone else or themselves. In that situation, even if you own your own business, the business still functions like a "job replacement".

That is in stark contrast to the situation where profit continues to be made even without the individual effort of the owner. We can see this at work each and every day among big business entities but small business owners can accomplish the same thing with foresight, planning and effort!

Leverage Your Skills

The first step in leveraging your skill is to establish a value for each skill and then determine which are essential or non-essential. For the sake of convenience, let's use $60 per hour as a marker. Your rate could be higher or lower so make the appropriate adjustments based upon your own calculations.

Now determine what activities you perform that are essential. Essential activities are those that must be performed by you or are better if performed by you. Non-essential are those activities that need to get done by someone – but not necessarily you.

Essential	Non-Essential
Therapy Sessions	Cleaning Bathrooms, Treatment Rooms Etc
Recording SOAP Notes	Scheduling, confirmation calls, other
Client concerns	Laundry
___________________	Ordering supplies
___________________	Stocking, Inventory, Sales
___________________	___________________
___________________	___________________
___________________	___________________
___________________	___________________
___________________	___________________
___________________	___________________

Great! By now you should have a list of essential and non-essential activities directly related to running your business. Now let's select one and calculate the cost. For this example we will use scheduling, confirmation calls and other related phone calls. Elsewhere in this book these calls were discussed in depth and represent important benefits to your practice building exercises by reducing no-shows, increasing client satisfaction and helping generate a solid foundation for a new relationship. Furthermore, research demonstrates these calls give results!

However, by taking an objective approach you can see how these calls often get lost in the shuffle of busy schedules. After putting in a full day of work you are tired. It's easy to let it slip once or twice. Then there is the trade-off between choosing to fit in another massage versus doing your scheduled phone work. Here is the crux of the situation. Let's say you schedule your phone calls every day at 6:30 PM but a very good client would like to book that slot. Does it make more sense to reject the client and make the phone calls or provide the massage and skip the phone calls?

The answer is neither! Both are important! In this case you have set a value of $60 per hour on your time. If you schedule the massage then you make the $60. If you make the calls you do not immediately make any money (however, we know from experience the long term benefit is much more. See the information on pricing elsewhere). However, what would it cost you to pay someone else to make these calls for you every day?

The rate for a Virtual Assistant begins as little as $8 an hour. With modern technology it's quite easy to update your schedule each day and transmit via email or fax pertinent information to someone working from home. This person works as an independent contractor from the convenience of their own home. It's a perfect situation for college students, retirees or others seeking a little additional income.

You can find virtual assistants locally or even nationwide through classified ads, craigslist, Guru.com or eLance. If you use Guru or eLance, you can automatically have the 1099 and other forms completed on your behalf as well.

Don't rule out distance employees. With Voice over IP and other long distance plans many virtual assistants have free long distance so one of the main obstacles has been all but eliminated.

Notice, if you can replace yourself for $8 or $10 an hour, what is your rate worth for that hour? It's no longer worth $60 an hour but rather $8 or $10!!! On top of that, you don't get to claim your time as a deduction against taxes when you make the calls yourself but it's a business expense when you pay someone else to do it for you.

In this situation it would make sense to delegate those non-essential duties to others at a lower rate and increase your billable hours by performing the additional sessions.

Express Example

Lynn decides to hire a virtual assistant for one hour a day to handle confirmation calls, first visit follow-up calls, courtesy calls and so forth. They contract for $10 per hour x 5 days per week or roughly $200 per month.

Lynn is able to replace that one hour per day with an average of 3 additional massage sessions per week while actually working less hours overall! The 3 sessions have a value of $180 per week or roughly $720 per month.

After paying the virtual assistant, Lynn is able to make an additional $500 per month while working 8 hours less each month!

Opportunity Cost

While writing this book I've had to make choices about what to do myself and what to have other do for me. Obviously, certain things were a necessity like doing the actual writing (leveraging my skill) but other things came down to a question of time.

For instance, the design of this book cover. In all likelihood I could have done it myself – eventually - but the reality is that I don't know how to design a book cover. It would take me much longer, and probably with less than satisfying results, to figure it all out. Even if the results were fantastic, I'm slow. It's not my area of specialization so it made much better sense for me to hire out the book design.

Likewise, there will be areas where you will need to pay more than what your time is worth because the other person can perform the same duties in much less time or with greater expertise than you would be able to. Common examples of this include repairs, accounting, legal advice or other issues.

This is because you have lost the opportunity to make better use of your time. For instance, let's assume you decided to paint your office. You make preparations in advance including buying paint and supplies, travel to and from the hardware store and so forth. Then you actually begin the painting. It takes you four days or 32 hours but it looks great! Saved a bundle right?

Not so fast. 32 hours at $60 per hour = $1920 plus you are tired and worn-out before your work week even begins!

Now for the sake of argument, let's just assume you find a top-notch handy-man who charges you $80 an hour which is more than your regular rate but he is able to get the job done in 25 hours because he has better tools and more skill. His rate is $2,000 so you paid him more for the job but wait...did you ?

First of all, you come to work Monday morning fresh rather than worn out. Next, even though you get to deduct the cost of your paint and supplies, you don't get to deduct anything for your time if you do it yourself. On the other hand, the cost of maintenance and paint may be deducted when you pay to have it done for you. In that situation, you may actually come out ahead after all!

Finally, you missed the opportunity to perform a weeks worth of sessions!

Leverage Your Time

On a closely related theme – it is also possible to leverage your time by providing "value added services" or products. Elsewhere in this book merchandising and how to select the perfect products for your practice is covered. That is one method to increase profit during the same period of time but there are other ways as well.

For instance, if you have the space, consider adding "self service" items to your practice. An example of this might be a hydro-massage bed like those found in shopping malls or "dry infrared" spas that have become quite popular. This can be particularly attractive if your location is near a shopping plaza or other frequently traveled area where people are likely to stop in casually while doing other errands.

Another common example is to form “clubs” or membership options for groups so you are literally able to serve more people at the same time or perhaps you book several sessions for a special event or demonstration and then hire other therapists to actually perform the massage.

Of course employees are one of the major methods used by all types of business large and small to leverage their time. These can be Independent Contractors, part-time employees, full-time employees or whatever best suits your needs.

There are a multitude of variations on this but the concept remains the same: Serving more than one person at a time!

Leverage Your Assets

Levering your assets can also take many various forms but let’s examine a common one – under utilized space! You pay for the space whether it’s used or not so it’s advisable to use it as much as possible.

I’ll use a real life example here. Several years ago a well known local therapist found a terrific deal on a strip plaza lease. It was in a great location and was quite affordable. It was also much more space than he needed so he used one room exclusively for the occasional group meeting which was a nice touch but generated zero additional income.

Even using the most conservative estimates he had enough extra space to create at least two more treatment rooms. If he had charged even $400 per month for each room or $9,600 per year it would have generated enough to put his children through college. Now this may seem like an extreme example but in reality, smaller versions of this take place all of the time.

Review your office layout and determine if you have additional space. Review your schedule and see if you can lease out office space during times when you won’t use it. How about early morning hours? Weekends? Late afternoon or early evening hours? Elsewhere in this book office rental rates, buy versus lease and other factors are discussed at length but look for ways to leverage your assets on a regular basis.

TIPS

Know your clients goal for treatment! Ask. Respond. Assess.

If you can double your practice between 8 AM and 10 AM or 4 PM to 6 PM you would bring in approximately double your current revenue but double your practice between 10 AM to 2 PM usually represents only 10% growth.

Chapter 12

"If we could sell our experiences for what they cost us we'd be millionaires"
Abigail Van Buren

Cost of Handling vs. Cost of Producing

As part of a clinical or therapeutic profession this can be a very difficult topic so I'd like to take a moment to clarify a few points. First, I strongly believe there is a proper place, time and response to each and every person in need of care. I also believe that individualized treatment is essential to the quality of ALL medical and health related care. Having said that, the reality is your practice is your livelihood. It is what allows you to provide for your own needs and those of your family and loved ones. It's also what allows you to select who and when you provide charitable care to others in need....whatever that need may be. As such, it's imperative to understand what comprises a "profitable" client. Toward that end, this segment of the discussion will be quite frank while providing a realistic assessment of your actual cost and capacity of "handling" versus "producing".

Now, I'm going to say something that superficially sounds negative but it's very important so keep reading...

All Clients are Not Equal...

Yes, all clients deserve the best treatment, respect and consideration available and all clients are equal when it comes to their human attributes...but they are not all equal when it comes to business and profit potential.

Some clients demand immense amounts of your time and energy. They fail to respect you as a professional. They present toxic or negative attitudes that leave you drained or even resentful by the end of the session...thereby jeopardizing your ability to fully serve other clients. Still other clients may have delightful personalities that are habitually late or chronically tend to cancel appointments at the last minute. Finally, there are those sporadic clients with very high preparation and other needs.

You may have heard it said that 80% of your business will come from 20% of your customers. That statistic tends to hold true through a variety of business relationships. What this means is the top 20% of your clients will generate approximately 80% of your revenue and in reverse, the bottom 20% of your clients will consume 80% of your time. For example, let's assume – for ease of numbers – you have 100 clients. A typical [and in 'real life' there isn't anything "typical" but rather approximations] breakdown would be as follows:

Top 20 Clients: These clients routinely and regularly schedule a massage almost like clockwork because massage is part of their routine and life. They tend to be on time for appointments, prefer a set schedule whenever possible, paperwork is minimal since they rarely change their schedules unless for emergency or travel, and they tend to generate positive referrals since they are enthusiastic about their massage experience. This is the type of client you want to attract! In fact, once you attract this type of client their word-of-mouth marketing makes it more likely for you to reduce your marketing expenses while still growing your business [remember, word of mouth marketing is one of the most cost effective and productive methods available to increase your business].

The Lifetime Value of a Client

Understanding the different types of clients is the first step but now you need to understand the "lifetime value" of each type of client. To calculate the lifetime value of a client there are several things you need to know and understand but everything revolves around time and money.

Since massage therapy is a service industry the lifetime value of a client is different from manufacturing or regular sales. For the sake of convenience, we will provide a few examples. To make this easy, the most simple estimates will be used. Your real life values will depend upon your total costs for marketing etc...for ease of numbers a flat $5 will be used in place of the gift card.

First, let's assume someone decides buy a gift certificate for a massage. That's great since someone thinks enough of your establishment to give a massage as a gift but it's also an unknown because the recipient of the gifted massage isn't a regular massage user [for the sake of this example]. So, you provide the massage and they don't come back.

1 Massage = $60
Minus cost [$5]
So, $60 - $5 = $55 Lifetime Value

Let's change the scenario slightly and assume they do come back but not until next year when they receive another gift certificate. This repeats itself (after all, they love getting a massage on their special day!) so the lifetime value of this client is now one massage per year for an average of 5 years (remember, on average, people move every 5-7 years)

1 Annual Massage = $60 with an average of 5 years = $600
$600 - $5 cost = $595 Lifetime Value

Instead, let's use the same example and assume this client enjoys the massage so much they begin to use your services each month.

12 Annual Massages @ $60 = $720 for an average of 5 years = $3,600
$3,600 - $5 cost = $3, 595

Finally, let's calculate this example for a weekly client.

50 Annual Massages @ $60 = $3,000 for an average of 5 years = $15,000
$15,000 - $5 cost = $14,995

Of course, this is based primarily on gross values....before operating expenses and other costs are deducted... and it doesn't include discounts, missed appointments and so forth but it should provide a working example of how to calculate the lifetime value of each client. This is a very important concept but before continuing, we must now include the next stage of lifetime value.

To this point, we have only discussed the actual lifetime value of each client without any referrals. In real life, the more often someone uses your services the more likely they are to tell someone else about it, further increasing the lifetime value through referrals.

Lifetime value of top 20% client with referrals

Your best clients who routinely and regularly use your services will provide the best referrals for several reasons. First, massage is a regular part of their life and they are highly engaged in it. The more frequently they use your services the more enthusiastic they are about it. Beyond that, people tend to know and interact with others who share similar interests, live in similar neighborhoods and have the same level of expendable income. They may even share the same hobbies or occupations if they know one another from work or socializing. In essence, your very best clients know other people very similar to themselves. If they try out massage and value it, then it's likely they in turn will also become excellent clients!

Middle 60% Clients: These clients are your average clients. Sometimes they come in, sometimes not. Schedules are less reliable. Many have time consuming paperwork, conditions or other situations that occasionally arise but in general...what you come to expect from doing business on a day to day basis.

Bottom 20% Clients: These clients are time consuming, toxic, disrespectful of your time, tend to miss appointments, present with complications and complaints on a regular basis and often have the therapist or other staff members "jumping hoops" to try to please. It doesn't take many of these to run a therapist into the ground both in terms of time, energy and finance! Just as the top 20% of clients will typically comprise 80% of your profits, the bottom 20% of clients will typically require 80% of your time.

As painful and counter-intuitive as it may seem to someone who had dedicated their life to helping others, it's important to identify - and then address – this situation when it arises. It is impossible to grow your business when all of your extra time and energy is spent "handling" issues rather than creating "productive" results for both you and your clients!

A Word About Negative Referrals

In addition to the positive aspects of creating a strong solid core foundation for your practice by actively pursuing clients with a high lifetime value [increasing productivity], reducing or eliminating the bottom 20% of clients [decreasing handling] results in one other very important consideration that I would be remiss by not mentioning.

Many therapists attempt to please everyone and work themselves ragged both physically and emotionally rather than setting limits or letting a client go. However, this is often a tragic mistake that can actually cost the therapist more than ever expected!

An unhappy client tends to tell – on average – 9 others! It doesn't take long for a less than desirable message to spread around town should you have just a few disgruntled clients. Instead of trying to be all things to all people, accept there are clients that will simply not "click"....and it's OKAY!!!

It happens in every profession and it does not mean you are less professional, nor competent; it only means there are personality or other differences which are simply not as compatible. Because of the close work required between therapist and client, massage is a career where normally insignificant issues can appear to be a much larger issue. Again, it's okay to accept – and indeed celebrate – these unique qualities between both the client and therapist for what they are...individual preferences.

Often people in all types of service related fields interpret this as rejection or feel guilty if they do not particularly enjoy the company of a client...or in fact, plain dislike a client. It's natural and acceptable. By recognizing these differences you can help your own practice grow, provide referrals to other respected professionals that may provide a better 'fit' and finally, assure the client receives the quality and level of care they are most comfortable with. It's a win-win situation all the way around and you do not end up fighting the ghost of an unhappy client who has generated 'negative referrals'.

When to Refer – Interactive Response Worksheet

There are appropriate times to refer a client. The most successful referral program is one that respects all parties involved. The first step is self-respect. Recognizing, establishing and then actually following through with your own personal boundaries as an extension of your professional ethics. Remember, these may be areas that another therapist is completely okay with and you may fully accept areas which other therapists find difficult.

Take a few minutes to consider your initial reaction to each of the following. If you are a veteran practitioner who has been in the field for a long period of time then it may be necessary for you to reflect back on your first reaction when initially presented with the idea or concept. Then consider whether this is something that you are completely comfortable with or simply have become resigned to deal with.

I want to challenge you to try this in your practice for six months and see for yourself if it doesn't alter your overall level of energy, positive attitude and responsiveness from clients while simultaneously increasing your standing in the community.

Remember, there are not any 'right' or 'wrong' answers. These are simply your personal preferences. Try to throw away the bias and individual "self talk" that may constrain your ability to recognize and legitimize your personal preferences.

For each of the following rank your order of preference from 1-10
1 = Dislike 5 = Neutral 10 = Favorite

Scalp/Head
1 2 3 4 5 6 7 8 9 10

Face
1 2 3 4 5 6 7 8 9 10

Neck
1 2 3 4 5 6 7 8 9 10

Shoulders
1 2 3 4 5 6 7 8 9 10

Armpits
1 2 3 4 5 6 7 8 9 10

Back
1 2 3 4 5 6 7 8 9 10

Stomach/Abdominal Region
1 2 3 4 5 6 7 8 9 10

Lumbar
1 2 3 4 5 6 7 8 9 10

Gluteal
1 2 3 4 5 6 7 8 9 10

Thighs
1 2 3 4 5 6 7 8 9 10

Legs
1 2 3 4 5 6 7 8 9 10

Feet
1 2 3 4 5 6 7 8 9 10

Hands
1 2 3 4 5 6 7 8 9 10

Whew! Time for a break. How are you doing so far? By now there are probably a few things that will have taken place...either you tend to be somewhere in the middle of each of the above or you have one or more extremes. Those extremes may be surprising to you or they may not be but let's take a moment to reflect on what this means and how it translate to your real life practice...and profitability.

First, let's tackle those things you do NOT like as much or overtly dislike. Begin by asking why? For example, let's assume someone ranked feet with a score of "1" essentially stating they actually dislike working with feet. Perhaps it's not the actual feet but rather the condition of hygiene encountered among the majority of the population. In that case, there is a "remedy" for their dislike. That remedy should become part of the office process and procedures. In this case, not necessarily for the comfort of the client although they will indirectly benefit because the therapist is working at a higher level of comfort, but for the benefit of the therapist.

That is a perfectly acceptable reason! Again, I encourage you to recognize and respect your own needs in order to address those of your client.

If you are like most people then it may be difficult for you to acknowledge that there are some parts of the body you are more comfortable with than others. As massage professionals it's even more difficult...after all, you work with people and their body all day long so the expectation is that everyone is equally comfortable and accepting of parts of the body. The reality is most people have preferences and that is perfectly acceptable.

Let's take the medical profession as an example. Physicians certainly have preferences and it is highly desired – even profitable – for them to be quite specialized. There are general practitioners who of course, serve a very real and truly valuable purpose. Likewise, when it comes time for brain surgery or a rare condition that would otherwise not allow the generalist enough exposure to become expert at, then that preference – translated into a specialization – is highly valued.

The same can apply to massage. There are generalist and specialists. If you find yourself STRONGLY drawn to specific areas of the body then use that as part of your foundation being sure to take into account the other lessons in this work book. Let's assume someone else ranked hands as a "10" above. Essentially hands are their favorite part of the body.

Great! Now by using the location information discussed elsewhere in this book they can establish whether or not there is the need for...and population to support a specialization in hands. A special note about specialization: The more specialized and the more valuable the results the further a client will travel.

So, what if you were relatively neutral or in the middle ground on all of the above? That is perfectly fine too. It simply means that the body is NEITHER a motivator or detractor for you. Other factors may be highly motivating or detracting to you such as environmental stimuli. Speaking of which, let's continue....

Again, for each of the following rank your order of preference from 1-10
1 = Dislike 5 = Neutral 10 = Favorite

Silence
1 2 3 4 5 6 7 8 9 10

Music
1 2 3 4 5 6 7 8 9 10

Productivity/Office
1 2 3 4 5 6 7 8 9 10

Machinery/Equipment
1 2 3 4 5 6 7 8 9 10

Sounds of Street/City
1 2 3 4 5 6 7 8 9 10

Environmental/Nature
1 2 3 4 5 6 7 8 9 10

Hospital/Clinical
1 2 3 4 5 6 7 8 9 10

Heat
1 2 3 4 5 6 7 8 9 10

Cold
1 2 3 4 5 6 7 8 9 10

Wind
1 2 3 4 5 6 7 8 9 10

Humidity
1 2 3 4 5 6 7 8 9 10

Day
1 2 3 4 5 6 7 8 9 10

Night
1 2 3 4 5 6 7 8 9 10

Large/Expansive Space
1 2 3 4 5 6 7 8 9 10

Small/Cozy Space
1 2 3 4 5 6 7 8 9 10

Again, let's review what this may indicate for your real life practice. Are there any extreme rankings? If not, it simply means that the environment is NEITHER a motivator or detractor for you. However, many people have very strong orientations toward certain environmental cues or other factors. Let's use a rather common area that people tend to have strong rankings on one way or another...space. This perfectly exemplifies how there is no 'right' or 'wrong' answer but rather preference and that preference can manifest itself in many ways.

Let's assume for just a moment that someone ranks the large expansive space as a "10" [favorite] and a small/cozy space as a "1" [dislike]. Now notice, it's not that they prefer a large space but are neutral toward a small space but rather they have an extreme response to both indicating not only a strong preference [motivator] but an active dislike [detractor] with the opposite. Perhaps this therapist suffers from a touch of claustrophobia or simply feels more freedom in a large area. In a situation such as this, the therapist may find it extremely challenging to work in a small office no matter how much they enjoyed everything else. Day after day after day to be confronted with a space that is felt to be uncomfortable becomes dreadful. Fine, accept that reality and try to find a place that suites your level of comfort.

By all means, be realistic about it as well. For instance, if a chiropractor had available office space for your practice but the room was implicitly small then it would eventually be a huge mistake for you to force yourself into this situation. I'll share a personal example that drives home this all important concept. Plain and simple, I have a strong response to windows. The room can be almost any size as long as the window is big and beautiful...and preferably able to be opened. I've had large office, small office, beautifully decorated office and utter dumps for an office – none of which impressed or depressed me until I had an office without a window.

It was a fine office in every other way – except for the window. The lighting was fine, it was comfortable. No big deal right? Wrong. I didn't learn to live with it but instead constantly wondered at my own state of general tension. I was thrilled when work took me out of the office even at the expense of having to travel long distances to visit clients. Even when sitting in traffic! I finally realized the sense of "freedom" I felt while sitting in traffic (which I normally despise) was only a symptom of something much larger. I really did not like what I thought was a perfectly acceptable office. I knew immediately what the problem was because it was the very thing I noticed the moment I first walked in...there wasn't a window.

I traded "down" to what had literally been a store-room...with a window...and was much happier almost immediately. Now, this might seem like nonsense to someone who is relatively neutral for environmental stimuli but for someone who has extreme rankings in either direction, it will border almost on a visceral response. Taking that strong visceral response and repeatedly exposing oneself to it – either positively or negatively – day after day and month after month then year after year....is it any wonder it either strongly motivates or detracts?

Of course not! Building your perfect practice should be a reflection of those things you most enjoy...and the elimination or remediation of those things you don't enjoy.

Just as most therapists will remain neutral for a majority of items, so will most clients. However, just as certain specific criteria will elicit a strong response in you...it will do the same in some clients. Yes, that may mean you refer them but it will equally mean that others will have just as strong of a positive response for the same reason you do which will reflect a stronger level of satisfaction.

Fearful that your clients won't like such a large area? You are probably correct – SOME won't like it at all but others will prefer it just as you do! Again, it's personal preference and there is no right or wrong answer. Many clients will be neutral on the majority of these factors but the same factors that you feel strong about will also naturally attract or detract other clients.

Those clients that have a strongly negative response should be immediately and professionally referred to another however, those that have an equally strong positive response will be that much more of a perfect "fit" for your practice.

The same goes for all of these criteria. For instance, the majority of massage establishments are open during standard business daylight hours however, there is evidence to support the need and interest [especially in large cities] for evening and weekend hours as well as very early morning hours. Again, your natural inclinations are very likely to gain clients that are strongly oriented in similar trends just as yourself.

In fact, using office hours as an example is a tremendous method to split or share an office with someone who has opposite or complimentary personal schedules to your own. For instance, split the cost with someone who would enjoy working a 6 AM to Noon shift, another from Noon to 6 PM and finally, someone else who is at their personal peak between 6 PM and Midnight. One office, three therapists. Less cost for all involved and a highly selective niche based upon time for those who indicate strong ranking in that area.

The same applies for other settings: dislike silence then perhaps sports massage in a gym setting or athletic events is more your style. Whatever your area of preference it is OKAY. Accept it, embrace it and let it help define your practice.

Continue the exercise for other areas of your personal preferences. For example

- Medical conditions including physical, disease, emotional and mental.

- Personality types

What About Clients that Don't "Fit"?

Ahhh, let's be realistic. Not everyone will be a perfect fit. You may just not "click". It's OKAY. Allow yourself to recognize the inherent differences among your clients and your own style! I challenge you to do this for six months and see if it doesn't actually result in growth rather than a diminishment of your practice!

First, generate a referral network with other practitioners. Never abandon a client or leave them "out in the cold". Basic integrity and respect owed to another human being dictates a professional attitude and the understanding that other practitioners may have a more suitable skill set or just different personality traits and abilities in keeping with the need of this particular client.

Next, make sure the referred professional is of the highest standard before making a referral!

Explain to the client how the other practitioner is better suited for their needs.

Be specific about what you specialize in, the vision for your practice, etc... ask the same for those in your referral network.

Finally, call the client to make sure the referral went well. If not, offer another referral based upon their feedback. Remember, do not leave the client "hanging"!!!

Analyze to Revitalize

So, the question is HOW do you determine which 20% to focus your efforts on? More importantly, How do you assure your marketing dollars are reaching the Right future clients...the type of client that will continue to use your service and spread the word about your practice?

Let's test the 80-20 rule...20% of your efforts will result in 80% of your profits and the top 20% of your clients usually represent roughly 80% of your profits . Again, this is roughly speaking. It will vary from practice to practice, town to town and even season to season but overall, it should be fairly close as this is a ratio that has been tested repeatedly. Despite this knowledge, many small business owners fail to capitalize on one of their greatest assets...their current client base!

Why it is imperative to Analyze your most profitable customers:

1. Your current clients require minimal to no "new client" acquisition cost; resulting in increased "net".
2. Your current clients represent the highest potential for "word of mouth" and "endorsement" advertising and marketing campaigns resulting in increased future profit potential.
3. Your current clients are "hungry" for your product or services and likely to purchase more IF you can demonstrate additional value resulting in greatly enhanced response rates for properly timed and placed campaigns.
4. By analyzing your best clients, you will be able to find new customers of the same type!

Large corporations have used the process of client or customer analysis for many years to grow their business but that data is within reach of small business owners like yourself. No, not quite as granular or specific, but enough to provide a working foundation for you to better understand this very important aspect of growing your practice!

The bulk of your past customers will probably be contained in only a few segments. Once you identify them you will be able to focus your effort and marketing budget to attract other people who fit into those segments and start really driving new customers—the most valuable customers—to your practice! Chances are, you and your clients will both be happier because the "fit" is just right!

Typically, clients fall into one of four general types:

Low Acquisition Cost **High Utilization of Services**	**High Acquisition Cost** **High Utilization**
Low Acquisition Cost **Low Utilization**	**High Acquisition Cost** **Low Utilization**

With modern technology it is possible to easily compile critical information about your clients and their purchasing/usage habits in order to create a “profile” of the type of individual who will most greatly benefit from your services BEFORE spending your hard earned dollars on a marketing campaign that may reach many people but fail to deliver the type of results desired.

Remember these pointers...

1. All clients are not equal when it comes to profitability.
2. It’s more important to reach the “right” people than “more’ people.
3. It’s better to spend more money to reach fewer people if they are the “right” fit.
4. 80% of your profit will come from 20% of your clients.
5. Integrate your preferences into your practice to attract and retain “best fit” clients.
6. Create and utilize referrals for clients that are not a good fit.
7. Reduce the risk of negative referrals by sending those clients to other practitioners who can better provide for the clients needs – physically, emotionally or mentally.

Target Marketing

Now that you understand the importance of identifying your perfect client profile it’s time to put it to use. It's important to remember the focus of marketing is people. If you're concentrating your efforts on your profit only, you'll miss the mark. The term target market is used because that market - that group of people - is the bull's eye at which you aim all your marketing efforts.

Don't forget a market is made up of people - people with common characteristics that set them apart as a group. The more statistics you have about a target market, the more precisely you can develop your strategy. The following are just a few ways to represent market segments (or groups).

Type of Market Segment	Shared Group Characteristics
Demographic Segment	Measurable statistics such as age, income, occupation, etc.
Psychographic Segment	Lifestyle preferences such as music lovers, vegans etc..
Use-based Segment	Frequency of usage such as drinking, traveling, etc.
Benefit Segment	Desire to obtain the same product benefits such as luxury, thriftiness, comfort from food, etc.
Geographic Segment	Location such as home address, business address, etc.

Here are examples of target segments that can be created using the above:

- Women business owners between the ages of 25 and 60 earning more than $25,000 annually form a demographic segment.

- People who drive compact cars due to their fuel efficiency form a benefit segment.

Be careful not to confuse a geographic market segment with a place. The market is the people who live in the Sunbelt area, not the Sunbelt area. This is a common mistake made by business owners that causes them to lose a marketing focus on their customers.

How To Design Marketing For Your Target Market

The reason we're concerned with identifying a target market is because it makes strategies for designing, pricing, distributing, promoting, positioning, and improving your service or idea easier, more effective, and more cost-effective.

For example, if research shows that a sturdy lift table appeals to your target market and if you're focused on that target market, you should choose that type of equipment. If, however, you're profit oriented - rather than people oriented - you might simply make purchase based upon price and standard functionality alone. In the long run, it will still hurt profit – it's better to spend more now than to loose clients because they are uncomfortable. In fact, it's advisable to go used rather than new if it brings you close to the needs and desires of your target market.

Here's another example: If you know your target market is 24- to 49-year-old men who like rhythm & blues, are frequent CD buyers, and live in urban neighborhoods, you can create an advertising message to appeal to those types of buyers. That may be an extremely different type of campaign than typically associated with massage but then again – it may attract an entirely new group to your services. A group completely ignored by other therapists! Additionally, you could buy local spots on a specific radio station or TV show that appeals to this type of buyer, rather than buying general media time to "cover all the bases." Make sense?

In summary, when you're making marketing decisions and trying to “cover all the bases” you are throwing away money. Everyone is different. Tailor your message with as much precision and accuracy as possible.

Tried and True Ways to Promote Your Practice

Every successful company uses some sort of promotion to influence certain audiences - usually customers or prospects - by informing or persuading them. Reasons for promoting a business include: increasing visibility, adding credibility to you or your company, enhancing or improving your image, and bringing in new business. The following cost-effective, easy-to-execute ideas have the power to increase sales in a way conventional advertising cannot. The key is to find the methods that are appropriate for your business, marketplace, and professional style.

1. Contests. As one example, a health food store decided to sponsor cooking contests. After sending out a press release announcing a competition for the best and most nutritious snack, a mailing went out to the store's customers soliciting entries. Food editors, professional chefs, and cooking teachers were invited to be judges. Both the winners and the winning recipes were publicized. As a therapist your practice could sponsor this in conjunction with a health food or vitamin store –saving both of you advertising costs while opening up new sources of revenue and gaining new clients.

2. Newsletters. Another good way to promote your practice is through newsletters. They demonstrate how much you know about your field and do it in a low-key, informative way. They help keep your business high in the consciousness of your prospects. The key is to provide information your clients find valuable.

3. Demonstrations. Demonstrations are an option to attract people to your place of business and establish your credibility. A chiropractic related establishment holds ergonomic demonstrations once a month featuring a proper lifting, posture and injury prevention techniques. These are sponsored through several large employers who deal with back related work injuries and are well received by the employers who help cover catering costs and openly promote the workshops among their employees. These workshops attract substantial crowds. Activities and demonstrations, food and drink, and an overall level of fun is established while creating a true value in the community.

4. Seminars. Often more appropriate for business-to-business marketing, seminars are the commercial side of demonstrations. If you hold a seminar, follow these rules for success: Schedule the event at a time convenient to most attendees; Be specific in the invitation about when the event begins, and ends, who will be there, and what the agenda is.; Follow up the invitations with personal phone calls; Charge for the seminar to give it a higher perceived value; Follow up after the event to get people's reactions.

5. Premiums. Also called an advertising specialty, a premium is a gift of some kind that reminds your customer of you and your service. There are thousands from which to choose: key chains, coffee mugs, refrigerator magnets, baseball caps, paperweights - just about anything that can be engraved, imprinted, silk-screened, or embroidered with your company name and phone number.

6. Speeches. Depending on your topic and market, you might want to speak before Chambers of Commerce, trade associations, health related groups, senior citizens, or other local organizations.

7. Articles. Another possibility is to write an article, reprint it, and mail it off to your friends, customers, and prospects. This positions you as an expert, and is a particularly good way to promote your business.

8. Bonuses. Give just a little bit more. Samples, freebies and new items are a nice touch but so are small gift certificates or complimentary items.

9. Coupons. For best results, the price break should be significant - at least 15 percent. This is one of the least expensive ways to develop new business and an excellent tool for evaluating advertising. However, one theory holds that coupons

draw people who only buy discount and never become regular customers, so be sure to monitor the results.

10. Donations. Donating your service to a charitable cause often results in positive exposure to community leaders, charity board members, PTAs, and civic groups. Many organizations look for donations of professional service time.

11. Free Services. If you can't afford to give away products, offering your services as a way of generating new business can also pay off. For example, send out a flyer offering customers a free consultation to draw them.

12. Special Benefits, Rates, or Notices. Smart organizations go out of their way to make customers feel important and appreciated. Frequent flyer clubs are the most pervasive example of loyalty-building benefits for customers only; this method has been adapted by many kinds of businesses.

13. Say Thanks. One of the best ways to let customers know you value their business and encourage their continued patronage is also one of the easiest. It boils down to saying thank you in letters, mailers, surveys, statement stuffers, receipts, invoices, and in person.

Chapter 13

The Sphere of Influence

Everyone has a Sphere of Influence. You have one. Your clients have one. Your banker has one. Your dry-cleaner has one. So does the waitress at your favorite restaurant. In the most simplistic terms the Sphere of Influence is simply that realm where you are able to influence another person's perception or decision-making process. This is not negative but rather a general tendency for all human beings. We learn from others and therefore it is only natural when we seek out trusted sources of information and experience before making decisions.

The Sphere of Influence is in motion when someone you trust gives you good advice or feedback. It is usually a small circle or network of highly valued, trustworthy friends or family which comprise your "inner circle" of influence. Your opinion matters to them and is likely to be highly regarded whether positive or negative. In turn, their opinion is typically appreciated by you.

Others who hold high levels of influence are typically people in a variety of professional situations or setting: for example, physicians are noted as typically having a high level of influence over their patients – especially once proper trust has been established.

The next level of influence is generally those people you know and work with on a less intimate basis. When they agree [or disagree] you are likely to take notice although it probably doesn't hold the same level of weight or validation as if it came from either an authority or a very close person. Nonetheless, it is still likely to be influential in your decision-making process...particularly if it's negative information.

The progression continues until the information is on the basis of rumor, gossip or just general reputation. In this situation, you may not know the person who made the original statement directly but have heard the information from a 'friend of a friend' or other similar situations. Still, the information itself tends to work "for" or "against" you as a business owner.

Using the Sphere of Influence to Attract and Retain Clients

The first step is to use your own sphere of influence to attract and build your client list. If you tend to be a bit shy this can be difficult but it's an important part of building a successful practice. Fortunately, one of the first places to begin is in your own inner circle and that will give you some practice before moving onward. Let's see how this works...take the time while reading this to fill in names beside each.

Sphere of Influence I Worksheet

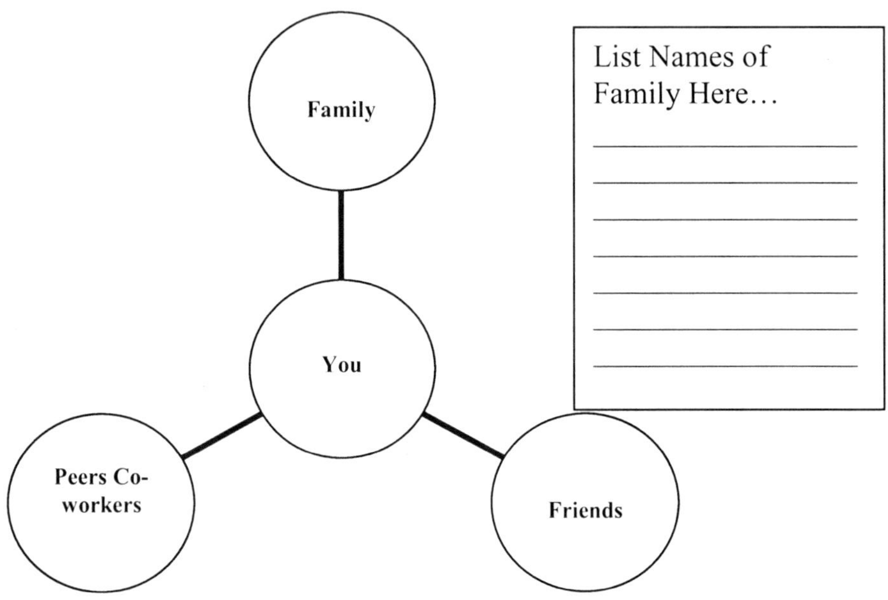

List Names of Peers Here…

List Names of Friends Here…

Great! You should now have a list of family, close friends and peers or co-workers that find YOU to be a source of information and expertise. It's now time to begin the process of communicating your USP [Unique Selling Proposition], your vision and goals for the practice, how it will look and much more.

Notice – This is VERY Important! – You are NOT asking for their opinion!!! I can't emphasize this enough! Everyone has opinions or preferences but there is a time and place for everything. Don't be tempted to ask for one at this stage. That is not the purpose of this exercise or activity. Stay Focused!

You are asking for them to spread the word about your business and your expertise, professionalism, mode of ethics and personal character. These are the people who know you best and trust you so they can attest to others about your trustworthiness, values and work ethic.

Seven Steps to Ignite Your Personal Sphere of Influence Worksheet

Here is what you need to do step by step. Take a few minutes to fill this out and try it out a few times before actually communicating it to anyone else. Begin with the people you listed above and actually go through this process several times. Remember – actually putting something in writing and going through these steps solidifies the commitment and substantially increases the likelihood of your personal success!

1. Introduce them to your career! This will sound silly for those of you who have been in business for awhile but one of the biggest problems that people encounter is the PERCEPTION that others understand exactly what they do and why. Assume absolutely Nothing! In fact, take this opportunity to "refresh" others about your life's work...chances are in so doing you will add a new spark back into your own vision! Briefly describe your career in meaningful terms.

   ____
   ____
   ____
   ____
   ____
   ____

2. State your USP [Unique Selling Proposition] and explain how it is different than others. Keep it simple yet clear and meaningful.

3. State your preferences as a therapist. Briefly tell them your perfect client.

4. States your goals for the business. Remain focused yet concise.

5. Ask them to refer you to three or five people. Don't just ask for "a referral" but instead, ask for a specific number of referrals from them. How many & Why?

6. Give them a "tool" to use to do the job...for example, a business card with a discount. List what tool you will use here with brief wording/description.

7. Show your appreciation by rewarding them! Yes, of course they will all be happy to help you because they are your family or friends but far to often in life we neglect those we care about the most. Make this a rewarding experience for them by showing your appreciation. Perhaps by giving them a free 30 minute massage or other special sign of appreciation. List rewards that they will appreciate.

____

____

____

____

____

____

So for instance, if you started with only three people and ask for three referrals. From those three new referrals you asked for three more and so forth....take a look at what would happen to your practice! Each of those 3 new contacts will have contacts and so on. Of course, not everyone will make 3 referrals each.

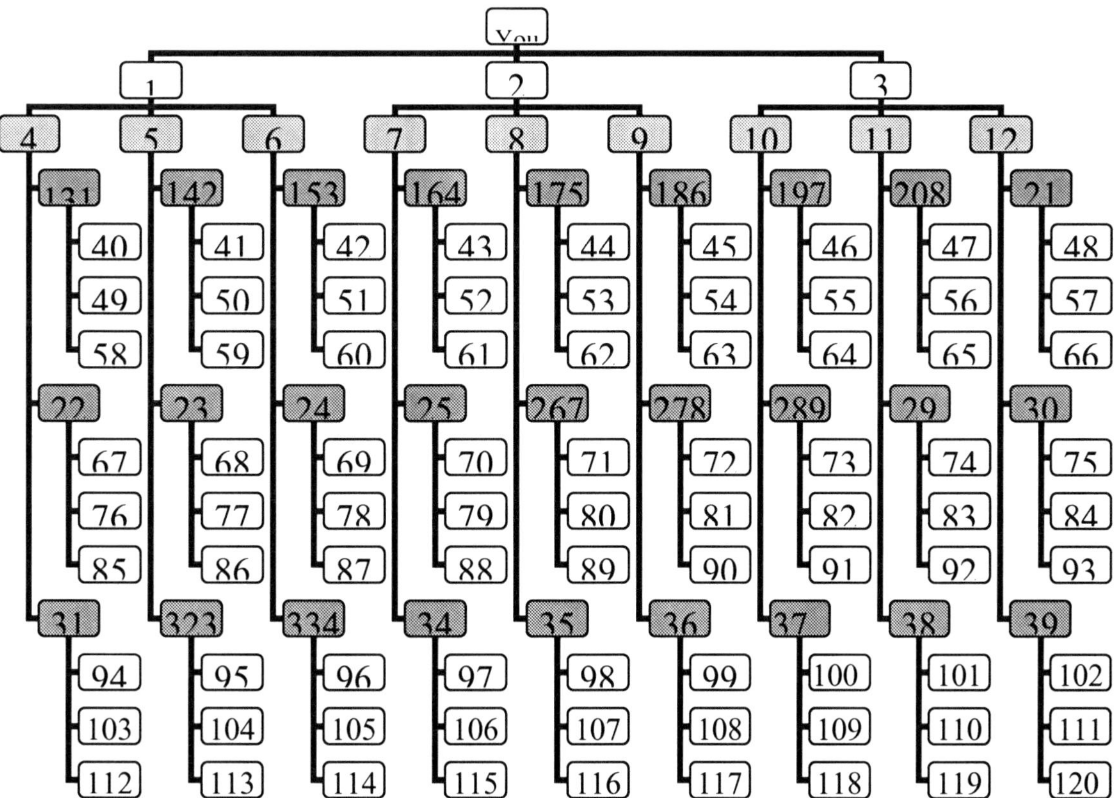

Sphere of Influence II

Wonderful! Now you should have worked through this a few times until it flows both on paper and when speaking. You should also have a good idea of the ***potential*** this strategy has for building your practice. Next you are ready to approach those outside your immediate sphere.

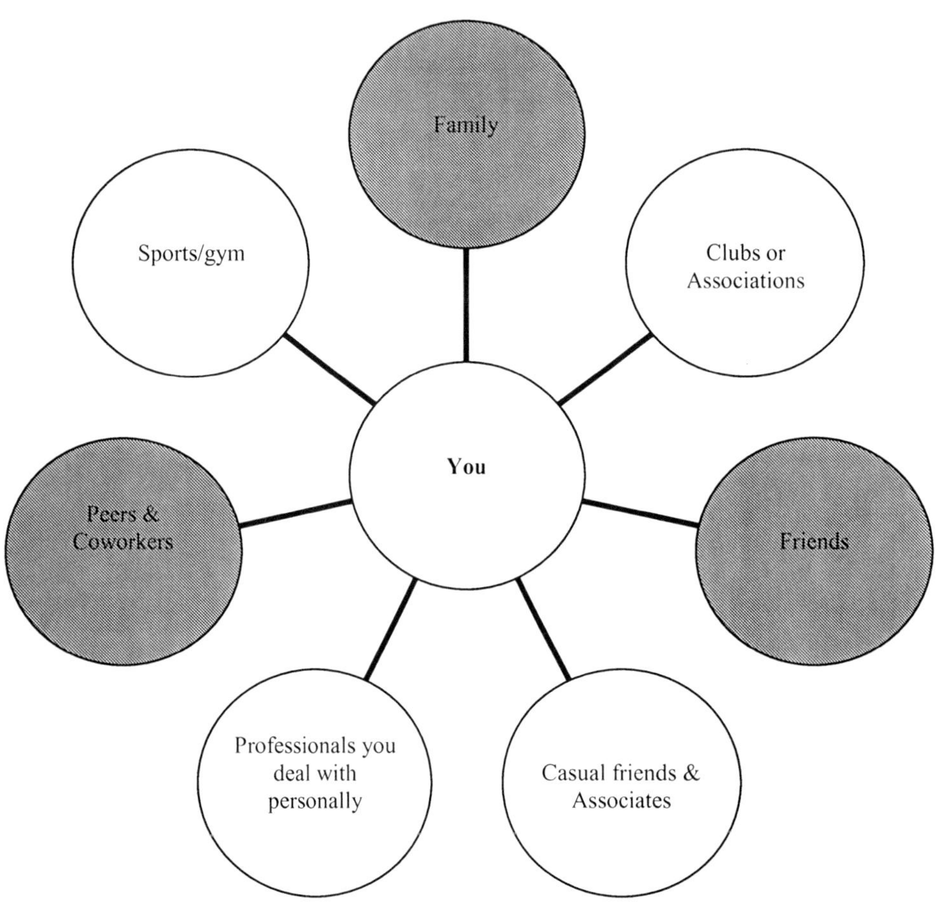

Five Steps to Ignite Your 2nd Sphere of Influence

These people are not as close or familiar but are still recognize who you are and have a familiarity and affinity for you. However, because they are not as directly involved with your personal life, you need to modify your message to be more concise yet still able to clearly communicate the primary points.

Again, take a few minutes to fill this out and try it out a few times before actually communicating it to anyone else. Begin with the people you listed above and actually practice several times before approaching others. This will need to be more clearly articulated and able to be communicated in 3-5 minutes. That means each point should take no longer than approximately 30 to 60 seconds each.

1. Introduce your business. Again, assume nothing. Be very precise. Don't just say "I'm a Massage Therapist" ...indeed you are, but that is what you do...not your business. Instead, tell them about your business. For example; "I own AnyTown Massage at 123 Street". I/We specialize in [state your USP]. If you are running a special be sure to include it. Be brief but concise.

   ____
   ____
   ____
   ____
   ____
   ____

2. State your preferences and goals as a therapist. Explain WHY you are requesting their assistance and what you hope it leads to for your practice.

   ____
   ____
   ____
   ____
   ____
   ____

3. Ask them to refer you to three or five people. Don't just ask for "a referral" but instead, ask for a specific number of referrals. Tell them How many & Why.

   ____
   ____
   ____

4. Give them a "tool" to use to do the job...for example, a business card with a discount. List what tool you will use here with brief wording/description.

5. Show your appreciation by rewarding them! Yes, once again you need to reward them. Unlike your close family and friends, this group will be less involved in your life and success. It's easy for them to walk away and forget. Instead, create a memory of a reward or act of appreciation they can look forward to by helping. List rewards that they will appreciate. It must be something of value to them.

Sphere of Influence III

Now you are ready for the outer range. This group consists of people that you know "of" but probably don't know personally. The focus now turns to people who have influence or access to many others in the general community. Remember the information about location – this is an area where it will apply so keep that in mind while working through this section.

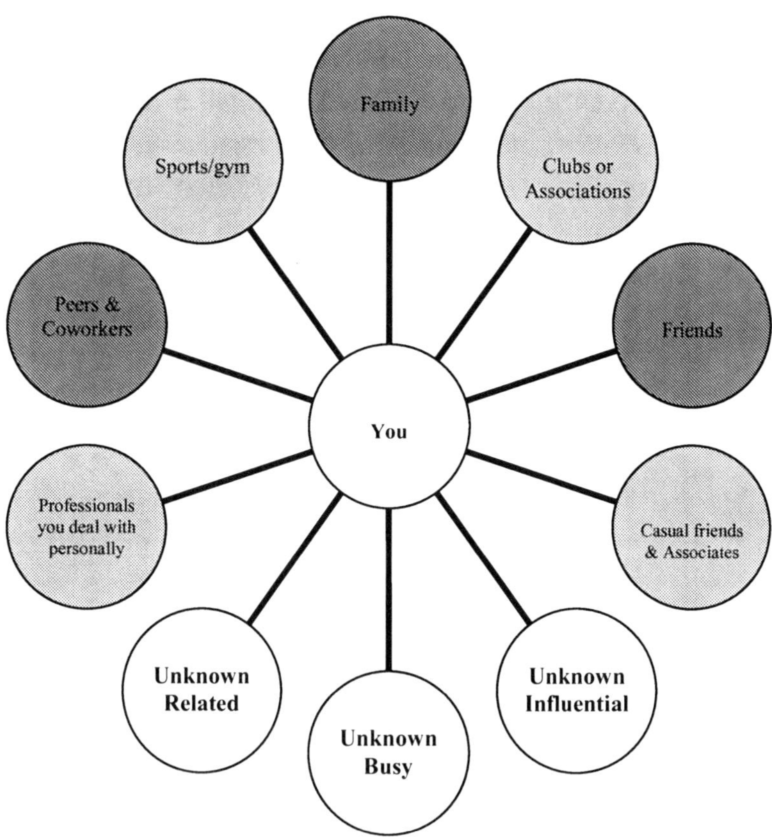

The three "types" consists of ...

1. Unknown Influential: Unknown Influential are people you do not personally know – or barely know – but who are well known in the local area or community. These may be local politicians, doctors, board members or others that are active and visible in the local community. Location is important to the level that they must be recognized by others in the general vicinity.

Take a moment and quickly jot down people that you know "of" that are active in your local community:

2. Unknown Busy: Unknown busy are people you do not personally know – or barely know – who are in positions that deal with people a lot. Examples would include restaurant service staff, police and fire rescue, beauticians and barbers, spa owners, golf or other amusement staff, dry cleaners and other small business owners that deal with a large number of people on a daily basis.

   This only applies to those people within a 15 mile radius of your practice location! Take a moment to jot down potential places to visit:

3. Unknown Related: Unknown related include "complimentary" business types or individuals. These would include Chiropractors or physicians if you address medical related massage, perhaps psychologists and psychiatrists for stress related specialization. Local athletic clubs, colleges and university sports coaches/teams for sports massage and so forth. Location is still important but within approximately a 35 mile range since they are directly complimented by your specialization.

Three Steps to Ignite Your 3rd Sphere of Influence

These people are known to you but for all practical purposes, essentially strangers. However, they hold visible positions in the local community and interact with large number of people on a daily basis. Because they do not know you and are certainly not involved with your business or goals, you need to modify your message to be even more concise yet still able to clearly communicate the primary points.

Again, take a few minutes to fill this out and try it out a few times before actually communicating it to anyone else. Begin with the people you listed above and actually practice several times before approaching others. This will need to be more clearly articulated and able to be communicated in 1 minute. That means each point should take no longer than approximately 15 to 30 seconds.

1. Introduce your business. Be very precise and don't include any additional words. Don't just say "I'm a Massage Therapist" ...indeed you are, but that is what you do...not your business. Instead, tell them about you business. For example; "I own AnyTown Massage at 123 Street". I/We specialize in [state your USP].

   ____

   ____

   ____

   ____

2. Invite them to visit you with either a free or deeply discounted massage. Give them your business card and let them know why you are doing this. It is perfectly acceptable to say that you are new and just starting out.

   ____

   ____

   ____

   ____

3. If they enjoy the service then hand them your referral tool and ask them to provide referrals. Again be specific.

   ____

   ____

   ____

   ____

   ____

A Note About the 3rd Sphere...

You will want to use this realistically and strategically. It will be essential to make a very good first impression so only do this when you are really ready and able to show your best work. Because these people have such widespread contact in the community, they are likely to have much more extensive personal Sphere's of Contact so will be able to make many more referrals than typical if they desire to do so. On the other hand, it can work in reverse just as easily. A negative referral from one of these power-house sources could wreck havoc on your reputation.

Use caution and gradually build up to this level.

Why are Referrals so Important?

- Because they come from a credible "endorser" who has experienced the benefits your company provides.
- They are low cost and tend to have much higher "conversion" rates
- According to research, up to 45% of service oriented business will be selected based upon recommendations of others.
- Dunn & Bradstreet research demonstrates it is one of the most popular and profitable ways to acquire new business.
- It builds loyalty among your current clients. Research indicates your clients are more likely to report higher satisfaction ratings, remain a client for a longer period of time and complete more sales when they recommend a company.

Startling Statistics

- If you are like most small business owners, you will loose between 15 to 20 percent of your clients each year. It's even higher for retail vendors.

- Depending upon your market, a large majority of your customers are dormant...they only make one or two transactions with you. This is usually around 50 to 60 percent.

- That leaves roughly the top 20% of your loyal, repeat, and highly profitable clients...remember the 20% rule!

- Out of that 20% you will have a few who are the "hyper-responders". They use your services constantly and make frequent referrals.

Lost Clients

Let's examine the Lost 20% of your clients that we mentioned above. As we have already established from the prior example, understanding and analyzing your best performing current clients will tremendously assist in acquiring the right type of New clients but don't neglect the lost clients.

What you Need to Know...

- The average business looses 20% of their client base each year
- Research indicates the average business spends 6x MORE to attract NEW customers than it does to keep an old one.
- To achieve a 10% increase in sales you must add 30% more customers!

Now-what are those lost clients costing you each year!!!

Why clients leave...

Of the 20% of clients that stop doing business with you research indicates

- 3% move
- 5% develop another relationship
- 9% leave for competitive reasons
- 14% are unhappy with the product or service
- 68% leave because of a "run in" with an employee or other perceived problem.

That translates to over 80%
who stop doing business with you because they are simply

UNHAPPY

But it doesn't stop there!!

The Research Institute of America found the average business will not hear from 96% of unhappy clients...they will just leave....
BUT, they will TELL at least 9 other people!

Word of Mouth Working Against You is NOT good thing!

Chapter 14

Testimonials

Testimonials are a valuable asset that should be respected, treasured and cultivated as an important part of business communication. They carry the respect of a referral but on a more personal and permanent basis. They can be the voice of a person even when that person cannot speak directly to a potential client.

Testimonials are so important that modern technology has recognized the value of placing "product reviews" on promotional sales items. Take Amazon as an example, this mega online bookstore turned into a mega shopping outlet in large part due to the product reviews where actual people freely express their opinions about a large variety of books and products. Clearly the written form of a "review" or "testimonial" can prove to be an exceptional method of communicating the prior experience of people who are happy with your services.

Testimonial versus Endorsement

Like many things, not all testimonials carry equal weight. In fact, a good testimonial is more than a simple endorsement. Endorsements are met with cynicism and outright skepticism in modern society. Glib marketing, paid sponsorship and the practice of "buying" good reviews has created an atmosphere or hostility toward those who attempt a "hard sale" or other "tactics"....with good cause. The value of a testimonial must be established on the fundamental integrity of the reviewer or person providing the testimonial. If they can be "bought" or have something to gain from the endorsement then it deserves to be scrutinized.

It has become increasingly common to see celebrities endorse a product for profit rather than enthusiasm. Professional services have started using these same tactics; just recently a local service provider presented a well known athlete on his commercial advertisements. I will leave it to the discretion of each individual practitioner to decide the appropriateness of this option however, in general, my professional opinion is that a testimonial based upon true enthusiasm and benefit will remain far superior – and much less costly – than that of an endorsement. Particularly a paid endorsement!

Celebrate and Educate

Every practice should have a small "library" of testimonials! If you are a new practitioner then begin building this while performing your internship. You can never start early enough! The testimonial library should include sections for each of the following:

- Each modality you perform
- Your area of specialization
- Client related testimonials
- Professional related testimonials
- Community related testimonials
- Special situation testimonials
- Referral testimonials

Ask for a Testimonial

Okay, it's time for some plain talk here. Many of you may find asking for a testimonial difficult. It may superficially seem like asking someone to critic or analyze your service. You may even risk rejection. It can feel uncomfortable, risky, needy.

Many people skip testimonials and wait for someone to send an unsolicited "thank you" or letter of appreciation. This is NOT a testimonial – at least not for business purposes! Yes, it is a testament to your skill or service but unsolicited letters of gratitude are usually more personal and can rarely be reproduced without potentially breeching privacy and confidentiality.

You are still faced with the task of asking the person for permission to reproduce what began as a letter of gratitude for use as a generalized communication device which can actually seem less than gracious if not overtly callous! Even worse, the unsolicited letter of gratitude or appreciation is rarely appropriate for use as a specific testimonial purpose due to the personal nature.

It's perfectly acceptable – and much more desirable – to openly ask for a testimonial! Yes, you may get rejected but that is usually due to other situations such as an increased need for personal privacy or other factors rather than "passing judgment" on your skills.

How to Ask for a Testimonial

It's actually quite easy once you muster up a little courage. Simple ASK and then tell them why and what you intend to use it for. Three steps...

1. Ask for the testimonial
2. Tell them why it is important
3. Explain what you intend to use it to accomplish

For those of you who have implemented other items in this book, this will be much easier as it fits perfectly with allowing your clients to share in your professional goals. It also allows your clients to celebrate their own health and progress while sharing this with others in the community!

For example, perhaps you work with a few pregnant clients but desire to expand this portion of your services. You would like to approach pregnant clients but also professionals including obstetricians and mid-wives. One of your current clients experienced very satisfying results and is quite enthusiastic about your services. During her next visit you simple ASK.

"Jan, I'm thrilled this provided so much relief. Would you be willing to write a testimonial? I would like to use it to help inform and educate others about this service and would like to specifically use it to expand my work with obstetricians and mid-wives."

Then wait for a response. If you are declined; Don't Take it Personally! Again, many people have a need for additional privacy. Respect that need. It is not a reflection on you, your skill level or practice. On the other hand, if they agree then knowing how to create a testimonial is the next lesson.

How to Create a Meaningful Testimonial

"He's Great"

"Very nice"

"She's Awesome"

While these are all very nice sentiments and opinions they do very little to install confidence or meaning in others. Now here is where things become difficult. Asking for a testimonial is a slight imposition upon your client. It requires time, thought and effort upon their part. Most people will be quite happy to help but writing is a lot like speaking in public...especially writing for an audience. It can quickly turn stressful for some people and the last thing you want to do is stress your client. Especially when they are doing you a favor!

On the other hand, you want and need meaningful testimonials. It's even worse to get a testimonial that you can't use – now your client may feel rejected by you! Even people with the best of intentions can get rushed and feel obligated to write something out – anything – before the next visit. Or they may feel guilty about not having done it so avoid you. Still others become frozen with the equivalent of "stage fright" when trying to craft a testimonial that they know will be read by others.

It's up to YOU at the therapist to remove these obstacles and make the process completely painless, rewarding and meaningful. It is not your clients responsibility to do all of this. You must take full responsibility for the quality and success of testimonials.

Qualities of a Meaningful Testimonial

A meaningful testimony should have three basic parts:

1. Life before massage
    a. Pain
    b. Medication
    c. Suffering
    d. Other treatments that failed
2. Personal massage encounter
    a. Feelings about massage in general

   b. Feelings about the therapist/practice
   c. Treatment received
   d. Quality of treatment
   e. First impressions
   f. When first began to feel better
3. Their life since massage
   a. how feeling now
   b. what can they do now that they couldn't do before
   c. impact on other therapy
   d. changes in medication, mobility or other measures
   e. personal feelings about overall health
   f. would they recommend massage for others

Testimonial Rules

1. Have a set form with questions for them to complete. If you do not have one, a draft is below. Personalize it for your practice and use it as a template. Not only will this eliminate the stress or stage fright experienced by some of your clients who suddenly find it difficult to think of what to say but it also provides the foundation for a meaningful testimonial.

2. Make sure the client completes the testimonial at the office. Do NOT send it home with them. If their schedule is tight then wait for another time but sending it home makes it suddenly feel like "homework". It creates an obligation, a stress, another "to do" on their long list. Remember, you do not want to stress your client or create any additional work.

3. Keep the form short but with enough space for them to expand upon if desired. Provide a pencil or pen, writing surface and quiet area. Let them know in advance approximately how long it should take. Usually 5 – 10 minutes should be sufficient.

4. Let them know you will provide a copy of the letter form for their approval at their next visit (more on this shortly).

5. Show your appreciation. You may have a short gift certificate for a chair massage or discount. Perhaps a special card of appreciation. This should NOT be anything of substantial value or else you risk the question of a paid endorsement however, a small token of gratitude and appreciation is certainly warranted.

Testimonial Worksheet

Help Us Help Others!

Share Your Massage Story!

You can help others discover the benefits of massage! Now that you have been helped by massage, don't you wish others knew about this drugless, natural, non-surgical way to improve their health? Now you can share your story of better health through massage.

Please take a few minutes to write in your own words, your massage story. Use the questions provided as a guide but feel free to attach a blank sheet of paper if you need more space.

There are many people who are not aware of the variety of conditions that massage is able to help. On behalf of future clients and our staff, we thank you for sharing your story!

1. Describe the condition or problem which brought you to massage including:

- Name of disorder or primary problem:

  ____

  ____

- Symptoms:

  ____

  ____

- Location of Pain if applicable:

  ____

  ____

- Duration and Severity:

  ____

  ____

2. Describe previous treatment and results:

   ____

   ____

   ____

3. What drugs or medications were you taking – if any:

   ____

   ____

4. What led you to the decision to try massage?

____

____

5. Had you been to a massage therapist previously?

____

____

6. Did you have any doubts whether massage would help you or not?

____

____

7. What were your first impressions of massage, the office and the therapist?

____

____

8. Describe your results including the time involved:

____

____

9. In your opinion what has been the most valuable thing you obtained from the massage experience?

____

____

10. What would you recommend to others who are suffering?

____

____

11. How many others have you told about massage?

____

____

12. How do you feel about massage now that you have experienced its benefits?

____

____

I give permission for all or any part of the above statements to be reproduced with or without my name, to be used in the interest of telling others about the benefits of massage therapy. Your information is never sold to marketing companies!

Signature: _______________________________________

Date:_______________

TIPS

Determine who your customers are and their needs and desires. Tell them how your service satisfies their wants or needs.

Direct your message to where your prospects are listening, viewing or reading.

Create a place of business that is unique and different from all others in some way.

Chapter 15

Professional Referral Program

We've already discussed the importance of general referrals in prior sections. Professional referrals are important for many of the same reasons but with the added benefit of establishing a strong support system and potentially steady foundation for your area of specialization. There are some important distinctions to make in your professional referral program.

Why Professionals Refer Clients

There are many reasons each with a various strengths and weaknesses which are important to understand as a therapist. All professional relationships are not equal so it's important to determine the type of relationship and quality of referral.

Convenience: You may be the only therapist in the general vicinity so by default they simply try to make it convenient for their clients. This may work for awhile but should a problem arise or another therapist provide a better "fit" for services then you would be at risk of loosing that relationship without further establishing a more meaningful foundation.

Examples of this type of referral include casual relationships based upon convenience. For example, a few months ago while on a day trip I ran over a piece of metal on the highway which caused a terrible gash in my tire that could not be safely repaired. The temporary tire wasn't something I felt comfortable driving long distances with so I located a tire dealership to purchase new tires. My regular mechanic wasn't in the area and the choice of tire dealership was simply a matter of convenience at that point.

In this situation the referral holds little value because there is no loyalty or differentiation attributed to your practice but rather the function itself. The personal making the referral recognizes the value of massage but NOT the value of the provider of that massage!

If you encounter a referral based upon convenience then recognize it as a point of tremendous potential! The professional making the referral may have done so purely from convenience but they understand the value of massage – now let them understand the value of your business!

Personal Relationships: Closely related to convenience is that of personal relationships. Many business and professional referrals are based upon the underlying friendship of the parties involved. There is nothing wrong with that and in fact, it can prove quite rewarding as people tend to share similar values, interest and other commonalities. However, problems can arise if the relationship is expected to be more friendly than professional (or worse, if you don't hit it off personally!). More importantly, liking someone is not the same as respecting them – especially in the realm of professional service.

An example of this type of referral is a hair stylist I know. You simply couldn't find a more friendly, outgoing and personable individual to spend an hour with. Unfortunately, the actual service was never up to par. Yes, the person is incredibly likeable but the resulting hair cut was a disaster. It became an uncomfortable situation of not wanting to hurt the persons feelings while avoiding having to sport a less than stylish haircut!

This situation places more value on the person rather than skill or ability. Here the personal making the referral recognizes what a terrific person you are but may not appreciate your professional criteria. Worse, if a dispute arises or a situation where there is a relationship issue, it can jeopardize the referral process. Aside from all of that, the final factor is the emphasis is on the wrong person!

The client – not the referring provider or massage therapist - should be the determining factor. In this case, the relationship between the therapist and referring provider is taking precedent.

When faced with this situation, once again recognize it as a tremendous opportunity to build a real foundation upon!

Expertise. Your practice is recognized as THE authority or the best. Plain and simple this is the type of referral that holds the most value. People will travel further, remain more loyal and seek out those experts who represent the highest form of practice. The emphasis is on that quality of service, skill, knowledge and attributes that form the foundation for all the rest.

Professional Referral Checklist

1. Make a list of all existing complimentary professionals that work with clients in your specialization. For example, if your specialization is medical massage then your list may include Chiropractors, Osteopaths, Podiatrists, Dentists or even Optometrists. You may have a very tight niche or quite wide but however it is divided, the professional referral will include those professionals with a wider geographic location than your typical clients.

2. Sign up for New Business listings and keep abreast of changes, additions to staff and other developments in the area. This is a Tremendous area of potential that few massage therapists use. When a newly graduated or relocated chiropractor, physician or other provider comes to town they also have to file appropriate licensure, certifications, business permits and so forth just like massage therapists. They will be actively recruiting new clients and professional affiliations. Most states have licensing information that you can purchase which will inform you of professionals that may be coming to your area. The local business or community section of the newspaper or other media may also issue press release or notifications of the addition of members to the practice. Immediately make contact with them!

3. Let them know you exist! Awareness is critical. They cannot refer anyone to you if they aren't aware of your existence. Be concise yet thorough. Let them know your specialization, USP, hours of operation, location and contact information.

4. Establish a relationship. Awareness alone will lead only to referrals based upon convenience but people have a natural desire to know who they are working with. Don't take up much time but be sure to make personal contact in some small way, shape or form so they know and understand who and what you and your business is about.

5. Establish your credentials and demonstrate the proper "fit". If you are not used to tooting your own horn this can be difficult at first but it's necessary to establish your credentials AS THEY RELATE TO THE REFERRING PARTY. Not just any credentials will do – the credentials must be meaningful to the professional. So, for instance returning back to the medical massage

specialization, if you are approaching a traditional orthopedic surgeon then do not take additional time explaining your certification in modalities that do not correspond to his/her client population. Remain concise and relevant at all times while speaking directly to your expertise in their area of need.

6. Ask for referrals! Yes, I know this sounds like a "no-brainer" but people often assume presenting the information is enough. It's not. Ask and then tell them Why you are asking. Research has found people tend to personalize a request with a reason much more than a simple request. For instance, "If you have clients that may benefit from xyz service(s) then I would appreciate the referral because I am building a new practice" or "...expanding my practice" etc as the case may be. You are not only asking but telling them the reason for the request.

7. Always thank them for their time. Follow-up with a personalized note or small token of appreciation even if they do not immediately make a referral. It will begin the process of building a relationship which may eventually lead to a referral basis in the future.

"Innovation is the ability to see change as an opportunity not a threat"

"If you're not failing every now and again, it's a sign you're not doing anything very innovative."

Chapter 16

Pricing Your Services

Service Types & Arrangements

Service pricing can be difficult and confusing however, it's one area that has a tremendous impact on your "bottom line". Many people ask if there are actually pricing formula and the answer is a resounding "sort of". Yes, there are formulas, but even the very best formulas used by the largest companies require "tweaking" and analysis to accurately reflect your specific location, market and type of service provided.

The good news is there are methods to determine your maximum and minimum price points – simple methods that may allow you to substantially increase your earnings while doing the same number of sessions per year.

Does it Really Matter?

Before exploring various pricing methods and options let's take time to establish whether it's really that important. Plain and simple - Yes. Don't make the mistake of thinking a small difference won't matter. It can make a huge difference in the lifetime of your earnings!

For the sake of convenience, I will use a standard $60 per session rate and assume a therapist does an average of 20 sessions per week for 50 weeks of the year or a total of 1,000 sessions annually without deducting for expenses, taxes or other.

In the table below I present the difference in $ amounts beginning with $1 below [$59] versus $1 above [$61] and compare the difference price makes on profit annually. This assumes all other factors are exactly the same – costs, same number of sessions and so forth.

$1	$5	$10	$15
59/61	55/65	50/70	45/75
$59k to 61k	55k to 65k	50k to 70k	45k to 75k
$ +/- $1k Yr	+/- 5k Yr	+/- 10k Yr	+/- 15k Yr
$2,000	$10,000	$20,000	$30,000

Methods of Determining Price

Determining a fair rate can be difficult and a common mistake among massage practice owners and new therapist is to compete on price alone. Below are the most common methods to determine pricing so you remain competitive yet without 'leaving money on the table'.

Below represent the major methods used to determine rates.

Price Comparison: What Others are Charging

By far the most common method used to derive a rate schedule is simply to find out what others are charging in the area. This usually entails calling or driving by, word-of-mouth and general shopping for rates. Essentially price is the major comparative factor with features, benefits and other attributes playing a secondary function.

This method assumes that what others are charging is fair and equitable. It also assumes all services and styles are more or less equally 'valuable' and that amenities are all fairly standard. Finally, it assumes minimal variation in preference for individual style, effectiveness and skills of the therapist. For obvious reasons this is rarely the case and as we have seen elsewhere in this book, a therapist should have an arsenal of differentiating factors, USP, location, skill level, expertise and other amenities of interest to their target audience.

In general, the price comparison method is inadequate. Variations in skill levels, cost of doing business and a multitude of other factors make this a problematic and relatively crude method to determine rates.

Break-Even Analysis

This method is used to try and ensure you cover the essential costs. This should always be the first step in developing a pricing strategy because failure to meet your basic business and living expenses will put your out of business no matter how great your therapeutic skill and talent!

To begin, write down all your costs for the year and Divide that number by the effective number of working days a year. This gives you a breakeven pricing structure based on an expected number of days worked. Remember, you personally cannot work seven days a week, 365 days a year. Even if you wanted to do so, or managed to do so for a short period of time, it is not realistic [or desirable!] for a long term basis. Later in this book we will discuss viable options for extending your profit and revenue without requiring you to give up all of your free time. In the meantime, make sure this is realistic and desirable. After all, it's not a Perfect Practice if it leaves you exhausted and burned out.

Allow for adequate leisure days, holidays and even a few sick or mental health days particularly if you have family members or others to care for. Also, it's important to keep your skills up to date so be sure to allow for time spent training and learning. Yes, online learning is wonderful and convenient but there are still times when you may simply want to attend a conference or other training in person without having to be concerned over lost revenue. Calculate this in from the beginning. In the "worst case" scenario, it will provide a small additional "buffer" for you during the early years in the event of other situations.

A commonly overlooked but very important function is to allow time for marketing activities! Although it may sound great to be 100% occupied with "billable hours" or direct customer contact, it's not as desirable as it may seem. Marketing is an ongoing process that should NEVER be neglected! A percentage of clients will move away from the area, have a change in circumstance or a host of other unexpected situations. In consultancy circles this is called the "feast and famine" effect and it's routinely found across a wide range of service related fields. Plan on it so it doesn't take you by surprise!

Calculating Productive Days

So, by now you may be wondering "What is the maximum number of chargeable days you could work if there was an abundant supply of clients?" That's a good question! Let's examine it in more detail. Keep in mind, we are looking for the annual average but that will consist of portion from a daily, weekly and monthly basis.

Many people start out by thinking in terms of a 52 week year but this can be deceptive! Let's borrow an example from large companies in deciding how they calculate productive days.

For employees, a company would normally expect to achieve roughly 200 effective "production" days. This is based on a calculation such as:

- Working weeks = 50 (allowing for two weeks annual leave)
- Public holidays = 15 days (three 5-day weeks), leaving 47 weeks
- Training, sickness and other non-production time, say 3 weeks, leaving 44 weeks.
- Multiplied by 5 days per week gives 220 working days per year.

In your case, being a highly motivated self-employed person you might achieve more than 220 days but don't forget, as an employee, you are responsible for going to the job and performing it. As a self employed professional or business owner, you will also need to set aside time for marketing, accounting, cleaning and more. Using a very conservative estimate, it would be wise to allow at least 25% of your time for this. So if you want to do 220 days of "work" you would still need to include an allowance for 55 days for marketing, cleaning, books, and the rest. This leaves the equivalent of 165 days of "earning" or "productive" time" - a lot less than 220!

Calculate Your Personal Days of Productivity Worksheet

Use the following worksheet to calculate your personal days of productivity per year. For each of the questions, use the equivalent number of days. So for example, if you intend to work 5 days per week then you would take 2 days off per week x 52 weeks or 104 days off per year. If you then decided to take 3 weeks vacation per year then you would use your normal work week of 5 days multiplied by 3 weeks or 15 days off per year.

365 days per year   52 weeks per year   7 days per week   8 hrs day

1. How many days off will you take each week? ____________
2. How many weeks vacation do you intend to take? ____________
3. How many sick days will you plan for? ____________
4. Number of holidays? ____________
5. Training, conferences, other? ____________
6. Equivalent marketing, office work. ____________
7. Hours per day you will work ____________

Calculating Hourly or Daily Rate Benchmarks

Divide your total costs by the number of days or hours you expect to work.

So for example, if your total cost is $70,000 per year and you expect to have an average of 165 productive days per year at an average of 8 hours per day then you would need to earn $424 per day or $53 per hour to reach that goal.

Express Example

Kate is calculating her personal days of productivity.

Kate works 5 days per week and takes 2 days per week off [365 – 104 = 261 days].

She would like to increase to 3 weeks vacation. At her standard 5 day work week that equals an additional 15 days off. [261 – 15 = 246]

Although she hopes to not have any sick days, just in case Kate includes 10 days. If she doesn't use them then it will act as a nice buffer or bonus [246 – 10 = 236]

Kate only recognizes 8 holidays per year but the majority of her clients celebrate 12. Kate realizes business is likely to be slower on the majority of these days so calculates the holidays based upon her clients [236 – 12 = 224]

Training is important to Kate and she enjoys the personal interaction of going in person. Kate would like to attend more frequently but for the time being, hopes to attend one major conference per year and perhaps a few smaller local ones. She calculates 5 days [224 – 5 = 219]

Daily equivalent. Kate works with medical reimbursement claims which are time consuming. She also handles all of her own accounting, cleaning, laundry and other duties associated with the office. Additionally, Kate sets aside time each week for marketing and other efforts required to grow her business as she's still relatively new. Kate estimates that she can perform 4 one hour sessions per day with another 4 hours required to take care of office and other duties while remaining in her allocated 40 hour work week. Kate is much higher than her friend Joe who is highly established and only uses 25% of his time for these duties but because she is new, her percentage is higher. [219 days – 50% = 110 Productive Day equivalent]. Joe, who is established, has 165 Productive Days annually which would be in accordance to most business levels once established.

Expect the Best but Plan for the Worst

Whenever calculating any forecasts or models, it's advisable to do three versions: A pessimistic version so that you can survive the worst scenario; an optimistic version for when things go well; and a realistic scenario which falls somewhere in between and should serve as a guideline for your general progress. Use this to measure your situation. If you are doing well and far beyond the original forecast, don't get excited just yet! Remember, seasonal fluctuations or other economic indicators can lead to large upward and downward trends. Use it month to month and year to year to track progress!

Elsewhere in this book you have calculated your costs. The following are for example only but replace these calculations with your own.

Office costs: Let's imagine that your office costs (utilities, telephone and other bills) add up to $1500 per month or $18,000 annually.

Equipment depreciation, loan payback [if any] and sunk costs:
Let's assume you purchased $5,000 worth of equipment and will need to replace it every 5 years leaving you with $1,000 toward depreciation expense. If you borrowed any money to start your business or purchase equipment, computers or other be sure to include it. For a general number we will use $2,000 for the purpose of this example.

Research and learning:
Let's assume you spend $2,000 a year on items such as subscriptions to associations, purchase of books and reports, attendance at training sessions and conferences.

Salary equivalent:
The money you intend to take out of the business to meet your own personal living expenses. Let's use a conservative estimate of $36,000 or $3,000 per month.

To this you need to add appropriate amounts to provide for your retirement, taxes, and insurance. Remember, as a self employed person you have larger potential write-off's but you also may have a larger percentage of self employment taxes and other expenses. Let's make this roughly 35% of the salary equivalent or $12,000 for the sake of convenience. Again, feel free to use your own numbers.

So the baseline total of your fixed costs would be $70,000. This is the actual minimum you should be striving toward. But, what if you aren't making that yet?

The Pessimistic Rate

Let's assume you are not bringing in this amount and may need time to ramp up to this level. To reach your breakeven level you need to consider: "How can I cut back on these items if I really needed to?" You might then decide that in order to get the business going you could initially cut back on your living expenses or minimize the first year of training by using other methods. Go through and calculate the absolute "essentials" that cannot be done without. This is the pessimistic figure.

Express Example

Kate has calculated her baseline to be $70,000 per year to cover her basic living expenses and business costs. She has also calculated her personal productivity days to be 110 multiplied by an average 8 hour day or 880 total billable hours. Kate needs to make an average of $636 per day or $79 per hour.

Currently Kate is only making an average of $50 per hour which is far below what she needs to cover her basic costs or "break even". Since Kate is new and working in a time intensive area, her only options are to increase fees, reduce costs, work more hours or increase productive hours by hiring someone else to handle many of her other administrative, marketing and other duties [which will increase her total costs]. Chances are, a few years of this and Kate will either go out of business or face potential burn-out from longer than average work hours.

Like many small business owners, Kate needs to pay close attention to her energy level and cash flow by calculating what she can do, what is better to pay for someone else to do and how to maximize her billable hours.

Perceived Value Pricing

This is where you consider the benefit or value to your client. Essentially, you are trying to decipher what the job is "worth" to your customer and your own "position" in the market. You understand the time, effort, training and preparation that goes into providing a session but beyond that, take into account your reputation and skill level based upon the needs of the client.

Value Pricing is highly dependent upon a Unique Selling Proposition as discussed elsewhere in this book. This can translate into Premium or Discount Pricing models. For obvious reasons, it's not advisable to compete on price alone however, premium services may be your entire service offerings or only a small selection of your service menu. To begin, take the following questions into account...

What is the scarcity value of your service?

If your skills and experience are in high demand, and there are relatively few people who can deliver in this field then customers may be prepared pay substantially more than the break even cost or your average rate.

Let's take an example from another service industry... veterinarian practice. Those of you who are animal lovers understand the value of a kind, gentle vet who works well with our furry friends and will often pay slightly higher than average office visits based upon personality alone. Many towns also have premium services where the vet will make house calls or holds weekend and evening hours. Still even higher rates apply to specialized veterinarian services such as surgery. Finally, off hours emergency surgery and specialized care may result in prices that rival those of human emergency rooms simply due to the fact that there are few other providers (scarcity) for an urgent need (demand) with high value (safety or concern for pet).

What is the leveraged value to the customer?

The client – by default – thinks that what you charge is of value or else they would not bother to contact you to begin with! However there may be significant extra "leverage value" for the customer depending upon their own personal needs and your skill, training and expertise.

For example, a few years ago I took up running with the goal of participating in a local distance run. About two months before the scheduled date, I experienced foot pain while running that only increased overnight. After a visit to the emergency room to rule out a stress fracture via X-ray, I began trying to schedule appointments with local professionals to assure mobility and function would be restored as soon as possible. Most Podiatrists in my area were booked 2-3 months in advance...far in excess of my personal need to compete in the local race. Likewise, finding a MT who specialized in sports massage rather than general massage became an imperative.

In this situation, someone who could meet my needs and assist me in reaching my personal goal became worth much more than I might have normally paid which brings us to the next topic...

Is Your Service A Life Saver?

No, it doesn't mean you literally must save a life but sometimes if you are able to assist someone in saving their dream, their job, or even as much as a good nights sleep due to pain then it just may qualify!

If your service is required at short notice, in an emergency, overnight etc. the perceived value of your service is now greater than normal. You should have a pricing structure that reflects this demand for emergency situations. One characteristic of the new economy is to accelerate the pace of business change and create more opportunities for people and companies that can offer fast response.

Conservative pricing structures for emergency services begin at 10% with 25% premium representing a fairly universal standard among most service related business providers.

Seven Step Conclusion

1. Get organized.
2. Have a clear understanding of your true capacity and potential - in days or hours - allowing for holidays, retraining, leisure time etc.
3. Set your breakeven price based on daily, hourly or monthly rates.
4. Check your breakeven price against what the customers perceived value increase your price as much as possible, whenever possible. The "right" price is the price that the customer will pay, while feeling that they are getting value for money.
5. Check the competition. Open your mind up to think of all possible competitors especially if you work in a specialized area. For instance, perhaps you specialize in back pain and charge more than other massage therapists in your area but much less than acupuncturist or traditional medical providers. Check your position against them and adjust your price accordingly.
6. Establish a range of pricing options for your entire menu of services that cover your costs and allow you to earn a good living while building positive relationships with satisfied clients.
7. Finally, write down your pricing approach and track it over time. Be flexible while growing your business but remain cognitive of the resulting profit or loss.

Optimized Pricing Projections

The optimized pricing projection worksheet can help you determine the best rates compared against your time and cost. However, since this worksheet is based on your "best estimates" it will only be as accurate as the information you use to make those estimates. It's like the old saying "garbage in – garbage out". Use the most reliable data at your disposal but also be prepared to use a good dose of common sense. At best, this provides a guideline for you to consider various strategies.

The first step is to determine the size of your target market. We have discussed that elsewhere in this book so you should have a fair estimate if you have done your homework to date.

As a rule of thumb, the lower the cost of something the more people will be able and willing to purchase a service or item. That would be terrific if you were selling widgets – the more people, the more sales! It's not that easy for service providers. What would happen if you ran a special "One Hour Massage for $5". Wow! I bet you would have people lined up at your door and scheduled six months in advance. I certainly would book as many sessions at that price as I could!

But at that rate you would work yourself into the ground and still not pay your basic necessities. A dozen sessions each day would only gross – before taxes and expenses - $60! It wouldn't take long for you to discontinue that advertisement!

On the other hand, some areas are able to charge much higher than average rates but let's use an extreme. How many sessions would you estimate scheduling if you increased your per hour rate to $500 per hour. The majority of therapists would have a lot of extra time on their hands and still not pay their bills.

This worksheet can be used for each service on your menu. This example has been deliberately simplified for the sake of convenience but it still demonstrates how working more can still lead to less money while raising prices above a certain extent reduces overall profit.

The first worksheet is for an existing business and the second is for a new business.

But First – A Reality Check!

Folks, burn-out is rampant and the cost of housing, groceries, transportation, insurance and medical bills has escalated rapidly in recent years. Many small business owners are working themselves to the point of exhaustion because they fear loosing business. I recently encountered a man who had a highly specialized niche, tremendous testimonials, a very loyal client base and a virtual celebrity list of clients yet he had not increased his rates in over a decade! Even after doubling his rates he would still have been one of the best values in town, however Never spring a huge price increase on customers. If you are severely under-priced then calculate your target goal range and begin implementing small progressive changes until you reach the desired level.

Are You a Candidate for Rate Increase? Checklist

Yes	No	It has been more than three years since I increased my rates.
Yes	No	My rates are more than 10% below competitors
Yes	No	I provide a highly specialized service and have minimal / no competition
Yes	No	I have more clients or work more hours than I can comfortably handle

Existing Business – Raise or Lower Prices

Let's determine whether or not Lou should raise his rates or not. Lou has a strong following and hasn't increased his rates in several years. Lou currently charges $60 per 1-hour session and performs a total of approximately 1,000 sessions annually.

Reading the chart from bottom to top, we see that Lou first wants to see if lowering his prices would be better than increasing them. He estimates a 25% reduction would increase his number of sessions by a hefty 15%. Although that is a lot more work, Lou quickly dismisses this option as it actually reduces his earnings by over $8,0000 annually.

Lou then calculates his price increases compared to those of competitors or other practitioners in the area. Since Lou has been charging $60 which is exactly the same medium price level, he changes that to $65 to see what impact a small price increase would have on his existing workload.

At the $65 level, Lou feels pretty confident that the majority of clients would remain with him as his clients are very satisfied. However, he knows a few may be unhappy so includes a .03% decrease in total sessions. Despite working less hours, Lou sees the result would be a $3,000 increase in his earnings!

Lou continues to calculate estimates based upon the high rates others are charging in the area. Because Lou understands that increases will cause a disproportionate decrease in his number of sessions, Lou uses a .07% reduction at $75 and estimates .18% at $90. At this point Lou expects to be performing substantially fewer sessions throughout the year yet his income continues to increase until he reaches a point when so many clients would drop out that his earning would decline. Every business should calculate this type of scenario's before making major changes to your pricing. Always use conservative numbers. If you are brand new and offer a generalized menu of services then your % of clients who leave due to a price increase would be substantially higher than someone who is highly specialized with a loyal and satisfied client roster.

Retail Price Range	Retail Price	% of current clients that change visits +/-	Anticipated # of Annual Sessions	Sales
Maximum Retail Price (1.5 x Highest Retail Price of Competitor in your area)	$135 per 1 hour session	- 60%	400	$54,000
Highest Retail Price of Competitor	$90 per 1 hour session	- 18%	820	$73,800
Intermediate High Retail Price	$75 per 1 hour session	- 7%	930	$69,750
Medium Retail Price	$65 per 1 hour session	- 3%	970	$63,050
Low Retail Price	$45 per 1 hour session	+ 15% increase	1150	$51,750
Current Situation	$60 per 1 hour session	Current Status	1000	$60,000

Optimized Pricing Projections Worksheet New Business

Estimated Size of Target Market: 10,000

Retail Price Range	Retail Price	% of target population who will buy at this price	Anticipated # of Annual Sessions	Sales
Maximum Retail Price (1.5 x Highest Retail Price of Competitor in your area)	$135 per 1 hour session	1%	100	$13,500
Highest Retail Price of Competitor	$90 per 1 hour session	2%	200	$18,000
Intermediate High Retail Price	$75 per 1 hour session	4%	400	$30,000
Medium Retail Price	$60 per 1 hour session	7%	700	$42,000
Low Retail Price	$45 per 1 hour session	9%	900	$40,500
Minimum Retail Price (break-even point as discussed elsewhere)	$35 per 1 hour session	11%	1100	$38,500

Chapter 17

Computing and Comparing Room/Office Rental Rates

As mentioned elsewhere, one "win-win" situation for both a Massage Practice Business owner and new or expanding therapist is the situation of providing or renting a room. This worksheet is primarily geared toward the practice owner who would like to incorporate this into their business plan but it also can be used by a newly established or expanding therapist to comparison "shop" for the best values in room rentals as well as decide when it makes financial sense to grow to the next stage and leave a specific setting.

Before beginning, it's important to note, this discussion is based upon the business and financial aspects of this type of arrangement. As with any situation, it's important to know the state and local laws governing rent, leasing and other contractual relationships in your area. It's also a very good idea to have your contract drawn up and reviewed by a competent legal advisor who is familiar with the regulations in your area...particularly when you are new to this type of situation and unsure what your rights and responsibilities may be.

Types of Arrangements

At first glance this might seem straightforward enough but in reality, there are actually many ways to determine a fair rate but it depends upon what is being offered. There are actually several ways to rent or lease space. It may be decided to rent/lease a room for a fixed amount per month. It may or may not include use of reception area, desk, laundry facilities, off-hours use etc or it may be completely inclusive of everything with the therapist having full range and use of that room at any time for any reason. Some rooms may have higher rates due to various amenities and therefore are available by the hour or for a specified number of hours per month according to each therapist needs. Still other arrangements may not indicate a specific room but rather access to “a room” during business hours with rooms being continually rotated.

Normally it would be expected that a fully “private” room used exclusively by one therapist and available at any time would be the most expensive. In fact, this type of situation may or may not stipulate whether the therapist is able to sub-lease the space to another therapist as they essentially have full and exclusive ‘rights’ to the room. Often they are able to decorate as desired [within the specification of the lease] and may sub-lease the space to another therapist.

At the low end of the spectrum would be the non-exclusive use of available rooms on a per appointment basis. Rooms are constantly rotated in order to maximize scheduling and minimize “down time’ between clients. The therapist is not able to select the room but is instead, provided a room based solely upon availability. Minimal to no personalization is offered and sub-leasing rare.

Extensive variations exist between these two extremes including the provision – either as part of the monthly lease/rental fee or in addition to as an ‘add-on’ fee of equipment or other service rentals including secretarial services, laundry etc...

Methods of Determining Rental and/or Lease Rates

Determining a fair rate can be difficult and a common mistake among massage practice owners and new therapist is to compare rates on price alone. One office may offer exceptionally low rates due to a low client rate...essentially the therapist doesn’t have enough work to keep busy so to reduce their own cost, they rent out the space. As mentioned elsewhere, a bad location is a major handicap to building a thriving business as many exceptional therapists have failed to thrive duc to poor location.

Other offices may subsidize the room rate through expecting other unpaid contributions such as working the reception desk, helping with housecleaning chores throughout the office and so forth. This is not necessarily bad particularly for a new therapist but these are non-billable hours nonetheless and should be calculated into the total cost.

Still other offices may simply have far to many amenities that sound enticing yet fail to deliver real results. For instance, it’s wonderful to walk into a posh new office with the latest and greatest of everything...it’s even more enticing to have full use of custom designed lift tables or other devices. The question remains, will this make you more profitable or are you paying more than it's worth to you as an individual therapist?

If your clients are such that mobility is a major factor then it could in fact, result in more revenue and increased client satisfaction. Likewise, if you yourself experience lower back pain or another physical condition that is alleviated then it could be a wise investment. It's necessary to establish each on a case by case basis to determine the best course of action and optimum pricing.

Other issues arise with setting rent and lease rates. For example, rising cost of insurance, utilities and other bills may lead to prices having been set to low so it's necessary to "build in" a reserve to account for these types of contingencies in advance. A good rule of thumb is to establish a 10% reserve for price increases. Be aware that rate hikes are not always evenly distributed so one year your utility bills may remain steady whereas the following year may result in rates in excess of a 10% increase. If you have implemented a steady "buffer" beginning the first year then it should average out without resorting to very large increases that only hurt all involved. On the other hand, if you have a reserve built in for several years and rates remain steady then by all means, pass it along. There is nothing that demands you always increase the rents. Just be aware to build in a buffer for the 'just in case" scenario especially when first starting out.

Below are the most common methods to determine pricing so you remain competitive yet without 'leaving money on the table'. If you are shopping for rooms or rentals then this will also provide a method of comparing rentals so you can better understand the full cost and benefit derived from each.

One final word, if you are a practice owner who opts to build this method into your business model – a quite viable method by the way – then remember, you now have two very different and distinct "clients"...your traditional massage clients and the therapists who pay rent or lease from you. Just as your massage clients have certain expectations and rights – with corresponding duties and obligations from you...so do your therapist clients who pay rent or lease from you. This can be a very rewarding and financially sound business decision with long term reward and high profit potential but likewise, there is risk, additional responsibility and an added complexity of time and energy required.

Below represent the major method of determining rate. Each should be considered depending upon the situation and circumstance.

Collective Comparison: What Others are Charging

One of the more common methods used to derive a rate is to simply find out what other are charging in the area. This would entail calling or driving by, word-of-mouth and general shopping for rates. Essentially price is the major comparative factor with features, benefits and other attributes playing a secondary function.

This method assumes that what others are charging is fair and equitable. It also assumes that all locations are more or less equally 'valuable' and that amenities are all fairly standard.

There are three potential pitfalls with using this method.

1. Charging what others are charging may not be fair. Remember tenants and practice owners are in the same position as you. They are looking for someone to tell them what rental rate is fair and equitable. If you use this method, compare your rate to many other rates and then take the median or mean average among all of the offices.

2. Rumors about rent may be quite different than the actual rates - especially in a rapidly changing market. There are two variations on this to be aware of. The first if for those offering to rent or lease a room or office....remember, "Asking Ain't Getting". The recent boom in the real estate market over the past few years comes to mind as people drive by their neighbors home for sale at a hugely inflated asking price and erroneously believe that is the value received. However, just like real estate transactions are negotiated with lower offers, contingencies to pay certain fee's or repairs and so forth, so are many rental and lease agreements.

   It may sound great that a certain office is charging double for their office rental than what you originally considered charging until you start asking questions about what is included and find out they are doing everything except the actual massage for each of their therapists who rent from them. A superficial glance might sound great until you include the cost of the additional laundry, supportive massage, sick coverage and more.

   For the person searching for a rental the variation is the exact opposite and may include a 'down –sell or 'up-sell'. This is a common practice among many real estate or used car sales people...they show you a few over priced options and then show you the slightly inflated asking price that is in keeping with what you can afford. After the initial panic, you are so happy to find something in your price range that a sense of desperation has set in. The sense of urgency and desperation has led more than one person to over pay for a house or car. Instead, make a list of what is and is not included in the price. Ask about separating out each feature.

3. Differences in the quality of location should also be taken into account when comparing your rental rate to those of others. Many people make the mistake of assuming all locations are more or less of equal productivity but as we have previously established, nothing could be further from the truth.

In general, the price comparison method is usually not well suited for either the person renting or the practice owner attempting to establish and equitable rate. It simply does not take variations into account and can easily end up costing more than what it is worth or significantly under-charging for premium services. This method should only be used when there are limited choices in a very similar location with minimal variations....and then, both parties need to be aware of much larger potential issues!

Potential Profitability Average

A rental rate can also be based on the profit potential for a given room or space. In the most simple terms, let's assume an office is open 10 hours per day from 9 AM to 7 PM for 6 days per week with a 25% reduction for cleaning leaving 7.5 billable hours per day multiplied by 6 days per week for a total of 45 billable hours at a rate of $60 per hour or $2700 per week profit potential.

In this case, the potential profit average is over $10,000 per month capable of being generated by this room. Of course, the majority of that will be kept by the therapist actually doing the work but the practitioner renting the room can calculate a percentage of the total profit potential for his/her share. Let's assume this owner decides to go with 25% which includes room and all maintenance, laundry and reception services to the therapists. All the therapist must do is focus on providing the actual massage and building their client list. In this case the rent would be over $2500 per month...a steep rental rate for only one therapist!

Of course, what immediately comes to mind is that the average practitioner would simply collapse from exhaustion trying to fill that number of billable hours each week. Indeed, it's not a realistic work schedule. However, this is a profit potential

model that will provide a foundation for those practice locations that do NOT offer exclusive room rentals but rather a rotating schedule of room availability.
Since the room is not exclusive, during the course of an average day there would likely be at least three or more therapists sharing the room. In fact, it could be “rented’ by blocks of time for only a few hours a week to as much – or as little - time was required by the therapist.

There are many benefits to this for both the practitioner and practice owner. First, if a therapist has a bad month then his/her cost is greatly reduced. They pay for what they use and little else. The practice owner realizes the maximum rent for each location or space based upon realistic earning potential. With three rooms, the practice would realize nearly $8,000 per month in rent...while providing an affordable and flexible option to those therapists who rent the space!

However, there are some potential problems as well [nothing is perfect!]. First, this requires dealing with a large number of therapists to keep the rooms filled. Many therapists desire a personalized space rather than a rather ‘generic’ room and scheduling must be diligent to assure availability as promised.

Overall, this can be a viable option with a win-win proposition for both parties IF the limitations and potential are fully understood and agreed upon.

Return on Investment

Another method is to simply calculate how much the room “costs” after pro rating for utilities, insurance, and all other expenses and then include in the desired rate of return.

For example, Val has a three room practice and calculates the average monthly cost of each room at $1,000 which includes the pro-rated per foot of space cost of rent or mortgage, utilities etc... Val decides she wants to make a 25% return which would equal $250 per month. Val sets the room rate at $1250 per month.

If Val is uncertain about vacancies or increasing cost of variable costs such as utilities then she may add in between 10% to as high as 25% based upon local conditions and historic vacancy rates.

Productivity Share Equivalent

Another method of determining rental rates is by comparing the rental rate to the return that would be received from a split of profits. With a productivity share equivalent lease, the amount of rent is automatically adjusted by changes in earnings. However, to compute a rental rate using this method it is necessary to have detailed knowledge of the number of clients, services performed and so forth. The amount of knowledge could open the average practice owner up to questions regarding employee/employer status among other things.

There are variations of this model that may provide some level of benefit in certain situations. For example, Tom is an Independent Contractor who leases space in a Chiropractic office. The office has several Chiropractors and Tom generates the majority of his business from the combined efforts of the Chiropractic staff who send him a constant stream of referral business. Tom operates independently and is able to advertise and serve other clients however, for the purpose of this arrangement, Tom is charged a base monthly rental fee of $400 and then a 5% charge of all clients to cover his share of laundry, trash collection, reception fee's and so forth.

In January Tom grossed $5,000 so his total rent was $400 base plus 5% of $5,000 or $250 for a total of $650.

In February Tom grossed $8,000 so his total rent was $400 base plus 5% of $8,000 or $400 for a total of $800.

In March Tom was ill so he only grossed $1,500. His total rent was $400 base plus 5% of $1,500 or $75 for a total of $475.

As can be quickly discerned from the above example, this is rarely a viable alternative for either party! First, it is difficult to establish a budget when the fluctuations rise and fall with regularity. Next, it's even worse when a hardship or other case arise. Yes, Tom owed less money but as a percentage of earnings, the $475 represented well over ¼ of his entire income for what was a difficult month financially!

On the other hand, a purely sliding scale could have resulted in Tom owing much less but with greatly increased risk for the practitioner who is now sharing in the loss of productivity experienced by Tom.

Although superficially these can appear to be attractive arrangements, the reality is the increased legal exposure combined with increased risk to both parties can create difficulties in the long run.

Replacement Rate

Another approach is to calculate how much the same amenities would cost to replace or duplicate. This is a particularly good method for brand new therapists who are short on cash but need to build a client base and for practitioners who have been in business for quite some time and may have failed to adjust their rental rates to keep pace with inflation or other costs...especially if you happen to own or have a long term lease for the building or space your business occupies!

I'm going to use an example here because this may be more prevalent given the recent increases in real estate over the past few years. Xavier owns an older house that he converted into his massage practice several years ago. The house was like most standard modest homes with three bedrooms, two bathrooms, a kitchen, living area that serves as a reception and waiting area. The three former bedrooms make perfect treatment rooms and since he's owned it for 20 years, his mortgage payment and utilities plus insurance and taxes are approximately $850 combined. {Yes, this is a real example!). Xavier charges $300 per month to three other therapists which covers all of his base expenses. He's not raised his rates in nearly a decade.

However to buy the same house in the same area today would cost over $3,000 per month. With all other services, equipment, location and the rest exactly the same, Xavier should be charging more than double his current rates based upon the current cost of a mortgage. Xavier could easily increase his rates to $750 per month while remaining below any competitors who would still need to charge $1,000 a month to break even. It would still be a win-win situation for both parties and Xavier could put an additional $1350 a month into his retirement account.

Rental Amenities Comparison Checklist

Use this form to compare different rental rates so you don't forget important features of the different places you visited or the features that you include in your rental rates.

	Rental A	Rental B	Rental C	Rental D
Date available	_______	_______	_______	_______
Rent amount	_______	_______	_______	_______
Rent due	_______	_______	_______	_______
Deposit	_______	_______	_______	_______
Late Payment charges	_______	_______	_______	_______
Length of lease	_______	_______	_______	_______
Penalty for breaking lease	_______	_______	_______	_______
Physical changes allowed	_______	_______	_______	_______
Subletting	_______	_______	_______	_______
Utilities Included	_______	_______	_______	_______
Water Sewer	_______	_______	_______	_______
Phone/Internet	_______	_______	_______	_______
Garbage/Recycling	_______	_______	_______	_______
Laundry	_______	_______	_______	_______
Sq footage	_______	_______	_______	_______
Shared Receptionist/Other	_______	_______	_______	_______
High speed internet	_______	_______	_______	_______
Website	_______	_______	_______	_______
Yellow Page/Other Ads	_______	_______	_______	_______
Storage	_______	_______	_______	_______
Furniture	_______	_______	_______	_______
View	_______	_______	_______	_______
Water pressure	_______	_______	_______	_______
Overall Cleanliness	_______	_______	_______	_______
Age of equipment/appliances	_______	_______	_______	_______
Counter space/drawers	_______	_______	_______	_______
Equipment Provided	_______	_______	_______	_______
Equipment Required	_______	_______	_______	_______
Community	_______	_______	_______	_______
Parking	_______	_______	_______	_______
Noise level	_______	_______	_______	_______
Appearance	_______	_______	_______	_______
Elevators/stairs	_______	_______	_______	_______
Neighborhood	_______	_______	_______	_______
Highway access	_______	_______	_______	_______
Distance to commute	_______	_______	_______	_______
Other	_______	_______	_______	_______

TIPS

Begin the process early to allow yourself maximum flexibility and negotiation

Never fall in love with just one property. You wont get the best deal available

Always create several viable leasing alternatives. Get proposals from each. Don't give a positive indication to any landlord until you have in your hands a fully executed new lease or lease renewal document.

Chapter 18

When to Lease or Buy Your Office Space

To Buy or Not to Buy: That is the Question. Every small business will eventually be faced with the question of whether or not to buy versus lease/rent your office space. Depending upon the local and nationwide market, interest rates, available credit line and tax considerations it is uncertain what the future will bring and there is not a "one size fits all" solution. Creating the Perfect Practice may or may not involve this all important consideration so you need to carefully weigh the pros and cons of leasing or buying office space.

Pros of Buying Your Own Office

Fixed Costs: Locking in your commercial mortgage long-term can give your business clear, fixed costs. In recent years the cost of buying real estate has dramatically increased while rental rates remained relatively lower however, whenever you rent, you are somewhat at the "mercy" of the terms of the lease. Once the lease expires, rates can often fluctuate – sometimes a great deal.

Tax Deductions: The associated costs of owning your own property can provide expense deductions in the form of mortgage interest, property taxes and other items.

Additional Income: Owning your office can offer the advantage of renting out extra office space and adding another source of income.

Retirement Fund: The prospect of owning the property allows it to appreciate over time. Many owners have found real estate a tremendous advantage when it comes to renting or selling to fund their retirement.

Cons of Buying Your Own Office

Lack of Flexibility: A new or growing business may experience unexpected needs in the future. If your business continues growing, your owned office space may become inadequate forcing a sale of the property.

Upfront Costs: Buying commercial space costs more at the beginning. Then there are maintenance costs, down payments, property improvements, taxes and other considerations.

Pros of Renting or Leasing Office Space

Prime Property: In some areas leasing may be the only way to secure a prime location. This can be particularly true in large cities.

Free-up Working Capital: Real estate often requires large down payments and up front costs that can take away funds from expansion or needed reserves.

More Time: Any type of ownership comes with headaches. A leasing option affords the time to focus solely on running your business.

Cons of Office Space Leasing

Variable Costs: With a leasing option you may be subject to annual rent increases and higher costs at the time when your lease expires.

No Equity: While leasing you will be funding someone else's retirement with your lease payments.

The answer to lease or buy office space is not clear-cut. Your decision will hinge on financial, tax, and personal issues. Do not make this decision sparingly. Bring in your accountant and financial planner to guide you with the best advice but keep in mind that this can be a valid part of your diversification and overall financial planning for the Perfect Practice.

Express Example

Let's use a conservative estimate. Luis found a fixer-upper property in 1990 that was originally a residential property but in the process of being rezoned due to widening of the road. It was offered for sale by owner with almost zero down. The property needed approximately $10,000 of work and was priced for a quick sale at $40,000 which was a fair price for the area at that time.

The monthly mortgage at a commercial loan rate of 9.5% for 20 years was $380 for the life of the loan and would be paid in full by the year 2010. The rental rate was competitive with rental rates in the area if not slightly higher due to repairs, taxes and insurance. Luis originally lost approximately $100 per month compared to renting a similar office space however, due to depreciation and other tax incentives, the overall rate was fairly competitive and Luis wanted the ability to make certain changes to the office and surrounding grounds that would not have met his criteria by leasing alone.

The property was fixed up and over the years, taxes and insurance continued to increase. The property experienced steady but minimal appreciation until 2001 at which point all real estate grew tremendously. The current property value is estimated at a minimum of $150,000. The taxes and insurance have gone up but the total combined cost is now far less than the average rental rates for comparable property in the area which is substantially higher. In fact, minimum rental rates are now far in excess of $1,000 monthly. In three short years the current property will be paid in full resulting in an additional monthly mortgage savings of $380 [a monthly payment which now seems very small indeed!].

Luis intends to retire at about the same time the mortgage is paid in full at which point he can rent to another therapist and generate a solid monthly rental income or sell – realizing a tidy profit for what would have been a growing monthly rental expense for all of these years. Not only has Luis saved on the increased rental rates but also has positioned himself to have a tidy rental income or large lump sum profit via the sale of the property.

Buy or Lease Worksheet

_________ What is your current monthly rent?

_________ What is your expected yearly % rent increase?

_________ For how long will you be in business?

_________ Total estimated cost of renting?

_________ What is your federal income tax bracket?

_________ What is the term of the loan in years?

_________ What is the loan rate?

_________ How much do you expect to borrow to purchase?

_________ What is the expected property purchase price?

_________ How long do you expect to own the property?

_________ What is the estimated annual appreciation of the property?

_________ How much do you expect to pay in annual property taxes?

_________ Estimated maintenance and repairs?

Totals:

_________ Estimated costs of renting
_________ Estimated gross costs of buying
_________ Estimated amount of tax related savings
_________ Estimated amount in increased equity
_________ Estimated net costs of buying

Check Your Zoning!

Zoning Ordinances and Regulations

Zoning ordinances and regulations are laws that define and restrict how you can use your property. Cities, counties, townships, and other local governments adopt zoning plans in order to set development standards to assure that land is used for the common good.

Why Zoning Is Such a Big Issue

Zoning laws come into play on every single real estate development, regardless of how big or small, so if you are thinking about buying property or making improvements to property you already own, you'd better be sure you understand the zoning restrictions before you commit to anything.

One zoning use is typically not compatible with another. For example, a commercial building usually cannot be constructed on property that's zoned for residential uses.

Getting the zoning changed on property is a very difficult process. It requires a process of giving public notice and then having a variance approved by government agencies that oversee enforcement of the zoning plan. Opposition to zoning changes by neighbors and other interested parties can be fierce.

You can find out how property is zoned by calling your local planning department. They can also explain what you would need to do to get a variance.

Before getting too involved in a zoning issue, it would no doubt be in your best interests to hire a local land use attorney to help you through the process.

Zoning Restrictions

Use requirements refer to how property can be used. Typical zonings categories include:

- Residential
- Commercial
- Industrial
- Agricultural
- Recreational

These categories usually break down into further subcategories. For example, there are subcategories for single-family (i.e., residences) and multiple-family (e.g., apartments or condominiums) residential use.

Zoning laws will set forth many use restrictions, such as:

- the height and overall size of buildings
- their proximity to one another
- what percentage of the area of a building lot may contain structures
- what particular kinds of facilities must be included with certain kinds of uses

For example, zoning ordinances will typically limit the number of stories and total height of a building, require a certain number of parking spaces for a commercial building, and require a driveway and garage on a suburban residential property.

The bulk requirements of a zoning ordinance refer to:

- the height and size restrictions on buildings
- the square feet of space which a building provides
- the percentage of area it covers on a building lot
- the minimum lot size requirements, if any

The setback and side-yard requirements of a zoning ordinance refer to the distance between the front and back property lines and from the side property lines.

Commercial Lease Checklist

Leasing a commercial space instead of committing yourself to owning commercial real estate can be an excellent move, but there are fewer tenant-friendly laws and no standard lease agreements. You'll need a lawyer's help to negotiate the best deal on a commercial lease.

Every commercial lease should be in writing and should include the following details:

How much rent is due, including any increases (called escalations). You'll want to know the going rate for space in the neighborhood before you begin negotiating. It also helps to let the landlord make the first offer, and ask for a lower rent than you think you can initially get. Escalations should be for specific dollar amounts or tied to a known method of calculation, such as cost of living indexes.

- How long the lease runs, when it begins, and under what conditions you can renew the lease. A shorter lease means less commitment, but less predictability for the long run. If location is very important — for example, if you have a retail store — you may want to opt for a longer lease. You can always attempt to renegotiate lower rents or improvements as time goes on. If you have a month-to-month lease, you'll want to make sure the landlord gives you as much time as possible when terminating the lease.

- Whether your rent includes utilities, such as phone, electricity, and water, or whether you'll be charged for these items separately.

- Whether you'll be responsible for paying any of the landlord's maintenance expenses, property taxes, or insurance costs, and if so, how they'll be calculated.

- Any required deposit and whether you can use a letter of credit instead of cash.

- A description of the space you're renting, square footage, available parking, and other amenities.

- A detailed listing of any improvements the landlord will make to the space before you move in. Your landlord may be more willing to make lots of expensive improvements if you're signing a longer lease.

- Any representations made to you by the landlord or leasing agent, such as amount of foot traffic, average utility costs, restrictions on the landlord renting to competitors (such as in a shopping mall), compliance with Americans With Disabilities Act requirements, and so forth. These may come in handy later when you want to renegotiate your lease.

- Assurances that the space is zoned appropriately for your type of business. Of course, you'll also want to check out this information with local zoning authorities.
- Whether you'll be able to sublease or assign the lease to someone else, and if so, under what conditions. You'll want to negotiate the ability to sublease so that you can move with as little financial pain as possible.

- How either you or the landlord can terminate the lease and the consequences.

When it comes time to renegotiate your commercial lease, you'll want to document your reasons for a lower rent or more space improvements with hard facts regarding lower foot traffic than represented, a downturn in your industry, and so forth. Some landlords will even be willing to take a percentage of your sales instead of a flat rental fee when economic times are slow.

As a tenant, you have far more leeway when negotiating a commercial lease rather than with a residential lease, which is one reason why having your own lawyer to represent you in negotiations is so important. A lawyer can also research zoning laws and local ordinances and fill you in on the local real estate market conditions and customs.

Chapter 19

Merchandising

You probably understand the need to create "passive" streams of income for your business. As a service provider, your greatest asset is also your most limited...Time! There is a very real limit on how much time you have available, and how much energy you have to dedicate to your business versus the rest of your life. You can always increase the "price" of your time but at some point, it will lead to reduced competitiveness as there will be a limit on the amount that the majority of people are willing and able to pay [although I cover many issues surrounding maximum value in another article]. That leads to the natural conclusion of a very real cap on your income without expanding your service offerings beyond the traditional.

Average Earnings from Merchandising

According to Census data, the average practice earns 10% of their revenue via the sale of products and merchandise. Keep in mind, that is an average. Many practice providers do not sell any items while others make much more than 10% from the sale of products. Next time you go to a service provider take a look around you. At the beauty salon there is usually a wide variety of hair care products to select from, ditto for many Chiropractic offices and increasingly traditional medical offices. Even the mechanic offers automobile embellishments for sale. There is a reason...it's profitable. People tend to buy more once they are buying anything. Yes, I know that sentence sounds a bit odd but it's the same reason there are those long lines stuffed full of small impulse purchase items at the checkout isle. The general attitude is that $1 or $2 [or $5 or more] dollars isn't worth the effort to pay for individually but if they are already in line to pay for another product then sure, it's a quick impulse purchase.

This is even true in restaurants. Ever been asked if you would like to increase the size of your order from huge to enormous at the local fast food restaurant? Of course you have. What about desert or an after dinner espresso at your favorite fine diner?

Same concept. Curious what the profit potential can lead to? Industry averages indicate an over all of 10% but that combines ALL practice providers...those that sell a lot with those that sell nothing whatsoever.

Profit Potentials

Let's do a little quick math by using a few different denominations and see if it would be worthwhile or not. We'll use Tim, Jim and Ken as our hypothetical therapists. Each perform an average of 20 massage sessions per week for 50 weeks out of the year or roughly 1,000 per year.

Tim isn't very good at this but decides to give it a try and sets the very modest goal of making $1 extra on average for each massage performed. Of course, that is an average. Some sessions he makes zero – in fact, that is usually the situation for Tim. However, at the end of the year he has indeed averaged $1 per session and has made an additional $1,000 or just over $80 per month. It's not a lot but it helps offset some of the increased utility and other bills that have been eating into his profit margins.

Jim sets his goal to match the practice average of 10% or roughly $6 per session. Jim also performs 1000 sessions during the year and made an additional $6,000 per year or $500 per month. Jim is thrilled with his progress as it allows him to purchase health insurance and begin a personal retirement account. Ken is an old veteran at this and has several exceptional product lines with exclusive territories so he's approaching 20% of his revenue through sales or roughly $12 per session average. Of course, this is a combination of many small sales with some very large sales as Ken has a variety of products to offer. Ken performs 1,000 sessions with earnings of $12,000 for the year or $1,000 per month from his sales.

Before we finish, let's take this one step further to see what type of long term impact it has one each. Again, for the sake of simplicity basic numbers are used.

Over a 20 year career	Over a 30 year career
Tim made an extra $20,000	$30,000
Jim made an extra $120,000	$180,000
Ken made an extra $240,000	$360,000

There are very real pro's and con's to the decision to carry an inventory, collect sales tax and so forth. However, the potential reward can be substantial enough to fund a retirement account. For instance, let's take a look at what would happen to each of the above accounts if invested in a very safe and conservative rate of return of 5% which is an approximate average for U.S. Treasury Bonds or other quite secure investments. Most retirement planners and investor accounts typically use an 8% or higher rate of return which would place Ken at well over $1 million and Jim approaching $1 million.

Tim 30 Years $80 per month @5%	Jim 30 years $500 per month @5%	Ken 30 years $1,000 per month @5%
1 : 982.31	1 : 6139.43	1 : 12278.86
2 : 2014.87	2 : 12592.96	2 : 25185.92
3 : 3100.27	3 : 19376.67	3 : 38753.34
4 : 4241.19	4 : 26507.44	4 : 53014.89
5 : 5440.49	5 : 34003.04	5 : 68006.08
6 : 6701.14	6 : 41882.13	6 : 83764.26
7 : 8026.29	7 : 50164.33	7 : 100328.65
8 : 9419.24	8 : 58870.26	8 : 117740.51
9 : 10883.46	9 : 68021.60	9 : 136043.20
10 : 12422.58	10 : 77641.14	10 : 155282.28
11 : 14040.45	11 : 87752.84	11 : 175505.67
12 : 15741.10	12 : 98381.86	12 : 196763.73
13 : 17528.75	13 : 109554.70	13 : 219109.39
14 : 19407.86	14 : 121299.15	14 : 242598.30
15 : 21383.12	15 : 133644.47	15 : 267288.94
16 : 23459.42	16 : 146621.40	16 : 293242.81
17 : 25641.96	17 : 160262.26	17 : 320524.52
18 : 27936.16	18 : 174601.01	18 : 349202.02
19 : 30347.74	19 : 189673.36	19 : 379346.72
20 : 32882.69	20 : 205516.83	20 : 411033.67
21 : 35547.34	21 : 222170.89	21 : 444341.79
22 : 38348.32	22 : 239677.01	22 : 479354.01
23 : 41292.60	23 : 258078.76	23 : 516157.53
24 : 44387.52	24 : 277421.99	24 : 554843.98
25 : 47640.78	25 : 297754.85	25 : 595509.71
26 : 51060.48	26 : 319127.99	26 : 638255.97
27 : 54655.14	27 : 341594.61	27 : 683189.21
28 : 58433.71	28 : 365210.66	28 : 730421.33
29 : 62405.59	29 : 390034.96	29 : 780069.92
30 : 66580.69	30 : 416129.32	30 : 832258.64

Express Example

Maria specializes in sports related massage and has been in business for ten years in a mature but stable location. Her annual earnings are approximately $45,000 after expenses but she would like to begin adding more to her personal retirement account. Maria is not readily able to work more hours but would like to expand her earning potential.

Maria is aware of an excellent product line which compliments her services while providing an attractive source of potential revenue. Athletic clients have high respect for the product line and it's not easy to find. Maria decides to obtain the necessary tax and other information to become a distributor and reseller of the product line. The item is a repeated purchase and generates an additional $300 per month on average for Maria with very little effort.

Maria is quite satisfied with her initial efforts but would like to expand her product line to increase profits. She believes it is realistic to expect the industry average of at least 10% of revenue which would translate into another $150 to $200 per month income. Maria decides to keep her eyes open for another product.

One year later Maria is at a conference and discovers an exciting nutritional supplement line that would be very attractive to her athletic clients. Maria is already established as a vendor with appropriate tax identification and other forms so she applies once again to distribute and sell the new nutritional supplement line. In this situation, the products are not well known to Maria's clients. Distributors are encouraged to buy large quantities for resell to get the best possible price. Maria anticipates a strong acceptance and purchases a six month supply. Unfortunately, the supplements take up precious space and clients do not respond as expected. Maria further finds it difficult to discuss the product line without sounding like she is making a professional recommendation. Inventory remains stagnant and Maria slashes prices in an attempt to get rid of the supplements before expiration dates.

Maria is confused and dazed; she's unsure what went wrong and how to prevent it from happening again.

Selecting the Perfect Products for Your Practice

Perfect Products for Your Practice: A 20 Point Checklist

Yes	No	Characteristic
_____	_____	Demand for the product already exists among qualified customers
_____	_____	Product benefits are easily understood and recognized.
_____	_____	Product is unique with few competitors providing same product
_____	_____	Sale of Product is not regulated by government
_____	_____	Product has no potential legal liabilities
_____	_____	Product has high perceived value and can justify a higher selling price
_____	_____	Product has repeat business potential
_____	_____	Product has minimal acquisition costs.
_____	_____	Product is easy to package and easy to store/display.
_____	_____	Product has a long shelf life and will not break, expire or go bad.
_____	_____	Product requires a minimum of "handling" for sale.
_____	_____	Product requires little or no after sales support
_____	_____	Product appeals to wide range of your current clients.
_____	_____	Product compliments your current service offering
_____	_____	Product enhances your respectability and meets high standards.
_____	_____	Product is always paid at time of purchase
_____	_____	Product is always available – no backorders required.
_____	_____	Product is never discounted and not available via discount chains, eBay
_____	_____	Product is easy to handle with a low initial cost [ie: impulse purchase].
_____	_____	Product is likely to make a good gift

Scoring

Search for products that will allow you to check "Yes" to each item on the list. If you find a "No", consider the item carefully before offering it as a potential enhancement of your service line. If a prospective product receives more than a few "No's" then reject it and continue searching.

Appendix 1

Where to Obtain a Business License Alphabetical State List

Alabama
http://www.ador.state.al.us/licenses/authrity.html

Alaska
http://www.dced.state.ak.us/occ/buslic.htm

Arizona
http://www.revenue.state.az.us/license.htm

Arkansas
http://www.arkansas.gov/business_res.php

California
http://www.calgold.ca.gov/

Colorado
http://www.state.co.us/oed/industry-license/index.cfm

Connecticut
http://www.state.ct.us/

Delaware
http://www.state.dc.us/revenue/services/Business_Tax/Step3.shtml

District of Columbia
http://www.dcra.dc.gov/

Florida
http://sun6.dms.state.fl.us/dor/businesses/

Georgia
http://www.sos.state.ga.us/corporations/regforms.htm

Hawaii
http://www.hawaii.gov/dbedt/business/start_grow/

Idaho
http://www.idoc.state.id.us/Pages/BUSINESSPAGE.html

Illinois
http://www.business.illinois.gov/licenses.cfm

Indiana
http://www.state.in.us/sic/owners/ia.html

Iowa
http://www.iowalifechanging.com/business/blic.html

Kansas
https://www.accesskansas.org/businesscenter/index.html?link=maintain#licenserenewals

Kentucky
http://www.thinkkentucky.com/kyedc/ebpermits.asp

Louisiana
http://www.louisiana.gov/wps/portal/.cmd/cs/.ce/155/.s/1114/_s.155/1110/_me/1110

Maine
http://www.maine.gov/portal/business/licensing.html

Maryland
http://www.dllr.state.md.us/

Massachusetts
http://www.state.ma.us/sec/cor/coridx.htm

Michigan
http://medc.michigan.org/services/startups/index2.asp

Minnesota
http://www.dted.state.mn.uss

Mississippi
http://www.olemiss.edu/depts/mssbdc/going_intobus.html

Missouri
http://www.missouribusiness.net/docs/license_registration_checklist.asp

Montana
http://www.state.mt.us/sos/biz.htm

Nebraska
http://assist.neded.org/licensed.html

New Hampshire
http://www.nhsbdc.org/startup.htm

New Jersey
http://www.state.nj.us/njbiz/s_lic_and_cert.shtml

New York
http://www.dos.state.ny.us/lcns/licensing.html

New Mexico
Not available at this time

Nevada
http://secretaryofstate.biz/comm_rec/index.htm

North Carolina
http://www.secstate.state.nc.us/secstate/blio/default.htm

North Dakota
http://www.nd.gov/sos/businessserv/registrations/business-search.html

Ohio
http://www.sos.state.oh.us/sos/businessservices/corp.aspx

Oklahoma
http://www.okonestop.com/

Oregon
http://www.filinginoregon.com

Pennsylvania
http://www.paopenforbusiness.state.pa.us

Rhode Island
http://www.dlt.ri.gov/lmi/jobseeker/license.htm

South Carolina
http://www.state.sd.us/STATE/sitecategory.cfm?mp=Licenses/Occupations

South Dakota
http://www.sdreadytowork.com/community/resources/startup/step8.asp

Tennessee
http://www.tennesseeanytime.org/business/index.html

Texas
http://www.tded.state.tx.us/guide/

Utah
http://www.commerce.state.ut.us/web/commerce/admin/licen.htm

Vermont
http://www.sec.state.vt.us/

Virginia
http://www.dba.state.va.us/licenses/

Washington
http://www.wa.gov/dol/bpd/limsnet.htm

West Virginia
http://www.state.wv.us/taxrev/busreg.html

Wisconsin
http://www.wdfi.org/corporations/forms/

Wyoming
http://soswy.state.wy.us/corporat/corporat.htm

Appendix 2

Where to Obtain Workers Compensation, Department of Labor, and Other Business Information – Alphabetical State Contact List

U.S. Department of Labor (DOL):http://www.dol.gov/
200 Constitution Avenue NW
Washington, District of Columbia 20210
(202) 693-6000

Alabama

State of Alabama: http://www.al.gov/
Department of Industrial Relations:
http://dir.alabama.gov/
Workers' Compensation Division:
http://dir.alabama.gov/wc/
Industrial Relations Building
649 Monroe Street
Montgomery, Alabama 36131
(800) 528-5166, (334) 242-2868
Fax: (334) 353-8262 (Self-Insurance)
(334) 353-8228 (Examiners/Ombudsman)
(334) 353-0840 (Claims)
(334) 353-8490 (Compliance/Drug Free/Medical/Education)
Fraud: (800) 923-2533
Ombudsman: (800) 528-5166

Alaska

State of Alaska: http://www.state.ak.us/
Department of Labor and Workforce Development:
http://www.labor.state.ak.us/home.htm
Workers' Compensation Division:
http://www.labor.state.ak.us/wc/wc.htm
Post Office Box 25512
Juneau, Alaska 99802-5512
(907) 465-2790; Fax: (907) 465-2797

Workers' Compensation Board:http://www.gov.state.ak.us/boards/factsheet/fact110.html
Department of Labor
Post Office Box 25512
M/S 0700
Juneau, Alaska 99802-5512
(907) 465-2790, Fax: (907) 465-2797

Arizona

State of Arizona: http://www.state.az.us/
Industrial Commission of Arizona:
http://www.ica.state.az.us/
800 West Washington
Phoenix, Arizona 85007

Post Office Box 19070
Phoenix, Arizona 85005-9070
(602) 542-4411
Fax: (602) 542-7889
Ombudsman: (602) 542-4538
Fax: (602) 542-4350
Arizona workers' compensation forms courtesy Interface Technologies:
http://www.interfacetec.com/

Industrial Commission Review Board
State Compensation Fund:
http://www.statefund.com/
3031 North Second Street
Phoenix, Arizona 85012
(602) 631-2000; Fax: (602) 631-2213

Arkansas

State of Arkansas: http://www.state.ar.us/
Workers' Compensation Commission:
http://www.awcc.state.ar.us/
Street Address:
324 Spring Street
Little Rock, Arkansas 72203
Mailing Address:
Post Office Box 950
Little Rock, Arkansas 72203-0950
(800) 622-4472, (501) 682-3930;
Fax: (501) 682-2777
Legal Advisor Direct: (800) 250-2511

California

State of California: http://www.ca.gov/state/portal/myca_homepage.jsp
Department of Industrial Relations:http://www.dir.ca.gov/
Commission on Health and Safety and Workers' Compensation (CHSWC):http://www.dir.ca.gov/CHSWC/
1515 Clay Street, Room 901
Oakland, California 94612
(510) 622-3959, Fax: (510) 622-3265

Division of Workers' Compensation (DWC):http://www.dir.ca.gov/dwc/
Street Address:
1515 Clay Street, 17th Floor
Oakland, California 94612
Mailing Address:
Post Office Box 420603
San Francisco, California 94142
(800) 736-7401, (510) 286-7100
California workers' compensation forms:http://www.interfacetec.com/

Division of Workers' Compensation Medical Unit:http://www.dir.ca.gov/IMC/imchp.html
Street Address:
1515 Clay Street, 18th Floor
Oakland, California 94612
Mailing Address:
Post Office Box 420603
San Francisco, California 94142
(800) 794-6900 (in California), (510) 286-3700, Complaint Line: (800) 999-1041

Workers' Compensation Appeals Board (WCAB):http://www.dir.ca.gov/WCAB/
Street Address:
455 Golden Gate Avenue, Suite 9328
San Francisco, California 94102-3660
Mailing Address:
Post Office Box 429459
San Francisco, California 94142-9459
Information and Assistance Division: (800) 736-7401, (415) 703-5020

Self-Insurance Plans (SIP):http://www.dir.ca.gov/SIP/
2265 Watt Avenue, Suite 1
Sacramento, California 95825
(916) 483-3392, Fax: (916) 483-1535

State Compensation Insurance Fund (SCIF):http://www.scif.com/
1275 Market Street
San Francisco, California 94103
(415) 565-1234, Claims Reporting Service (toll free): (888) 222-3211, Fraud Hotline: (888) 786-7372

Colorado

State of Colorado:http://www.colorado.gov/
Department of Labor & Employment:http://www.coworkforce.com/
633 17th Street, Suite 200
Denver, Colorado 80202-3660
Division of Workers' Compensation: http://www.coworkforce.com/dwc/
633 17th Street, Suite 400
Denver, Colorado 80202-3660
(888) 390-7936 (English), (800) 685-0891 (Spanish), (303) 318-8700, Fax: (303) 318-8710
Colorado workers' compensation forms courtesy Interface Technologies:http://www.interfacetec.com/

Industrial Claims Appeals Office (ICAP):http://www.coworkforce.com/icao/
633 17th Street, Suite 600
Denver, Colorado 80202-3660
(303) 318-8131, Fax: (303) 318-8139

Connecticut

State of Connecticut: http://www.state.ct.us/index.asp
Workers' Compensation Commission: http://wcc.state.ct.us/
Capitol Place
21 Oak Street, Fourth Floor
Hartford, Connecticut 06106
(860) 493-1500, Fax: (860) 247-1361
Connecticut workers' compensation forms courtesy Interface Technologies:http://www.interfacetec.com/

Compensation Review Board (CRB):http://wcc.state.ct.us/index2.htm
Capitol Place
21 Oak Street, Fourth Floor
Hartford, Connecticut 06106
(203) 493-1500, Fax: (203) 247-1361

Delaware

State of Delaware:http://delaware.gov/
Department of Labor:http://www.delawareworks.com/
4425 North Market Street
Wilmington, Delaware 19802
Division of Industrial Affairs:
http://www.delawareworks.com/industrialaffairs/
4425 North Market Street, Third Floor
Wilmington, Delaware 19802
(302) 761-8200 (Wilmington), (302) 422-1134 (Milford)
Office of Workers' Compensation:http://www.delawareworks.com/industrialaffairs/services/WorkersComp.shtml
State Office Building, Sixth Floor
820 North French Street
Wilmington, Delaware 19801
(302) 761-8200 (Wilmington), (302) 422-1134 (Milford)

District of Columbia

District of Columbia:http://www.dc.gov/
Department of Employment Services:
http://www.does.dc.gov/does/site/default.asp
Government of the District of Columbia
64 New York Avenue, N.E.
Washington, District of Columbia 20002
(202) 724-7000, Fax: (202) 724-5683,
TDD/TYY: (202) 673-6994

Labor Standards Bureau
64 New York Avenue, N.E., Room 3129
Washington, District of Columbia 20002
(202) 671-1555, Fax: (202) 673-6412

Office of Workers' Compensation:http://www.does.dc.gov/does/cwp/view.asp?a=1232&Q=537428
Mailing Address:
Post Office Box 56098
Washington, District of Columbia 20002
Street Address:
64 New York Avenue, N.E., Room 2909
Washington, District of Columbia 20002
(202) 671-1000, Fax: (202) 671-1929

Office of Hearings and Adjudication:http://www.does.dc.gov/does/cwp/view.asp?a=1232&Q=537904
64 New York Avenue, N.E., Room 2011
Washington, District of Columbia 20002
(202) 671-2233, Fax: (202) 673-6938

Florida

State of Florida:http://www.myflorida.com/
Florida Department of Financial Services:http://www.fldfs.com/
Division of Workers' Compensation:
http://www.fldfs.com/WC/
301 Forrest Building
2728 Centerview Drive
Tallahassee, Florida 32399-0680
(850) 921-6966; Fax: (850) 922-6779; Fraud: (800) 742-2214 (in Florida) (Department of Insurance, Bureau of Workers' Compensation Fraud: (850) 413-3116); Safety: (800) 367-4378 (in Florida), (850) 488-3044
Florida workers' compensation forms:http://www.interfacetec.com/

Workers' Compensation Oversight Board:http://www.doi.state.fl.us/wc/pdf/2kAR_OversightBoard.PDF
100 Marathon Building
2574 Seagate Drive
Tallahassee, Florida 32399-2152
(850) 487-2613, SunCom: 277-2613; Fax: (850) 487-3232

Florida Division of Administrative Hearings:
http://www.doah.state.fl.us/internet/
Office of Judges of Compensation Claims:
http://www.jcc.state.fl.us/jcc/default.cfm
Petition for Benefits:
Post Office Box 8000
Tallahassee, Florida 32314-8000
Filing:
Post Office Box 6350
Tallahassee, Florida 32314-6350
Request for Assignment of Case Number:
Post Office Box 6410
Tallahassee, Florida 32314-6410
(850) 487-1911, SUNCOM 277-1911

Florida Department of Education:http://www.fldoe.org/
Florida Division of Vocational Rehabilitation:http://www.rehabworks.org/
2002 Old Saint Augustine Road, Building A
Tallahassee, Florida 32301-4862
(800) 451-4327 (Voice/TDD), (850) 245-3399 (Voice/TDD)

Georgia

State of Georgia:http://www.georgia.gov/
Georgia State Board of Workers' Compensation:http://sbwc.georgia.gov/

270 Peachtree Street, NW
Atlanta, Georgia 30303-1299
(800) 533-0682, (404) 656-3875, Fax: (404) 656-7768, Enforcement Division: (404) 657-1391, Safety Library: (404) 656-9057
Georgia workers' compensation forms courtesy Interface Technologies:http://www.interfacetec.com/

Georgia Subsequent Injury Trust Fund:http://sitf.georgia.gov/
Suite 500, North Tower
1720 Peachtree Street, NW
Atlanta, Georgia 30309-2420
(404) 206-6360, Fax: (404) 206-6363, TDD: (404) 206-5053

Hawaii

State of Hawaii: http://www.hawaii.gov/portal/
Department of Labor & Industrial Relations (DLIR):http://hawaii.gov/labor/
830 Punchbowl Street
Honolulu, Hawaii 96813
(808) 586-8842, Fax: (808) 586-9099,
Disability Compensation Division: http://hawaii.gov/labor/dcd/index.shtml
830 Punchbowl Street, #211
Honolulu, Hawaii 96813
(808) 586-9151, Fax: (808) 586-9219,
Labor & Industrial Relations Appeals Board: http://hawaii.gov/labor/hlirab/index.shtml
830 Punchbowl Street #404
Honolulu, Hawaii 96813
(808) 586-8600, Fax: (808) 586-8599,

Idaho

State of Idaho:http://www.idaho.gov/
Idaho Industrial Commission:http://www.iic.idaho.gov/
317 Main Street
Post Office Box 83720
Boise, Idaho 83720-0041
(800) 950-2110, (208) 334-6000; Fax: (208) 334-2321; TDD: (800) 950-2110

State Insurance Fund:http://www.idahosif.org/
1215 West State Street
Post Office Box 83720
Boise, Idaho 83720-0044
(800) 334-2370, (208) 334-2370 (in the Boise area); Fax: (208) 334-2262 (Policyholder Services, Administration, Management Services, Legal), (208) 334-3253 (Claims), (208) 334-3254 (Underwriting); Fraud: (800) 448-ISIF (4743)

Illinois

State of Illinois:http://www.il.gov/
Illinois Workers' Compensation Commission:http://www.iwcc.il.gov/
100 West Randolph Street, Suite 8-200
Chicago, Illinois 60601
(866) 352-3033 (toll free within Illinois), (312) 814-6611, Fax: (312) 814-6523, TDD: (312) 814-2959
Illinois workers' compensation forms courtesy Interface Technologies:http://www.interfacetec.com/

Office of Self-Insurance Administration:http://www.state.il.us/agency/iic/selfinsurance.htm
701 South Second Street
Springfield, Illinois 62704
(217) 785-7084, Fax: (217) 785-6557

Indiana

State of Indiana:http://www.in.gov/
Workers' Compensation Board of Indiana:http://www.in.gov/workcomp/
Government Center South
402 West Washington Street, Room W-196
Indianapolis, Indiana 46204
(317) 232-3808; Claims/Statistics: (317) 233-4930; Fax: (317) 233-5493; Insurance: (317) 233-3910; Ombudsman: (800) 824-COMP (2667), (317) 232-5922

Indiana Compensation Rating Bureau (ICRB):http://www.icrb.net/
Street Address:
5920 Castleway West Drive
Indianapolis, Indiana 46250
Mailing Address:
Post Office Box 50400
Indianapolis, Indiana 46250
(800) 622-4208, (317) 842-2800; Fax: (317) 842-3717

Iowa

State of Iowa: http://www.state.ia.us/
Iowa Workforce Development:http://www.iowaworkforce.org/
1000 East Grand Avenue

Des Moines, Iowa 50319-0209
(800) JOB-IOWA, (515) 281-5387
Iowa Division of Workers' Compensation:
http://www.iowaworkforce.org/wc/
1000 East Grand Avenue
Des Moines, Iowa 50319-0209
(800) JOB-IOWA (562-4692), (515) 281-5387; Fax: (515) 281-6501, TTD: (515) 281-4748

Kansas

State of Kansas:http://www.kansas.gov/
Department of Labor:http://www.dol.ks.gov/
401 SW Topeka Boulevard
Topeka, Kansas 66603-3182
(785) 296-5000
Division of Workers' Compensation:http://www.dol.ks.gov/WC/HTML/wc_ALL.html
800 SW Jackson, Suite 600
Topeka, Kansas 66612-1227
(800) 332-0353, (785) 296-2996; Fax: (785) 296-0839; Fraud: (800) 332-0353, (785) 296-6392; Industrial Safety & Health: (800) 332-0353, (785) 296-4386; Ombudsman: (800) 332-0353, (785) 296-2996

Kentucky

Commonwealth of Kentucky:http://kentucky.gov/
Kentucky Department of Labor:http://labor.ky.gov/
1047 U.S. 127S, Suite 4
Frankfort, Kentucky 40601
(502) 564-3070
Office of Workers' Claims:
http://www.labor.ky.gov/workersclaims/
657 Chamberlin Avenue
Frankfort, Kentucky 40601
(502) 564-5550 (Administrative Services, Open Records); Fax: (502) 564-8250 (Administrative Services), (502) 564-9533 (Ombudsman), (502) 564-5732 (Open Records), (502) 564-0916 (Security and Compliance); Ombudsman: (800) 554-8601 (Frankfort), (800) 554-8603 (Paducah), (800) 554-8602 (Pikeville); Security and Compliance: (502) 564-5550
Kentucky workers' compensation forms courtesy Interface Technologies:http://www.interfacetec.com/

Workers' Compensation Board
Division of Workers' Compensation Funds:http://www.labor.ky.gov/ows/workerscompensationfunds/
1047 U.S. 127 South, Suite 4
Frankfort, Kentucky 40601
(502) 564-3070; Fax: (502) 564-5112

Workers' Compensation Funding Commission:http://www.kwcfc.ky.gov/
Street Address:
#42 Millcreek Park
Frankfort, Kentucky 40601
Mailing Address:
Post Office Box 1228
Frankfort, Kentucky 40602-1228
(502) 573-3505, Fax: (502) 573-4023

Kentucky Workers' Compensation Law (via CompEd, Inc.):http://www.comped.net/

Louisiana

State of Louisiana:
http://www.louisiana.gov/wps/portal/
Department of Labor:http://www.laworks.net/
Mailing Address:
Post Office Box 94094
Baton Rouge, Louisiana 70804-9094
Street Address:
1001 North 23rd Street
Baton Rouge, Louisiana 70804-9094
(225) 342-3111, TDD: (800) 259-5154
Office of Workers' Compensation Administration:
http://www.laworks.net/wrk_owca.asp
Mailing Address:
Post Office Box 94040
Baton Rouge, Louisiana 70804-9040
Street Address:
1001 North 23rd Street
Baton Rouge, Louisiana 70802-9094
(225) 342-7555, Fax: (225) 342-5665, Fraud: (800) 201-3362 or Safety: (800) 201-2497

Maine

State of Maine:http://www.maine.gov/
Workers' Compensation Board:
http://www.maine.gov/wcb/
27 State House Station
Augusta, Maine 04333-0027
(207) 287-3751; Fax: (207) 287-7198
Maine workers' compensation forms courtesy Interface Technologies:http://www.interfacetec.com/

Maryland

State of Maryland:http://www.maryland.gov/
Maryland Workers' Compensation Commission: http://www.wcc.state.md.us/
10 East Baltimore Street
Baltimore, Maryland 21202-1641
(800) 492-0479, (410) 864-5100; Fax: (410) 333-8122; Fraud: (800) 846-4069; Maryland workers' compensation forms courtesy Interface Technologies:http://www.interfacetec.com/

Insured Workers' Insurance Fund:http://www.iwif.com/
8722 Loch Raven Boulevard
Towson, Maryland 21286-2235
(800) 264-IWIF (4943), (410) 494-2000; Fax: (410) 494-2001; Injury Reporting Hotline: (888) 410-1400; Fraud: (888) ANTI-FRAUD (268-4372),

Massachusetts

Commonwealth of Massachusetts: http://www.mass.gov/
Department of Industrial Accidents: http://www.mass.gov/dia/
600 Washington Street, Seventh Floor
Boston, Massachusetts 02111
(800) 323-3249, (617) 727-4900; Fax: (617) 727-6477; TTY: (800) 224-6196
Massachusetts workers' compensation forms courtesy Interface Technologies:http://www.interfacetec.com/

Massachusetts Workers' Compensation Advisory Council: http://www.mass.gov/wcac/
600 Washington Street, Seventh Floor
Boston, Massachusetts 02111
(617) 727-4900, ext. 378; Fax: (617) 727-7122

Workers' Compensation Rating and Inspection Bureau of Massachusetts: https://www.wcribma.org/mass/
101 Arch Street
Boston, Massachusetts 02110
(617) 439-9030, Fax: (617) 439-6055

Michigan

State of Michigan:http://www.michigan.gov/
Department of Labor & Economic Growth: http://www.michigan.gov/cis
Street Address:
611 W. Ottawa
Lansing, Michigan 48909
Mailing Address:
Post Office Box 30004
Lansing, Michigan 48909
(517) 373-1820, Fax: (517) 373-2129
Workers' Compensation Agency: http://www.michigan.gov/wca
Street Address:
State Secondary Complex
General Office Building
7150 Harris Drive
1st Floor, B-Wing
Lansing, Michigan 48913
Mailing Address:
Post Office Box 30016
Lansing, Michigan 48909
(888) 396-5041, (313) 456-2400, Fax: (313) 456-2424
Michigan workers' compensation forms courtesy Interface Technologies:http://www.interfacetec.com/

Board of Magistrates:http://www.michigan.gov/wca/0,1607,7-191-26919---,00.html
Post Office Box 30016
Lansing, Michigan 48909
(517) 241-9380, Fax: (517) 241-9379, TDD in Lansing: (517) 322-5987

Workers' Compensation Appellate Commission:http://www.michigan.gov/cis/0,1607,7-154-10576_17495---,00.html
Street Address:
Ottawa Building, 2nd Floor
611 West Ottawa Street
Lansing, Michigan 48909
Mailing Address:
Post Office Box 30468
Lansing, Michigan 48909-7968
(517) 373-8020, Fax: (517) 241-1396

Michigan Economic Development Corporation:http://medc.michigan.org/
300 North Washington Square
Lansing, Michigan 48913
(888) 522-0103, (517) 373-9808
Michigan Business Guide to Workers' Compensation:http://medc.michigan.org/services/workerscomp/
Compensation Cost Control Service:http://www.michigan.gov/wca/0,1607,7-191-26925-41305--,00.html
Victor Office Center, Fourth Floor
201 North Washington Square
Lansing, Michigan 48909-7968
(517) 373-9809, Fax: (517) 241-3689

Compensation Advisory Organization of Michigan (CAOM):http://www.caom.com/
Street Address:
17197 N. Laurel Park Drive, Suite 311
Livonia, Michigan 48152
Mailing Address:
Post Office Box 3337
Livonia, Michigan 48151-3337
(734) 462-9600, Fax: (734) 462-9721

Minnesota

State of Minnesota: http://www.state.mn.us/
Department of Labor and Industry:
http://www.doli.state.mn.us/
443 Lafayette Road North
St. Paul, Minnesota 55155-4307
(800) DIAL-DLI (342-5354), (651) 284-5005;
TTY: (651) 297-4198

Workers' Compensation Division:http://www.doli.state.mn.us/workcomp.html
443 Lafayette Road North
St. Paul, Minnesota 55155
(800) DIAL-DLI (342-5354) in Greater Minnesota, (651) 284-5005 in the St. Paul area, (800) 365-4584 or (218) 733-7810 in the Duluth area; Fax: (651) 284-5727
Minnesota workers' compensation forms courtesy Interface Technologies:http://www.interfacetec.com/

Workers' Compensation Court of Appeals:
http://www.workerscomp.state.mn.us/
405 Minnesota Judicial Center
25 Dr. Martin Luther King Jr. Boulevard
St. Paul, Minnesota 55155
(651) 296-6526, Fax: (651) 297-2520,
TTY/TDD: (800) 627-3529

Mississippi

State of Mississippi:
http://www.state.ms.us/its/msportal.nsf?Open
Mississippi Workers' Compensation Commission: http://www.mwcc.state.ms.us/
Street Address:
1428 Lakeland Drive
Jackson, Mississippi 39216
Mailing Address:
Post Office Box 5300
Jackson, Mississippi 39296-5300
(601) 987-4200, Fraud: (601) 359-4250

Missouri

State of Missouri:http://www.mo.gov/
Department of Labor and Industrial Relations:
http://www.dolir.missouri.gov/index.asp
Street Address:
3315 West Truman Boulevard, Room 213
Jefferson City, Missouri 65102
Mailing Address:
Post Office Box 504
Jefferson City, Missouri 65102-0504
(573) 751-9691, Fax: (573) 751-4135
Division of Workers' Compensation:
http://www.dolir.missouri.gov/wc/
Street Address:
3315 West Truman Boulevard, Room 131
Jefferson City, Missouri 65102
Mailing Address:
Post Office Box 58
Jefferson City, Missouri 65102-0058
(573) 751-4231, Fax: (573) 751-2012, Employee Hotline: (800) 775-2667, Employer Hotline: (888) 837-6069, Fraud and Noncompliance: (800)-592-6003, (573)-526-6630, Workers' Safety Program: (573) 526-3504
Missouri workers' compensation forms courtesy Interface Technologies:http://www.interfacetec.com/

Labor and Industrial Relations Commission:http://www.dolir.state.mo.us/lirc/index.htm
3315 West Truman Boulevard
Jefferson City, Missouri 65102

Montana

State of Montana:http://mt.gov/
Department of Labor and Industry:http://dli.mt.gov/
Post Office Box 1728
Helena, Montana 59624-1728
(406) 444-2840, Fax: (406) 444-1394

Employment Relations Division:http://erd.dli.mt.gov/

Workers' Compensation Claims Assistance Bureau:
http://erd.dli.mt.gov/wcclaims/wcchome.asp
Street Address:
1805 Prospect Avenue
Helena, Montana 59624
Mailing Address:
Post Office Box 8011
Helena, Montana 59624-8011

(406) 444-6543, Fax: (406) 444-3465, TDD: (406) 444-9696

Workers' Compensation Regulation Bureau: http://erd.dli.mt.gov/wcregs/wcrhome.asp
Street Address:
1805 Prospect Avenue
Helena, Montana 59624
Mailing Address:
Post Office Box 8011
Helena, Montana 59624-8011
(406) 444-6541, Fax: (406) 444-3465

Workers' Compensation Court:http://wcc.dli.mt.gov/
Street Address:
1625 11th Avenue
Helena, Montana
Mailing Address:
Post Office Box 537
Helena, Montana 59624-0537
(406) 444-7794, Fax: (406) 444-7798

Montana State Fund:http://www.montanastatefund.com/
Street Address:
5 South Last Chance Gulch
Helena, Montana 59601
Mailing Address:
Post Office Box 4759
Helena, Montana 59604-4759
(406) 444-6500, Claim Reporting/ Customer Service: (800) 332-6102, Fraud Reporting: (888) 682-7463

Self Insurers' Guaranty Fund
Post Office Box 4133
Missoula, Montana 59806
(406) 549-8849

Nebraska

State of Nebraska:http://www.nebraska.gov/
Workers' Compensation Court:http://www.wcc.ne.gov/
Street Address:
Lincoln, Nebraska 68509
State House, 13th Floor
Mailing Address:
Post Office Box 98908
Lincoln, Nebraska 68509-8908
(800) 599-5155 (in Nebraska only), (402) 471-6468 (Lincoln and out of state), Fax: (402) 471-2700

Nevada
State of Nevada:http://www.nv.gov/
Department of Business & Industry: http://dbi.state.nv.us/
In Northern Nevada:
788 Fairview Avenue, Suite 100
Carson City, Nevada 89701-5491
(775) 687-4250, Fax: (775) 687-4266

In Southern Nevada:
555 E. Washington Avenue, Suite 4900
Las Vegas, Nevada 89101
(702) 486-2750, Fax: (702) 486-2758

Division of Industrial Relations :http://dirweb.state.nv.us/
400 West King Street, Suite 400
Carson City, Nevada 89703
(775) 684-7260, Fax: (775) 687-6305

Industrial Insurance Regulation Section:http://dirweb.state.nv.us/iirs.htm
400 West King Street, Suite 400
Carson City, Nevada 89703
(775) 684-7270, Fax: (775) 687-6305
Workers' Compensation Section:http://dirweb.state.nv.us/WCS/wcs.htm
1301 North Green Valley Parkway, Suite 200
Henderson, Nevada 89014
(702) 486-9080, Fax: (702) 990-0364
Northern District:
400 West King Street, Suite 400
Carson City, Nevada 89703
(775) 684-7270, Fax: (775) 687-6305
Southern District:
1301 North Green Valley Parkway, Suite 200
Henderson, Nevada 89014
(702) 486-9080, Fax: (702) 990-0364

Nevada Attorney for Injured Workers:http://naiw.nv.gov/

2200 South Rancho Drive, Suite 230
Las Vegas, Nevada 89102
(702) 486-2830, Fax: (702) 486-2844

1000 East William Street, Suite 208
Carson City, Nevada 89701
(775) 684-7555, Fax: (775) 684-7575

Employers Insurance Company of Nevada:http://www.employersinsco.com/
9790 Gateway Drive, Suite 100
Reno, Nevada 89521

2550 Paseo Verde Parkway

Henderson, Nevada 89074-7117
(888) 682-6671; Claim Reporting: (888) 900-1455, Fax: (888) 527-3422; Underwriting/Insurance Services: (888) 682-6671

New Hampshire

State of New Hampshire: http://www.state.nh.us/
Department of Labor:
http://www.labor.state.nh.us/
95 Pleasant Street
Concord, New Hampshire 03301
(603) 271-3177
Workers' Compensation Division:
http://www.labor.state.nh.us/workers_compensation.asp
95 Pleasant Street
Concord, New Hampshire 03301
(603) 271-3174 (claims), (603) 271-2042 (coverage), (603) 271-6172 (self-insurance), (603) 271-3328 (vocational rehabilitation)
New Hampshire workers' compensation forms courtesy Interface Technologies:http://www.interfacetec.com/

New Jersey

State of New Jersey: http://www.state.nj.us/
Department of Labor:
http://www.state.nj.us/labor/
John Fitch Plaza
Post Office Box 110
Trenton, New Jersey 08625
(609) 292-2323, Fax: (609) 633-9271
Division of Workers' Compensation:http://www.nj.gov/labor/wc/wcindex.html
Post Office Box 381
Trenton, New Jersey 08625-0381
(609) 292-2515, Fax: (609) 984-2515
New Jersey workers' compensation forms courtesy Interface Technologies:http://www.interfacetec.com/

N.J. Compensation Rating and Inspection Bureau:http://www.njcrib.com/
60 Park Place
Newark, New Jersey 07102
(973) 622-6014, Fax: (973) 622-6110

New Mexico

State of New Mexico:http://www.newmexico.gov/
Workers' Compensation Administration:
http://www.workerscomp.state.nm.us/
Mailing Address:
Post Office Box 27198
Albuquerque, New Mexico 87125-7198
Street Address:
2410 Centre Avenue SE
Albuquerque, New Mexico 87125
(800) 255-7965, (505) 841-6000, Fax: (505) 841-6009
Help Line/Hot Line: (866) WORKOMP (967-5667), TTY/TDD: (505) 841-6043,

New York

State of New York:http://www.ny.gov/
New York State Workers' Compensation Board:
http://www.wcb.state.ny.us/
20 Park Street
Albany, New York 12207
(877) 632-4996, Fax: (518) 473-1415, Fraud: (888) 363-6001
New York workers' compensation forms courtesy Interface Technologies:http://www.interfacetec.com/

New York State Insurance Fund:http://ww3.nysif.com/
199 Church Street
New York, New York 10007
(888) 875-5790, (212) 312-9000, Fax: (212) 385-2073

North Carolina

State of North Carolina:http://www.ncgov.com/
Department of Commerce:http://www.nccommerce.com/
Mailing Address:
4301 Mail Service Center
Raleigh, North Carolina 27699-4301
Street Address:
301 North Wilmington Street
Raleigh, NC 27020-0571
(919) 733-4151

North Carolina Industrial Commission:
http://www.comp.state.nc.us/
Mailing Address:
4340 Mail Service Center
Raleigh, North Carolina 27699-4340
Street Address:
Dobbs Building (sixth floor)
430 North Salisbury Street
Raleigh, North Carolina 27603-5937
(919) 807-2500, Fax: (919) 715-0282

Fraud Investigations Section: (888) 891-4895 (in North Carolina):http://www.comp.state.nc.us/ncic/pages/fraud.htm
Safety Education Section: (919) 807-2603:http://www.comp.state.nc.us/ncic/pages/safety.htm
Workers' Compensation Information Specialists Section (formerly Ombudsman Section): (800) 688-8349:http://www.comp.state.nc.us/ncic/pages/ombudsmn.htm
North Carolina workers' compensation forms courtesy Interface Technologies:http://www.interfacetec.com/

North Dakota

State of North Dakota:http://www.nd.gov/
Workforce Safety & Insurance:http://www.WorkforceSafety.com/
1600 East Century Avenue, Suite One
Bismarck, North Dakota 58506-5585
(800) 777-5033, (701) 328-3800; Fax: (701) 328-3820; Fraud: (800) 243-3331; Safety and Loss Prevention: (701) 328-3886; TDD: (701) 328-3786
Workforce Safety & Insurance Board of Directors
Post Office Box 2174
Bismarck, North Dakota 58502-2174

Ohio

State of Ohio:http://ohio.gov/
Ohio Bureau of Workers' Compensation:http://www.ohiobwc.com/
30 West Spring Street
Columbus, Ohio 43215-2256
(800) OHIOBWC (800-644-6292); Fax: (877) 520-OHIO (6446); TTY: (800) BWC-4-TDD (800-292-4833); Authorized Consent for Release of Information: Fax: (614) 621-3376; Ombudsman: (800) 335-0996, Fax: (614) 644-1998, Ohio workers' compensation forms courtesy Interface Technologies:http://www.interfacetec.com/

Industrial Commission of Ohio: http://www.ohioic.com/index.jsp
30 West Spring Street
Columbus, Ohio 43215-2256
(800) 521-2691, (614) 466-6136, Fax: (614) 752-8304

Oklahoma

State of Oklahoma:http://www.ok.gov/
Oklahoma Workers' Compensation Court: http://www.owcc.state.ok.us/
Oklahoma City Location:
Denver N. Davison Court Building
1915 North Stiles Avenue
Oklahoma City, Oklahoma 73105
Tulsa Location:
440 South Houston, Suite 210
Tulsa, Oklahoma 74127
(800) 522-8210 (statewide), (405) 522-8600 (Oklahoma City) and (918) 581-2714 (Tulsa), Fax: (405) 522-8687 (administration)

Department of Labor: http://www.okdol.state.ok.us/
4001 North Lincoln Boulevard
Oklahoma City, Oklahoma 73105-5212
(888) 269-5353, (405) 528-1500 Fax: (405) 528-5751
Workers' Compensation Enforcement Unit:http://www.okdol.state.ok.us/workcomp/index.htm
Worker Safety Policy Council:http://www.okdol.state.ok.us/wspc/index.htm

CompSource Oklahoma:http://www.compsourceok.com/
Mailing Address (Oklahoma City):
Post Office Box 53505
Oklahoma City, Oklahoma 73152-3505
Street Addresses:
(Administration, Claims, Financial Services, Special Investigations)
1901 North Walnut Avenue
Oklahoma City, Oklahoma 73105-3295
(Policyholder Services, Information Systems)
410 North Walnut Avenue
Oklahoma City, Oklahoma 73104
(800) 347-3863, (405) 232-7663; Teleclaim (to report an injury): (800) 872-7015; Claims Information: (800) 462-7966, (405) 962-3872; Fax: (405) 962-3000, Fraud Hotline: (800) 899-1847
Street Addresses (Tulsa Branch Office):
1305 South Denver Avenue
Tulsa, Oklahoma 74119-3040
Mailing Address (Tulsa Branch Office):
Post Office Box 50580
Tulsa, Oklahoma 74150-0580
(800) 347-3863, (918) 295-1500

Oregon

State of Oregon:http://www.oregon.gov/
Department of Consumer & Business Services:
http://egov.oregon.gov/DCBS/
350 Winter Street NE
Salem, Oregon 97301-3878
(503) 378-4100, Fax: (503) 378-6444

Workers' Compensation
Division:http://wcd.oregon.gov/
350 Winter Street NE, Room 27
Salem, Oregon 97301-3879
(800) 452-0288 (Workers' Compensation Infoline); (503) 947-7810, Fax: (503) 947-7514; TTY: (503) 947-7993; Fraud Hotline: (800) 422-8778 (in Oregon); Small Business Ombudsman: (503) 378-4209, Fax: (503) 373-7639; Ombudsman for Injured Workers: (800) 927-1271, (503) 378-3351, Fax: (503) 373-7639

Workers' Compensation
Board:http://www.cbs.state.or.us/external/wcb/index.html
2601 25th Street SE, Suite 150
Salem, Oregon 97302-1282
(503) 378-3308

Workers' Compensation Management-Labor Advisory Committee:
http://www.oregon.gov/DCBS/MLAC/
Department of Consumer & Business Services
350 Winter Street, Room 200
Salem, Oregon 97301-3878
(503) 947-7867; Fax: (503) 378-6444

Ombudsman for Injured Workers:
http://egov.oregon.gov/DCBS/OIW/index.shtml
350 Winter Street NE, Room 160
Salem, Oregon 97310
(800) 927-1271, (503) 378-3351

Ombudsman for Small Business:
http://egov.oregon.gov/DCBS/SBO/index.shtml
350 Winter Street NE
Salem, Oregon 97301-3878
(503) 378-4209, V/TTY: (503) 378-4100

SAIF Corporation:http://www.saif.com/
400 High Street SE
Salem, Oregon 97312-1000
(800) 285-8525, (503) 373-8000

Pennsylvania

State of Pennsylvania: http://www.state.pa.us/
Department of Labor and Industry:
http://www.dli.state.pa.us/
Labor & Industry Building
Room 1700
7th and Forster Streets
Harrisburg, Pennsylvania 17120
(717) 787-5279
Bureau of Workers'
Compensation:http://www.dli.state.pa.us/landi/cwp/view.asp?a=138&Q=58929&landiPNav=|#1026
1171 South Cameron Street, Room 324
Harrisburg, Pennsylvania 17104-2501
(800) 482-2383 (inside Pennsylvania), (717) 772-4447 (local/out of state), TTY: (800) 362-4228 (for hearing and speech impaired only)
Pennsylvania workers' compensation forms courtesy Interface
Technologies:http://www.interfacetec.com/

State Workers' Insurance
Fund:http://www.dli.state.pa.us/landi/cwp/view.asp?a=151&Q=58236&landiNavDLTEST=|852|1065|2548|
100 Lackawanna Avenue
Scranton, Pennsylvania 18503
(570) 963-4635

Workers' Compensation Appeal Board
1171 South Cameron Street, Room 305
Harrisburg, Pennsylvania 17104-2511
(717) 783-7838

Rhode Island

State of Rhode Island: http://www.state.ri.us/
Workers' Compensation
Court:http://www.courts.state.ri.us/workers/defaultnew-workers.htm
One Dorrance Plaza
Providence, Rhode Island 02903
(401) 458-5000, Fax: (401) 222-3121

Medical Advisory
Board:http://www.courts.ri.gov/workers/medical/medical-advisory.htm
One Dorrance Plaza
Providence, Rhode Island 02903
(401) 458-3460

Workers' Compensation Advisory Council
194 Smith Street

Providence, Rhode Island 02908
(401) 751-7100

Department of Labor and
Training:http://www.dlt.ri.gov/
1511 Pontiac Avenue
Cranston, Rhode Island 02920-4407
(401) 462-8000
Workers' Compensation Division:
http://www.dlt.ri.gov/wc/
Street Address:
1511 Pontiac Avenue, Building 69, Second Floor
Cranston, Rhode Island 02920-0942
Mailing Address:
Post Office Box 20190
Cranston, Rhode Island 02920-0190
(401) 462-8100, Fax: (401) 462-8105, TDD:
(401) 462-8006
Rhode Island workers' compensation forms
courtesy Interface
Technologies:http://www.interfacetec.com/

South Carolina

State of South Carolina:http://www.sc.gov/
Workers' Compensation Commission:
http://www.wcc.state.sc.us/
Street Address:
1612 Marion Street
Columbia, South Carolina 29201
Mailing Address:
Post Office Box 1715
Columbia, South Carolina 29202-1715
(803) 737-5700, Fax: (803) 737-5768
South Carolina workers' compensation forms
courtesy Interface
Technologies:http://www.interfacetec.com/

South Carolina State Accident Fund:
http://www.myscgov.com/scoa/
Street Address:
800 Dutch Square Boulevard
Columbia, South Carolina 29221
Mailing Address:
Post Office Box 102100
Columbia, South Carolina 29221-5000
(800) 521-6576, (803) 896-5800

South Carolina Second Injury Fund
22 Koger Center
Winthrop Building, Suite 119220
Executive Center Drive
Columbia, South Carolina 29210
(803) 798-2722, Fax: (803) 798-5290

South Carolina Workers' Compensation
Uninsured Employers' Fund
22 Koger Center
Winthrop Building, Suite 119220
Executive Center Drive
Columbia, South Carolina 29210
(803) 798-2722, Fax: (803) 798-5290

South Dakota

State of South Dakota: http://www.state.sd.us/
Department of Labor:
http://www.state.sd.us/dol/dol.asp
Division of Labor and
Management:http://www.state.sd.us/dol/dlm/dlm
-home.htm
Kneip Building, Third Floor
700 Governors Drive
Pierre, South Dakota 57501-2291
(605) 773-3681, Fax: (605) 773-4211

Tennessee

State of Tennessee:http://www.tennessee.gov/
Department of Labor and Workforce
Development: http://www.tennessee.gov/labor-
wfd/
Workers' Compensation
Division:http://www.state.tn.us/labor-
wfd/wcomp.html
710 James Robertson Parkway
Gateway Plaza, Second Floor
Nashville, Tennessee 37243-0665
(800) 332-2667 (within Tennessee), (615) 532-
4812, Fax: (615) 532-1468
Tennessee workers' compensation forms
courtesy Interface
Technologies:http://www.interfacetec.com/

Texas

State of Texas: http://www.state.tx.us/
Department of Insurance
:http://www.tdi.state.tx.us/
Street Address
333 Guadalupe
Austin, Texas 78701
Mailing Address
Post Office Box 149104
Austin, Texas 78714-9104
(800) 578-4677, (512) 463-6169
Division of Workers'
Compensation:http://www.tdi.state.tx.us/wc/inde
xwc.html
7551 Metro Center Drive, Suite 100
Austin, Texas 78744-1609

(512) 804-4000, Commissioners: (512) 804-4435 fax: (512) 804-4431, Customer Relations/Services: (512) 804-4100 or 804-4636, Fax: (512) 804-4001, Fraud Hotline: (888) 327-8818 or (512) 804-4703, Injured Worker Hotline/Ombudsman: (800) 252-7031, Safety Violations Hotline: (800) 452-9595
Texas workers' compensation forms courtesy Interface Technologies:http://www.interfacetec.com/

Utah

State of Utah:http://www.utah.gov/
Labor Commission of Utah:http://www.laborcommission.utah.gov/
Division of Industrial Accidents:http://www.laborcommission.utah.gov/indacc/indacc.htm
Mailing Address:
Post Office Box 146610
Salt Lake City, Utah 84114-6610
Street Address:
160 East 300 South, 3rd Floor
Salt Lake City, Utah 84111
(800) 530-5090 (in state only), (801) 530-6800, Fax: (801) 530-6804, TDD: (801) 530-7685

Workers' Compensation Fund of Utah: https://www.wcfgroup.com/wcfWebsite/homePage.do
Salt Lake City Office
392 East 6400 South
Murray, Utah 84107
(800) 446-2667

Vermont

State of Vermont:http://vermont.gov/
Department of Labor:http://labor.vermont.gov/
Street Address
5 Green Mountain Drive
Montpelier, Vermont 05601-0488
Mailing Address
Post Office Box 488
Montpelier, Vermont 05601-0488
(802) 828-4000, Fax: (802) 828-4022

Workers' Compensation Division
FAQ for Injured Workers:http://labor.vermont.gov/Workers/Injured/tabid/110/Default.aspx
FAQ for Businesses:http://159.105.83.167/WorkersCompensation/tabid/114/default.aspx
National Life Building
Drawer 20
Montpelier, Vermont 05620-3401
(802) 828-2286, Fax: (802) 828-2195
Vermont workers' compensation forms courtesy Interface Technologies:http://www.interfacetec.com/

Virginia

Commonwealth of Virginia:http://www.virginia.gov/
Virginia Workers' Compensation Commission: http://www.vwc.state.va.us
1000 DMV Drive
Richmond, Virginia 23220
(877) 664-2566, Fax: (804) 367-9740, TDD: (804) 367-8600
Virginia workers' compensation forms courtesy Interface Technologies:http://www.interfacetec.com/

Washington

State of Washington:http://access.wa.gov/
Department of Labor and Industries:http://www.lni.wa.gov/
Labor and Industries Building
Post Office Box 44001
Olympia, Washington 98504-4001
(800) 547-8367, (360) 902-4200, Fax: (360) 902-4202
Workers' Comp Claims: http://www.lni.wa.gov/ClaimsIns/Claims/default.asp

Board of Industrial Insurance Appeals:http://www.biia.wa.gov/
Street Address:
2430 Chandler Court, SW
Olympia, Washington 98504-2401
Mailing Address:
Post Office Box 42401
Olympia, Washington 98504-2401
(800) 442-0447, (360) 753-9646, Fax: (360) 586-5611
Washington workers' compensation forms courtesy Interface Technologies:http://www.interfacetec.com/

West Virginia

West Virginia:http://www.wv.gov/
Insurance
Commission:http://www.wvinsurance.gov/

BrickStreet Mutual Insurance
Company:http://www.brickstreet.com/
Mailing Address:
Post Office Box 3824
Charleston, West Virginia 25338-3824
Street Address:
4700 MacCorkle Avenue
Charleston, West Virginia 25304
Administrative Services: (888) 4-WV-COMP and (304) 926-3400, Fax: (304) 926-5372;

Workers' Compensation Office of Judges:
http://www.wvinsurance.gov/ooj/
Mailing Address:
Post Office Box 2233
Charleston West Virginia 25328-2233
Street Address:
One Players Club Drive
Charleston West Virginia 25311-1638
(304) 558-1686, Fax: (304) 558-1021

Workers' Compensation Board of
Review:http://www.wvinsurance.gov/boardofreview/index.htm
Mailing Address:
Post Office Box 2628
Charleston, West Virginia 25329-2628
Street Address:
104 Dee Drive
Charleston, West Virginia 25301
(304) 558-5230, Fax: (304) 558-1322

Workers' Compensation Industrial
Council:http://www.wvinsurance.gov/wc/industrialcouncil/indcx.htm

Wisconsin

State of Wisconsin:
http://www.wisconsin.gov/state/home
Department of Workforce Development:
http://www.dwd.state.wi.us/
Workers' Compensation
Division:http://www.dwd.state.wi.us/wc/default.htm
Mailing Address:
Post Office Box 7901
Madison, Wisconsin 53707-7901
Street Address:
Room C100
201 East Washington Avenue
Madison, Wisconsin 53703
(608) 266-1340; Fax: (608) 267-0394; Fraud (608) 261-8486
Wisconsin workers' compensation forms courtesy Interface
Technologies:http://www.interfacetec.com/

Workers' Compensation Advisory
Council:http://www.dwd.state.wi.us/wc/councils/wcac/default.htm
(608) 266-6841
Frances Huntley-Cooper, Chairman

Wisconsin Compensation Rating
Bureau:https://www.wcrb.org/WCRB/wcrbhome.htm
Mailing Address:
Post Office Box 3080
Milwaukee, WI 53201-3080
Street Address:
20700 Swenson Drive, Suite 100
Waukesha, Wisconsin 53186
(262) 796-4540, Fax: (262) 796-4400

Wisconsin Labor and Industry Review
Commission: http://www.dwd.state.wi.us/lirc/
Mailing Address:
Post Office Box 8126
Madison, Wisconsin 53708-8126
Street Address:
Wisconsin Public Broadcasting Building
3319 West Beltline Highway
Madison, Wisconsin
(608) 266-9850 Fax: (608) 267-4409

Wyoming

State of Wyoming:http://wyoming.gov/
Department of Employment:
http://wydoe.state.wy.us/
Cheyenne Business Center
1510 East Pershing Boulevard
Cheyenne, Wyoming 82002
(307) 777-7672, Fax: (307) 777-5805
Workers' Safety and Compensation Division:
http://wydoe.state.wy.us/doe.asp?ID=9
Cheyenne Business Center
1510 East Pershing Boulevard
Cheyenne, Wyoming 82002
(307) 777-7159, Fax: (307) 777-5524.

To Report an Injury: (800) 870-8883 or (307) 777-7441, Fax: (307) 777-6552.

To Report Fraud: (888) 996-9226 or (307) 777-6552, Fax: (307) 777-3581.

Appendix 3

General Small Business Resources

Small Business Help from the IRS

At one time or another, every small business owner has tax questions. The IRS offers a variety of types of assistance to small business owners: publications, CD-ROMs, videos, Taxpayer Assistance Centers, toll-free tax assistance, classes, and workshops. To order these products, call (800) 829-3676

Publication 1066C, The Virtual Small Business Tax Workshop DVD

The DVD is designed to help new and existing small business owners understand and meet their federal tax obligations. The workshop consists of ten lessons that provide information and resources in an interactive format. You can view topics that apply to your type of business – it literally allows you to customize your lessons.

Publication 3207, Small Business Resource Guide CD

This CD contains important information including all the business tax forms, instructions, and publications needed by small business owners. The CD also provides valuable business information on a variety of government agencies, non-profit organizations, and educational institutions. The CD contains essential startup information needed to plan and finance a new business. The design of the CD makes finding information quick and easy.

The Business and Specialty Tax Line

The Business and Specialty Tax Line is available at 800-829-4933. The line assists small businesses with their business returns.

IRS Tax Forms and Publications CD

The CD containing current and prior year tax forms and publications, can be purchased from the National Technical Information Service (NTIS). Order the CD by calling toll free (877) 233-6767 or at the ordering page.

TeleTax

TeleTax ((800) 829-4477) is the IRS toll-free telephone service that provides recorded tax information and automated refund information. About 150 recorded topics provide basic tax information. For the directory of topics, listen to topic 123. This Touch-Tone service is available 24 hours a day, 7 days a week. It's also available in Spanish.

Tax Forms and Publications

To order IRS tax forms and publications, call (800) 829-3676.

Tax Assistance

Individual taxpayers can call (800) 829-1040, Monday through Friday, from 8:00 a.m. until 8:00 p.m. local time. Business taxpayers can call the Business and Specialty Tax Line at (800) 829-4933.

Miscellaneous Government Small Business Resources

Employee Benefits Security Administration (EBSA)
401(k) Plans, Retirement, Savings, Health Benefit Plans including COBRA
(202) 219-8776

Office of Federal Contract Compliance Programs (OFCCP)
Americans with Disabilities Act, Affirmative Action, Executive Order 11246, §503 of the Rehabilitation Act, Vietnam Veterans (202) 693-0023

Office of Workers' Compensation
(202) 693-0046

Wage and Hour Division
Contract Work Hours and Safety Standards Act, Copeland "Anti-kickback" Act, Davis-Bacon, Employee Polygraph Protection Act, Fair Labor Standards Act, Family and Medical Leave, Wage Garnishment Law, Service Contract Act, Migrant Seasonal Agricultural Workers, Walsh-Healey Public Contracts Act (202) 693-0067

Occupational Safety and Health Administration (OSHA)
Occupational Safety and Health Act of 1970 and OSHA's cooperative programs
(202) 693-221

Office of Small Business Programs
Small Business Regulatory Enforcement Act (SBREFA): Key Points for Small Business
202) 693-6489 or (888) 9-SBREFA

Small Business Help from Social Security

Social Security Administration
(800) 772-6270
(Employer Information Line)

Small Business Administration Answer Desk

6302 Fairview Road, Suite 300
Charlotte, North Carolina 28210
(800) U-ASK-SBA ((800)-827-5722)
Send e-mails to: answerdesk@sba.gov
Answer Desk TTY: (704) 344-6640

Small Business Help Line

1-800-UASK-SBA (1-800-827-5722) will connect you with a Nationwide Answer Desk staffed with multilingual personnel to assist you.
Send e-mails to: answerdesk@sba.gov
Answer Desk TTY: (704) 344-6640

Federal Small Business Resources

Department of Agriculture/Small Business Opportunities

Includes information on contract opportunities, business support programs, various loan programs, marketing information, and other useful links. Most people think of the USDA only as dealing with agriculture however, they provide small business information and loans in many areas. http://www.usda.gov/da/smallbus

Department of Commerce

Provides a wide range of information concerning economic and business development issues of interest to small business owners. http://home.doc.gov/

Department of Housing and Urban Development
http://www.hud.gov

The Office of Small and Disadvantaged Business Utilization (OSDBU)
http://www.hud.gov/offices/osdbu/index.cfm

The Department of Housing and Urban Development (HUD) is committed to ensuring that small businesses, small disadvantaged businesses and women-owned businesses participate fully in HUD direct contracting as well as in contracting opportunities generated by HUD grant funds.

HUBZone Empowerment Contracting
https://eweb1.sba.gov/hubzone/internet/

The HUBZone Empowerment Contracting program provides federal contracting opportunities for qualified small businesses located in distressed areas. Fostering the growth of these federal contractors as viable businesses, for the long term, helps to empower communities, create jobs, and attract private investment."

Department of Labor/Office of Small Business Programs
http://www.dol.gov/osbp/welcome.html

"The Office of Small Business Programs (OSBP) administers four programs:

- Procurement related utilization of small, small minority, and small women-owned businesses, and minority colleges and universities, by the Department of Labor.
- Department of Labor interaction with and support of Minority Colleges and Universities.
- Department of Labor's central point for Compliance Assistance Information and referral services for small entities.
- Administrative oversight of Department Advisory Committees and similar activities."

Department of Labor/Occupational Safety and Health Administration (OSHA)
Office of Small Business Assistance
http://www.osha.gov/dcsp/smallbusiness/index.html

Department of Veterans Affairs/The Center for Veterans Enterprise (CVE)
810 Vermont Avenue, N. W., Washington, D.C. 20420
Phone: (202) 565-8336
Toll Free: (866) 584-2344
Fax: (202) 565-4255 or (202) 565-8156
E-mail: VACVE@mail.va.gov
http://www.vetbiz.gov

If you're a service-disabled veteran interested in starting or growing your own business, the U.S. Small Business Administrations Veterans Business Outreach Program is designed to help you do just that.

Small Biz Assistance for Veterans & National Guard
http://www.score.org/veteran.html

America's service men and women can benefit from small business resources specifically for veteran, National Guard and reservist small business owners. SCORE has compiled a team of volunteer counselors with special expertise in helping this segment of entrepreneurs.

DisabilityInfo.gov
http://www.disabilityinfo.gov/

With just a few clicks, the portal provides access to disability-related information and programs available across the government on numerous subjects, including civil rights, education, employment, housing, health, income support, technology, transportation, and community life.

FIRSTGOV for the Self-Employed
http://www.firstgov.gov./Business/Self_Employed.shtml

An extensive portal for information on services and information available for workers in America.

General Services Administration/GSA Office of Enterprise Development
1800 F Street, NW, Washington, DC 20405
Phone: (202) 501-1021
http://www.gsa.gov/

GSA's advocate for small, minority, and women business owners.

Office of Personnel Management (OPM)/Federal Employment of People with Disabilities
http://www.opm.gov/disability/

This site provides a simple and straightforward mechanism to help Americans, with and without disabilities, better understand how to hire and retain persons with disabilities.

Start-Up USA
Self-Employment Technical Assistance, Resources, & Training
Virginia Commonwealth University
Worksupport.com
1314 West Main Street
P.O. Box 842011
Richmond, Virginia 23284-2011
http://www.start-up-usa.biz/

U.S. Equal Employment Opportunity Commission (EEOC)
"Small Employers And Reasonable Accommodation"
http://www.eeoc.gov/facts/accommodation.html

WomenBiz.Gov/The Gateway for Women-Owned Businesses Selling to the Federal Government
http://www.womenbiz.gov/

Whether you are just starting to think about bidding on your first government contract, or you are about to submit your tenth proposal, there are key pieces of information about selling to the federal government that can be useful to you at any stage of your business.

Women Entrepreneurship in the 21st Century
http://www.women-21.gov/

Rhe U.S. Department of Labor and the U.S. Small Business Administration have partnered to keep attention focused on women owned small business.

Women with Disabilities Entrepreneurship Project
U.S. Department of Labor - Women's Bureau
200 Constitution Avenue, NW, Room S-3002, Washington, DC 20210
Phone: (202) 693-6710 or Toll Free (800) 827-5335
Fax: (202) 693-6725
http://www.dol.gov/wb/media/newsletter/e-news10artl-04.htm

Appendix 4

Toll Free Health Hotlines – Speak to a Live Person!

AIDS/HIV Treatment, Prevention and Research	800-HIV-0440
Aging	800-222-2225 800-222-4225 (TTY)
Alcohol and Drug Abuse	800-729-6686 888-889-6432 (TTY)
Alcohol Abuse and Alcoholism	301-443-3860
Alzheimer's Disease	800-438-4380 800-222-4225 (TTY)
Arthritis and Musculoskeletal and Skin Diseases	877-22-NIAMS 877-226-4267 301-565-2966 (TTY)
Back to Sleep: Sudden Infant Death Syndrome (SIDS)	800-505-CRIB 800-505-2742
Basic Research on Cells, Proteins, and Genes	301-496-7301
Bladder Control for Women	800-891-5388
Cancer	800-4-CANCER 800-422-6237 800-332-8615 (TTY)
Child Health and Human Development *Bilingual staff available for information in English and Spanish*	800-370-2943 888-320-6942 (TTY)
Complementary and Alternative Medicine *Bilingual staff available for information in Spanish*	888-NIH-6226 866-464-3615 (Voice/TTY)
NIH Consensus Program	888-644-2667
Deafness and Other Communication Disorders	800-241-1044 800-241-1055 (TTD/TTY)
Diabetes **Diabetes Education Program** **Control Your Diabetes. For Life** **Small Steps, Big Rewards. Prevent type 2 Diabetes**	800-860-8747 800-438-5383 800-438-5383 800-438-5383
Digestive Diseases **Endocrine and Metabolic Disorders** **Hematologic Diseases**	800-891-5389 888-828-0904 888-828-0877
Drug Abuse	301-443-1124
Genetic and Rare Diseases	888-205-2311
Eye Diseases	301-496-5248
Extramural Research Grants	301-435-0714
Global Health	301-496-2075
Heart, Lung, and Blood	800-575-WELL

	800-575-9355 301-592-8573 240-629-3255.(TTY)
Human Genome Research	301-402-0911
Kidney and Urologic Diseases	800-891-5390
National Library of Medicine	888-346-3656
Network of Libraries of Medicine	800-338-7657
Mental Health and Mental Illness	301-443-4513 301-443-8431 (TTY)
Mental Health and Mental Illness **Real Men. Real Depression Campaign**	866-615-NIMH (6464) 866-415-8051
Neurological Disorders	800-352-9424 301-468-5981 (TTY)
Nursing Research	301-496-0207 866-910-3804 301-594-5605 (TTY)
Oral Health *Bilingual staff available for information in Spanish*	301-402-7364 301-496-6706
Osteoporosis and Related Bone Diseases	800-624-BONE 800-624-2663 202-223-0344 202-466-4315 (TTY)
Ovulation Research	888-644-8891
Clinical Center Patient Recruitment	800-411-1222 866-411-1010 (TTY)
Patient Recruitment and Public Liaison Office	800-411-1222 866-411-1010 (TTY)
Schizophrenia Research	888-674-6464
Smoking Cessation, NCI's Smoking Quitline	877-44U-QUIT 877-448-7848
Stroke	800-352-9424 301-468-5981 (TTY)
WE CAN (Ways to Enhance Children's Activity and Nutrition)	866-35-WE-CAN
Weight Control	877-946-4627
Women's Health	301-496-8176
Office of Research on Women's Health	301-402-1770
National Women's Health Information	800-994-9662 888-220-5446 (TTD)

Appendix 5

Toll Free Health Hotlines - Order Resources & Supplies

A

ABLEDATA, 800-227-0216

AdCARE Hospital Helpline, 252-6465

Aerobics and Fitness Foundation of America, 968-7263 (Consumers); 800-446-2322 (Professionals)

Agency for Healthcare Research and Quality Clearinghouse, 800-358-9295

AIDS Info, 448-0440; (888) 480-3739 (TTY)

Al-Anon Family Group Headquarters, 800-425-2666

Alcohol and Drug Helpline, 800-821-4357

Alliance for Aging Research, 800-639-2421

ALS Association, 800-782-4747

Alzheimer's Association Helpline, 800-272-3900

Alzheimer's Disease Education and Referral Center, 800-438-4380

American Academy of Allergy, Asthma and Immunology, 800-822-2762

American Academy of Facial Plastic and Reconstructive Surgery, 800-332-3223

American Alliance for Health, Physical Education, Recreation and Dance, 800-213-7193

American Association of Critical Care Nurses, 800-899-2226

American Association of Diabetes Educators, 800-338-3633

American Association of Kidney Patients, 800-749-2257

American Autoimmune Related Diseases Association, Inc., 800-598-4668

American Behcet's Disease Association, 800-723-4238

American Brain Tumor Association, 800-886-2282

American Cancer Society, 800-227-2345 (Voice/TDD/TT)

American Chiropractic Association, 800-986-4636

American Cleft Palate-Craniofacial Association/Cleft Palate Foundation, 800-242-5338

American Council of the Blind, 800-424-8666

American Council on Alcoholism, 800-527-5344

American Council on Exercise, 800-825-3636

American Counseling Association, 800-347-6647

American Dental Association, 800-947-4746 (Catalog Sales and Service)

American Diabetes Association, 800-342-2383; 232-6733 (Fax Order Fulfillment)

American Headache Society, 800-255-2243

American Health Assistance Foundation, 800-437-2423

American Heart Association, 800-242-8721

American Heart Association Stroke Connection, (888) 478-7653

American Institute for Cancer Research, 800-843-8114

American Juvenile Arthritis Organization, 800-283-7800

American Kidney Fund, 800-638-8299

American Leprosy Missions (Hansen's Disease), 800-543-3131

American Liver Foundation, 800-465-4837

American Lung Association, 800-586-4872; 800-528-2971 (Living Bank)

American Nurses Association, 800-274-4262

American Occupational Therapy Association, 800-729-2682; 800-377-8555 (TDD); 800-701-7735 (Fax-on-Request)

American Osteopathic Association, 800-621-1773

American Parkinson's Disease Association, 800-223-2732

American Podiatric Medical Association, Inc., 800-275-2762

American Running Association, 800-776-2732

American SIDS Institute, 800-232-7437

American Social Health Association, 800-230-6039

American Society for Deaf Children, 800-942-2732

American Society for Dermatologic Surgery, Inc., 800-441-2737

American Society of Plastic Surgeons, Inc. (888) 475-2784

American Speech-Language-Hearing Association, 800-638-8255

American Thyroid Association, 800-849-7643

American Trauma Society, 800-556-7890

American Urological Association Foundation, 800-828-7866

Americans with Disabilities Act Information Center, 800-949-4232 (Voice/TTY)

Americans with Disabilities Act Information Line, 800-514-0301 (English and Spanish); 800-514-0383 (TTY)

Amputee Coalition of America, (888) 267-5669

Angel Flight Mid-Atlantic, 800-296-3797

Aplastic Anemia and MDS International Foundation, Inc., 800-747-2820

ARC of the United States, The, 800-433-5255

Arthritis Foundation Information Hotline, 800-283-7800

Arthritis National Research Foundation, 800-588-2873

Association for Applied Psychophysiology and Biofeedback, 800-477-8892

Association of perioperative Registered Nurses, 800-755-2676

Asthma and Allergy Foundation of America, 800-727-8462

Asthma Information Line, 800-822-2762

B

Back to Sleep SIDS Information Campaign, 800-505-2742

Batten's Disease Support and Research Association, 800-448-4570

Bethany Christian Services, 800-238-4269

Blind Children's Center, 800-222-3566

Bradley Method of Natural Childbirth, 800-422-4784

Braille Institute of America, 800-272-4553

Brain Tumor Society, 800-770-TBTS

C

Calix Society, 800-398-0524

Cancer Hope Network, (877) 467-3638

Candlelighters Childhood Cancer Foundation, 800-366-2223

Captioned Media Program, National Association for the Deaf, 800-237-6213; 800-237-6819 (TTY); 800-538-5636 (Fax)

Caring Connections, 800-658-8898

CDC INFO, 800-232-4636; (888) 232-6348 (TTY)

CDC National Prevention Information Network, 800-458-5231; 800-243-7012 (TTY); (888) 282-7681 (Fax)

Center for Food Safety and Applied Nutrition, (888) 723-3366

Charcot-Marie-Tooth Association, 800-606-2682

Child Find of America, Inc., 800-426-5678; 800-292-9688

Childhelp USA® National Child Abuse Hotline, 800-422-4453

Children and Adults with Attention Deficit/Hyperactivity Disorder, 800-233-4050

Children's Brain Tumor Foundation, (866) 228-HOPE (4673)

Children's Craniofacial Association, 800-535-3643

Children's Hospice International, 800-242-4453

Children's Tumor Foundation, 800-323-7938

Christopher Reeve Foundation, 800-225-0292

College of American Pathologists, 800-323-4040

Cooley's Anemia Foundation, 800-522-7222

Cornelia de Lange Syndrome Foundation, 800-223-8355; 800-753-2357

Covenant House Nineline, 800-999-9999

Crohn's and Colitis Foundation of America, Inc., 800-932-2423; 800-343-3637 (Warehouse)

Cystic Fibrosis Foundation, 800-344-4823

D

DB-Link, 800-438-9376; 854-7013 (TTY)

DES Action USA, 800-337-9288

DHHS Inspector General's Hotline, 800-447-8477

Dial A Hearing Screening Test, 800-222-3277 (Voice/TTY)

Drug-Free Workplace Helpline, 800-967-5752

Drug Help, 800-488-3784

Drug Policy Information Clearinghouse, White House Office of National Drug Control Policy, 800-666-3332

Dystonia Medical Research Foundation, 800-377-3978

E

Ear Foundation, 800-545-4327

Easter Seal Society, 800-221-6827

Eldercare Locator, 800-677-1116

Endometriosis Association, 800-992-3636

Environmental Justice Information Line, 800-962-6215

Epilepsy Foundation, 800-332-4050 (Library); 800-332-1000 (Publications)

Epilepsy Information Service, 800-642-0500

F

FACES: The National Craniofacial Association, 800-332-2373

Families of Spinal Muscular Atrophy, 800-886-1762

Federal Emergency Management Agency, 800-621-3362 (Disaster Assistance); 800-480-2520 (Publications)

Federal Information Center, GSA, 800-688-9889; 800-326-2996 (TTY)

Fibromyalgia Network, 800-853-2929

First Candle/SIDS Alliance, 800-221-7437

Food Allergy and Anaphylaxis Network, 800-929-4040

Foundation Fighting Blindness, 800-683-5555; 800-683-5551 (TDD)

Foundation for Ichthyosis and Related Skin Types, Inc., 800-545-3286

G

Gay, Lesbian, Bisexual, and Transgender Helpline, (888) 340-4528

Gay & Lesbian National Hotline, (888) 843-4564

Genetic Alliance, 800-336-4363

Genetic and Rare Diseases Information Center, (888) 205-2311; (888) 205-3223 (TTY)

Girls & Boys Town National Hotline, 800-448-3000; 800-448-1833 (TDD)

Glaucoma Research Foundation, 800-826-6693

Guide Dog Foundation for the Blind, Inc., 800-548-4337

Guide Dogs for the Blind, 800-295-4050

H

Health Care Services (National Kidney Foundation), 800-622-9010

Health Resources and Services Administration Information Center, (888) 275-4772; (877) 489-4772 (TTY)

Hear Now, 648-4327 (Voice/TDD)

Heart Information Service, 800-292-2221

Hepatitis Foundation International, 800-891-0707

Hill-Burton Free Medical Care Program, 800-638-0742; 800-492-0359 (in MD)

Histiocytosis Association of America, 800-548-2758

Hormone Foundation, 800-467-6663

Housing and Urban Development Drug Information and Strategy Clearinghouse, 800-955-2232

HUD USER, 800-245-2691; 800-927-7589 (TDD)

Human Growth Foundation, 800-451-6434

Huntington's Disease Society of America, 800-345-4372

I

Immune Deficiency Foundation, 800-296-4433

Indoor Air Quality Information Clearinghouse, 800-438-4318

Insure Kids Now Hotline, (877) 543-7669

International Childbirth Education Association, 800-624-4934 (orders only)

International Chiropractors Association, 800-423-4690

International Dyslexia Association, 800-222-3123

International Essential Tremor Foundation, (888) 387-3667

International Hearing Society, 800-521-5247

International Rett Syndrome Association, 800-818-7388

J

Job Accommodation Network, 800-232-9675 (Voice/TTY); 800-526-7234 (Voice/TTY)

John Tracy Clinic, 800-522-4582 (Voice/TDD)

Joseph and Rose Kennedy Institute of Ethics, 800-633-3849

Juvenile Diabetes Research Foundation, 800-223-1138

K

Kidney Cancer Association, 800-850-9132

L

La Leche League International, 800-525-3243

Lamaze International, 800-368-4404

Lambda Legal Defense and Education Fund, (866) 542-8336 x235 (Foster Care Helpline)

Les Turner Amyotrophic Lateral Sclerosis Foundation, Ltd., (888) 257-1107

Leukemia & Lymphoma Society, 800-955-4572

Liberty Godparent Home, 800-542-4453

Living Bank, 800-528-2971

Louisiana Center for the Blind, 800-234-4166

Lupus Foundation of America, (888) 385-8787

Lyme Disease Foundation, Inc., 800-886-5963

M

MAGIC Foundation for Children's Growth, 800-362-4423

Medical Institute for Sexual Health, 800-892-9484

MedicAlert Foundation International, 800-432-5378

Medicare Issues Hotline, 800-633-4227; 800-820-1202 (TDD/TTY)

Multiple Sclerosis Association of America, 800-532-7667

Multiple Sclerosis Foundation, (888) 673-6287

Muscular Dystrophy Association, 800-572-1717

Myasthenia Gravis Foundation, 800-541-5454

N

National Abortion Federation, 800-772-9100

National Adoption Center, 800-862-3678

National Alliance for the Mentally Ill, 800-950-6264

National Association for Continence, 800-252-3337

National Association for Parents of Children with Visual Impairments, 800-562-6265

National Association for the Education of Young Children, 800-424-2460

National Association of Hospital Hospitality Houses, Inc., 800-542-9730

National Association of Radiation Survivors, 800-798-5102

National Bone Marrow Transplant Link, 800-546-5268

National Brain Injury Information Center, 800-444-6443

National Brain Tumor Foundation, 800-934-2873

National Cancer Institute's Cancer Information Service, 800-422-6237, 800-332-8615 (TTY)

National Center for Complementary and Alternative Medicine Clearinghouse, (866) 464-3615 (TTY); (866) 464-3616 (Fax)

National Center for Lesbian Rights, 800-528-6257 (Youth Legal Information Line)

National Center for Missing and Exploited Children®, 800-843-5678; (877) 446-2632 (Voice Mail)

National Center for Stuttering, 800-221-2483

National Child Care Information Center, 800-616-2242; 800-516-2242 (TTY); 800-716-2242 (Fax)

National Clearinghouse of Rehabilitation Training Materials, (866) 821-5355

National Council on Alcoholism and Drug Dependence, Inc., 800-622-2255

National Council on Problem Gambling, 800-522-4700

National Criminal Justice Reference Service, 800-851-3420, (877) 712-9279 (TTY)

National Dairy Council, 800-426-8271; 800-974-6455 (Fax)

National Diabetes Information Clearinghouse, 800-860-8747

National Digestive Diseases Information Clearinghouse, 800-891-5389

National Dissemination Center for Children with Disabilities, 800-695-0285 (Voice/TTY)

National Domestic Violence Hotline, 800-799-7233; 800-787-3224 (TDD)

National Down Syndrome Congress, 800-232-6372

National Down Syndrome Society Hotline, 800-221-4602

National Family Association for Deaf-Blind, 800-255-0411

National Fire Protection Association, 800-344-3555

National Fragile X Foundation, 800-688-8765

National Gaucher Foundation, 800-925-8885

National Hansen's Disease Programs, 800-642-2477

National Headache Foundation, (888) 643-5552

National Health Information Center, 800-336-4797

National Health Service Corps, 800-221-9393 (Scholarships/Loan Repayment & Job Opportunities in underserved areas)

National Heart, Lung, and Blood Institute Health Information Line, 800-575-9355 (High Blood Pressure and Cholesterol Information Hotline)

National Hemophilia Foundation, 800-424-2634

National Hispanic Family Health Helpline, (866) 783-2645

National Hispanic Prenatal Helpline, 800-504-7081

National Hopeline Network, 800-784-2433

National Immunization Information Hotline, 800-232-4636; 800-232-6348 (TTY)

National Information Clearinghouse on Children Who Are Deaf-Blind, 800-438-9376; 800-854-7013 (TTY)

National Inhalant Prevention Coalition, 800-269-4237

National Institute for Occupational Safety and Health Information Inquiry Service, 800-356-4674

National Institute for Rehabilitation Engineering, 800-736-2216

National Institute of Arthritis and Musculoskeletal and Skin Diseases Information Clearinghouse,
(877) 226-4267

National Institute of Child Health and Human Development Information Resource Center, 800-370-2943

National Institute of Mental Health Information Center, (866) 615-6464, (866) 415-8051 (TTY)

National Institute of Neurological Disorders and Stroke, 800-352-9424

National Institute on Aging Information Center, 800-222-2225

National Institute on Deafness and Other Communication Disorders Information Clearinghouse,
800-241-1044; 800-241-1055 (TTY)

National Jewish Medical and Research Center, 222-5864

National Kidney and Urologic Diseases Information Clearinghouse, 800-891-5390

National Lead Information Center, 800-424-5323 (Clearinghouse)

National Lekotek Center, 800-366-7529; 800-573-4446 (Voice and TTY)

National Library of Medicine, (888) 346-3656

National Library Service for the Blind and Physically Handicapped, 800-424-8567

National Life Center/Pregnancy Hotline, 800-848-5683

National Lymphedema Network, 800-541-3259

National Marfan Foundation, 800-862-7326

National Marrow Donor Program®, 800-627-7692

National Mental Health Association Resource Center, 800-969-6642; 800-433-5959 (TTY)

National Multiple Sclerosis Society, 800-344-4867

National Organization for Albinism and Hypopigmentation, 800-473-2310, 800-648-2310 (Fax)

National Organization for Rare Disorders, 800-999-6673

National Organization for Victim Assistance, 800-879-6682

National Organization on Fetal Alcohol Syndrome, 800-666-6327

National Parkinson Foundation, Inc., 800-327-4545

National Patient Travel Helpline, 800-296-1217

National Pediculosis Association, 800-446-4672

National Pesticide Information Center, 800-858-7378

National Program for Playground Safety, 800-554-7529

National Psoriasis Foundation, 800-723-9166

National Rehabilitation Information Center, 800-346-2742

National Resource Center on Domestic Violence, 800-537-2238, 800-553-2508 (TTY)

National Resource and Training Center on Homelessness and Mental Illness, 800-444-7415

National Reye's Syndrome Foundation, 800-233-7393

National Runaway Switchboard, 800-786-2929; 800-621-0394 (TDD)

National Safety Council, 800-621-7619, 800-767-7236 (Radon Hotline)

National Spasmodic Torticollis Association, 800-487-8385

National Spinal Cord Injury Association, 800-962-9629

National Stroke Association, 800-787-6537

National Stuttering Association, 800-937-8888

National Technical Information Service, 800-553-6847

National Veterans Services Fund, 800-521-0198

National Women's Health Information Center, 800-994-9662

National Youth Crisis Hotline, 800-448-4663

Neurofibromatosis, Inc., 800-942-6825 (Hotline)

O

Office for Civil Rights, U.S. Department of Health and Human Services, 800-368-1019

Office of Minority Health Resource Center, 800-444-6472

Office of Orphan Products Development, 800-300-7469

Osteogenesis Imperfecta Foundation, 800-981-2663

Osteoporosis and Related Bone Diseases~National Resource Center, 800-624-2663

P

Paget Foundation for Paget's Disease of Bone and Related Disorders, 800-237-2438

Paralyzed Veterans of America, 800-424-8200

Parkinson's Disease Foundation, 800-457-6676

Peer Listening Line, 800-399-7337

Pension Benefit Guaranty Corporation, 800-400-7242

Phoenix Society for Burn Survivors, 800-888-2876

Planned Parenthood Federation of America, 800-230-7526; 800-669-0156 (Order line)

PMS Access, 800-222-4767

Poison Help Hotline, 800-222-1222

Polycystic Kidney Disease Foundation, 800-753-2873

Prader-Willi Syndrome Association, 800-926-4797

Prevent Blindness America, 800-331-2020

Prevent Child Abuse America, 800-555-3748

Pride Surveys, 800-279-6361

PRIDE Youth Programs, 800-668-9277

Project Inform HIV/AIDS Treatment Hotline, 800-822-7422

Public and Indian Housing Information and Resource Center, 800-955-2232

R

Rape, Abuse, and Incest National Network, 800-656-4673

Recording for the Blind and Dyslexic, 800-221-4792

Research to Prevent Blindness, 800-621-0026

Restless Legs Syndrome Foundation, (877) 463-6757

S

Safe Drinking Water Hotline, 800-426-4791

Safe Sitter, 800-255-4089

SAMHSA's National Clearinghouse for Alcohol and Drug Information, 800-729-6686; (877) 767-8432 (Spanish); 800-487-4889 (TDD)

SAMHSA's National Mental Health Information Center, 800-789-2647; (866) 889-2647 (TDD)

School Nutrition Association, 800-877-8822

Scleroderma Foundation, 800-722-4673

Scoliosis Association, 800-800-0669

Seniors EyeCare Program, 800-222-3937

Shaping America's Youth®, 800-729-9221

Shriners Hospital for Children Referral Line, 800-237-5055

Sickle Cell Disease Association of America, Inc., 800-421-8453

Simon Foundation for Continence, 800-237-4666

Sjogren's Syndrome Foundation, Inc., 800-475-6473

Smoking Quitline of the National Cancer Institute, (877) 448-7848; 800-332-8615 (TTY)

Smoking, Tobacco and Health Information Line, Office on Smoking and Health, 800-232-4636

Social Security Administration, 800-772-1213

Spina Bifida Association of America, 800-621-3141

Spondylitis Association of America, 800-777-8189

Starlight Starbright Children's Foundation, 800-274-7827

Sturge-Weber Foundation, 800-627-5482

Stuttering Foundation of America, 800-992-9392

Support Organization for Trisomy 18, 13 and Related Disorders, 800-716-7638

Susan G. Komen Breast Cancer Foundation, 800-462-9273

T

Thyroid Foundation of America, Inc., 800-832-8321

TOPS (Taking Off Pounds Sensibly) Club, Inc., 800-932-8677

Tourette Syndrome Association, Inc., (888) 486-8738

Trevor Helpline, (866) 488-7386

Tuberous Sclerosis Alliance, 800-225-6872

Turner Syndrome Society of the United States, 800-365-9944

U

United Cerebral Palsy Association, 800-872-5827

United Leukodystrophy Foundation, 800-728-5483

United Network for Organ Sharing, (888) 894-6361

U.S. Coast Guard InfoLine, Office of Boating Safety, 800-368-5647, 800-689-0816 (TDD/TTY)

U.S. Consumer Product Safety Commission Hotline, 800-638-2772; 800-638-8270 (TDD)

U.S. Department of Agriculture Meat and Poultry Hotline, (888) 674-6854

U.S. Fish & Wildlife Service, 800-344-9453

U.S. Food and Drug Administration, 800-332-1088 (Medwatch); (888) 463-6332 (Consumer Inquiries)

U.S. Pharmacopeia Center for the Advancement of Patient Safety, 800-233-7767

Us Too! International, 800-808-7866

Vasculitis Foundation, 800-227-9474

V

Vehicle Safety Hotline, National Highway Traffic Safety Administration, (888) 327-4236; 800-424-9153 (TTY)

Vestibular Disorders Association, 800-837-8428

Veterans Affairs Health Benefits Service Center, (877) 222-8387

Veterans Special Issue Helpline, 800-749-8387

Vision Connections Help Near You Information and Resource Service, 800-829-0500

Vision Council of America, 800-424-8422

W

Weight Control Information Network, (877) 946-4627

Well Spouse Association, 800-838-0879

Wilson's Disease Association, (888) 264-1450

Women's Health America, 800-558-7046

Women's Sports Foundation, 800-227-3988

Y

YMCA of the USA, 800-872-9622

Y-ME National Organization for Breast Cancer Information Support Program, 800-221-2141 (English); 986-9505 (Spanish)

Z

Zero to Three: National Center for Infants, Toddlers and Families, 800-899-4301

Appendix 6

Massage Related Resources

Associations

- American Massage Therapy Association www.amtamassage.org
- Associated Massage & Bodywork Professionals www.abmp.com
- American Medical Massage Association www.americanmedicalmassage.com
- International Massage Association www.imagroup.com
- Spa Massage Alliance www.spamassagealliance.com

Certification

National Certification Exam for Therapeutic Massage and Bodywork (NCETMB) www.ncbtmb.com

National Certification Board for Therapeutic Massage & Bodywork - NCBTMB is a nationally recognized credentialing body formed to set high standards for those who practice therapeutic massage and bodywork.

8201 Greensboro Drive, Suite 300, McLean, VA 22102

(800) 296-0664 or (703) 610-9015.

Insurance Providers

- American Massage Council (800) 500-3930
- American Massage Therapy Association (AMTA) (847) 864-0123
- Associated Bodywork and Massage Professionals (ABMP) (800) 458-2267
- International Massage Association (540) 351-0800

Magazines/Journals

Massage & Bodywork (Magazine of the ABMP). If you subscribe to only one – make it this one!

- www.massageandbodywork.com
- www.abmp.com

Massage Therapy Journal (AMTA)

- www.amtamassage.org

Massage Magazine

- www.massagemag.com

Appendix 7

Servant Leader Resources

World Business Academy
http://www.worldbusiness.org/

The Carter Center
http://www.cartercenter.org/default.asp?bFlash=True

The Robert K. Greenleaf Center for Servant-Leadership
921 East 86th Street, Suite 200 ~ Indianapolis, IN 46240 U.S.A.
Phone: (317) 259-1241 ~ Fax: (317) 259-0560

The Institute for Servant Leadership
http://www.servleader.org/
P.O.Box 1007
Hendersonville NC
Telephone: (828) 692-1694.

Barbuto and Wheeler, (2002). Becoming a Servant Leader: Do You Have What it Takes?. Nebraska Cooperative Extension G02-1481.A.

Buckingham, Marcus (1999). First, Break All the Rules: What the World's Greatest Managers Do Differently. © 1999 Simon & Schuster.

Geisler, Jill. (2000). I'm Your Leader—What Have I Done for You Lately?
Popper, Micha (2004). Hypnotic Leadership: Leaders, Followers, and the Loss of Self. *Book News, Inc., Portland, OR*

Greenleaf, Robert (2005). www.greenleaf.org

Poynteronline. http://www.potnter.org

Appendix 8

Massage Competency State Contacts

Not every state has requirements however, some still require other certifications, permits or associated items so be sure to check with your local and state small business agencies.

Alabama

Alabama Massage Therapy Board
Keith E. Warren, Exec. Director
610 S. McDonough Street
Montgomery, AL 36104
Phone: 334-269-9990
Fax: 334-263-6115
www.almtbd.state.al.us

Arizona

Arizona Board of Massage Therapy
1400 West Washington, #230
Phoenix, AZ 85007
Phone: 602-542-8604
Fax: 602-542-3093
www.massageboard.az.gov

Arkansas

Arkansas State Board of Massage Therapy
P O Box 20739
Hot Springs, AR 71903
Phone: 501-623-0444
Fax: 501-623-4130
www.arkansasmassagetherapy.com

Connecticut

Connecticut Massage Therapy Licensure
Dept. of Public Health & Addiction Service
150 Washington Street
Hartford, CT 06106
Phone: 860-509-7603

Delaware

Delaware Board of Massage & Bodywork
Cannon Building, #203
861 Silver Lake Blvd
Dover, DE 19904
Phone: 302-744-4537
Fax: 302-739-2711
www.dpr.delaware.gov/boards/massagebodyworks/

District of Columbia

District of Columbia Board of Massage Therapy
Department of Health
717 14th Street, NW
Washington, DC 20005
Phone: 877-672-2174
Fax: 202-727-8471
http://doh.dc.gov/doh/site/default.asp

Florida

Florida Board of Massage Therapy Florida
Department of Health
Medical Quality Assurance
4052 Bald Cypress Way - BIN # C06
Tallahassee, FL 32399
Phone: 850-245-4161
Fax: 850-921-6184
www.doh.state.fl.us/mqa/massage/ma_lic_req.html

Georgia

Georgia Board of Massage Therapy
Georgia Secretary of State
Macon, GA
Phone: 478-207-1300
www.sos.state.ga.us/plb/massage

Hawaii

Hawaii State Board of Massage Therapy
Dept. of Commerce & Consumer Affairs
P O Box 3469
1010 Richards St.
Honolulu, HI 96801
Phone: 808-587-3222
www.hawaii.gov/dcca/areas/pvl/boards/massage/

Illinois

Illinois Dept. of Financial & Professional Regulations
320 West Washington Street
3rd Floor
Springfield, IL 62786
Phone: 217-782-8556
Fax: 217-782-7645
www.ildfpr.com/dpr/who/masst.asp

Iowa

Iowa Board of Massage Therapy Examiners
Department of Public Health
Lucas State Office Bldg, 5th Floor
321 East 12th Street
Des Moines, IA 50319-0075
Phone: 515-281-6959
Fax: 515-281-3121
www.idph.state.ia.us/licensure

Kentucky

Kentucky Board of Licensure for Massage Therapy
P O Box 1360
Frankfort, KY 40602
Phone: 502-564-3296
Fax: 502-564-4818
http://finance.ky.gov/ourcabinet/caboff/

Louisiana

Louisiana Board of Massage Therapy
12022 Plank Road
Zachary, LA 70811
Phone: 225-771-4090
Fax: 225-771-4021
www.lsbmt.org

Maine

Maine Massage Therapy
Dept. of Professional & Financial Regulation
Office of Licensing & Registration
35 State House Station
Augusta, ME 04333-0035
Phone: 207-624-8613
Fax: 207-624-8637
www.state.me.us/pfr/olr/categories/cat26.htm

Maryland

Maryland Massage Therapy Advisory Committee
Board of Chiropractic Examiners
4201 Patterson Avenue - 5th Floor
Baltimore, MD 21215-2299
Phone: 410-764-4738
Fax: 410-358-1879
www.mdmassage.org

Mississippi

Mississippi State Board of Massage Therapy
P O Box 12489
Jackson, MS 39236-2489
Phone: 601-856-6127
Fax: 601-853-0336
www.msbmt.state.ms.us

Missouri

Missouri State Board of Therapeutic Massage
Division of Professional Registration
3605 Missouri Blvd.
PO Box 1335
Jefferson City, MO 65102-1335
Phone: 573-522-6277
Fax: 573-751-0735
http://pr.mo.gov/massage.asp

Nebraska

Nebraska Massage Therapy Board
Health & Human Services
Regulation & Licensure - Credentialing Division
P O Box 94986
Lincoln, NE 68509-4986
Phone: 402-471-2115
Fax: 402-471-3577
www.hhs.state.ne.us/crl/mhcs/mass/massage.htm

Nevada

Nevada Board of Massage Therapy
111 West Telegraph
Suite 200
Carson City, NV 89703
http://massagetherapy.nv.gov/

New Hampshire

New Hampshire Office of Program Support,
Licensing & Regulative Services
Board of Massage Therapy
129 Pleasant Street
Concord, NH 03301-3857
Phone: 603-271-4814
Fax: 603-271-5590
www.dhhs.state.nh.us/DHHS/LRS/

New Jersey

New Jersey Board of Nursing
Massage, Bodywork & Somatic Therapy
Examining Committee
124 Halsey Street
Newark, NJ 07102
Phone: 973-504-6430
Fax: 973-648-3481
www.state.nj.us/lps/ca/medical/nursing.htm

New Mexico

New Mexico
Massage Therapy Board
2550 Cerrillos Road
Santa Fe, NM 87505
Phone: 505-476-4870
Fax: 505-476-4645
www.rld.state.nm.us/b&c/massage/

New York

New York State Board of Massage Therapy
Office of the Professions
Division of Professional Licensing Services
89 Washington Avenue
Albany, NY 12234
Kathleen M. Doyle, Exec. Secretary
Phone: 518-474-3817 Ext. 150
Fax: 518-486-2981
www.op.nysed.gov/mtlic.htm

North Carolina

North Carolina Board of Massage
and Bodywork Therapy
P O Box 2539
Raleigh, NC 27602
Phone: 919-546-0050
Fax: 919-833-1059
http://www.bmbt.org

North Dakota

North Dakota State Board of Massage
PO Box 218
Beach, ND 58621
Phone: 701-872-4895
www.ndboardofmassage.com

Ohio

State Medical Board
Massage Licensing Division
77 S. High Street - 17th Floor
Columbus, OH 43266-0315
Phone: 614-466-3934
Fax: 614-728-5946
www.med.ohio.gov/MTsubwebindex.htm

Oregon

Oregon Board of Massage
748 Hawthorne Avenue NE
Salem, OR 97301
Patty Glenn, Executive Director
Phone: 503-365-8657
Fax: 503-385-4465
www.oregonmassage.org

Rhode Island

Rhode Island Department of Health
Division of Professional Regulation
3 Capitol Hill - Room 410
Providence, RI 02908-5097
Phone: 401-222-2827
Fax: 401-222-1272
www.health.ri.gov/hsr/professions/massage.htm

South Carolina

South Carolina Division of Professional
110 Center View
P O Box 11329
Columbia, SC 29210
Phone: 803-896-4490
Fax: 803-896-4484
www.llr.state.sc.us/POL/massagetherapy

South Dakota

South Dakota Board of Massage Therapy
P.O. Box 7251
107 W. Missouri
Pierre, SD 57501
Phone: 605-224-8803
www.state.sd.us/doh/massage

Tennessee

Tennessee Massage Licensure Board
Cordell Hull Bldg., 1st Floor
227 French Landing, Suite 300
Heritage Place Metro Center
Nashville, TN 37243
Phone: 800-778-4123 Ext. 3211
Fax: 615-532-5164
http://www2.tennessee.gov/health/

Texas

Texas Dept. of State Health Services
Massage Therapy Licensing Program
1100 W. 49th Street
Austin, TX 78756-3183
Phone: 512-834-6616
Fax: 512-834-6677
www.dshs.state.tx.us/massage/default.shtm

Utah

Division of Occupational & Professional Licensing
Board of Massage Therapy
160 East 300 South
Salt Lake City, UT 84145
Phone: 801-530-6628
Fax: 801-530-6511
www.dopl.utah.gov/licensing/massage.html

Virginia

Board of Nursing
Department of Health Professions
6606 W. Broad Street - 5th Floor
Richmond, VA 23230-1712
Phone: 804-662-9909
Fax: 804-662-9512
www.dhp.state.va.us

Washington

Washington State Dept. of Health
Massage Therapy Program
P.O. Box 47867
Olympia, WA 98504-7868
Phone: 360-236-4700
Fax: 360-236-4818
www.doh.wa.gov/massage/default.htm

Washington, DC

Department of Health
Board of Massage Therapy
717 14th Street NW - Suite 600
Washington, DC 20005
Phone: 877-672-2174
Fax 202-727-8471
http://doh.dc.gov/doh/site/default.asp

West Virginia

State of West Virginia
Massage Therapy Licensure Board
200 Davis Street #1
Princeton, WV 24740-7430
Phone: 304-487-1400
Fax: 304-487-1460
www.wvmassage.org/

Wisconsin
Wisconsin Department of Regulation and Licensing: Massage Therapy Board
1400 E. Washington Avenue
Madison, WI 53703
Phone: 608-266-2112
Fax: 608-261-7083
http://drl.wi.gov/prof/mass/def.htm

Glossary

Practice Planner Small Business Glossary

ACCOUNTING	The recording, classifying, summarizing and interpreting in a significant manner and in terms of money, transactions and events of a financial character.
ACCOUNTS PAYABLE	Trade accounts of businesses representing obligations to pay for goods and services received
ACCOUNTS RECEIVABLE	Trade accounts of businesses representing moneys due for goods sold or services rendered evidenced by notes, statements, invoices or other written evidence of a present obligation.
ACID RATIO	Current assets less inventories divided by current liabilities. Also known as "Quick Ratio."
ACQUISITION	The acquiring of supplies or services by the federal government with appropriated funds through purchase or lease.
ADA **Americans with Disabilities Act**	The Americans with Disabilities Act (ADA) gives federal civil rights protections to individuals with disabilities similar to those provided to individuals on the basis of race, color, sex, national origin, age, and religion. It guarantees equal opportunity for individuals with disabilities in public accommodations, employment, transportation, State and local government services, and telecommunications.
AFFILIATES	Business concerns, organizations, or individuals that control each other or that are controlled by a third party. Control may include shared management or ownership; common use of facilities, equipment, and employees; or family interest. The calculation of a firm's size includes the employees or receipts of all affiliates. Affiliation with another business concern is based on the power to control, whether exercised or not. Such factors as common ownership, common management and identity of interest (often found in members of the same family), among others, are indicators of affiliation. Power to control exists when a party or parties have 50 percent or more ownership. It may also exist with considerably less than 50 percent ownership by contractual arrangement or when one or more parties own a large share compared to other parties. The affiliated business concerns need not be in the same line of business.

AMORTIZATION Gradual reduction of term debt by periodic payment sufficient to pay current interest and to eliminate the principal at maturity.

ANCILLARY BOND A type of surety bond where the surety company guarantees other factors which are incidental and essential to the performance of a contract.

ANNUAL RECEIPTS Receipts are averaged over a firm's latest 3 completed fiscal years to determine its average annual receipts. "Receipts" means the firm's gross or total income, plus cost of goods sold, as defined by or reported on the firm's Federal Income Tax return. The term does not include, however, net capital gains or losses, nor taxes collected for and remitted to a taxing authority if included in gross or total income. The firm may not deduct income taxes, property taxes, cost of materials or funds paid to subcontractors. Travel, real estate and advertising agents, providers of conference management services, freight forwarders and customs brokers may deduct amounts they collect on behalf of another. If a firm has not been in business for 3 years, the average weekly receipts for the number of weeks the firm has been in business is multiplied by 52 to determine its average annual receipts.

APPRAISED VALUE The value placed on an item, product or business by an appraiser, recognized for experience in a particular field.

ASSETS The entire property of a person, association, corporation, or estate applicable or subject to the payment of debts.

ASSUMPTIONS The act of assuming/undertaking another's debts or obligations.

AUCTION A public sale of goods to the highest bidder.

BAD DEBTS Funds owing to a business which are determined to be uncollectible.

BALANCE SHEET Financial statement listing a company's assets, liabilities, and equity on a specific date.

BANKRUPTCY A condition in which a business cannot meet its debt obligations and petitions a federal district court for either reorganization of its debts or liquidation of its assets. In the action the property of a debtor is taken over by a receiver or trustee in bankruptcy for the benefit of the creditors. This action is conducted as prescribed by the National Bankruptcy Act, and may be voluntary or involuntary.

BEST AND FINAL OFFER For negotiated procurements, a contractor's final offer following the conclusion of discussions.

BID BOND A type of surety bond where the surety company guarantees the bidder will enter into a contract and furnish the required payment and performance bonds.

BOOK VALUE	The value of an item or property at a specific time after deducting depreciation from original cost.
BREAK-EVEN POINT	The point at which the volume of sales or revenues exactly equals total expenses. The break-even point represents the level of output or activity required before the business can make a profit; reflects the relationship between costs, volume and profits.
BUSINESS BIRTH	Formation of a new establishment or enterprise.
BUSINESS CARD(S)	A card identifying a business and an individual associated with that business.
BUSINESS CONCERN	A business concern eligible for assistance as a small business is a business entity organized for profit, with a place of business located in the United States, and which operates primarily within the United States or makes a significant contribution to the US economy through payment of taxes or use of American products, materials, or labor.
BUSINESS DEATH	Voluntary or involuntary closure of a firm or establishment
BUSINESS DISSOLUTION	For enumeration purposes, the absence from any current record of a business that was present in a prior time period
BUSINESS FAILURE	The closure of a business causing a loss to at least one creditor.
BUSINESS PLAN	A comprehensive planning document which clearly describes the business developmental objective of an existing or proposed business applying for financial or other assistance
BUSINESS START	A business with a name or similar designation that did not exist in a prior time period.
CANCELED LOAN	The annulment of an approved loan prior to disbursement.
CAPACITY TO REPAY	The determination made by a lender on whether a borrower can repay a loan after examining financial statements, financial ratios and operating data.
CAPITAL	Assets less liabilities, representing the ownership interest in a business or Accumulated possessions calculated to bring income.
CAPITAL EXPENDITURES	Business spending on additional plant equipment.
CAPITALIZATION	The basic resources of a company including the owner's equity, retained earnings and fixed assets. One of the "Five C's" of Credit
CAPITALIZED PROPERTY	Personal property of the business which has an average dollar value of $300.00 or more and a life expectancy of one year or more. Capitalized property is depreciated annually
CARRYING COSTS	Inventory costs associated with capital, storage, handling expenses, insurance, taxes and obsolescence.

CASH CONVERSION CYCLE	The length of time between the payment of payables and the collection of receivables.
CASH DISCOUNT	An incentive offered by the seller or business owner to encourage the buyer to pay within a stipulated time. For example, if the terms are 2/10/N 30, the buyer may deduct 2 percent from the amount of the invoice (if paid within 10 days) otherwise, the full amount is due in 30 days.
CASH FLOW	The movement of money into and out of your business.
CASH FLOW STATEMENT	An accounting presentation showing how much of the cash generated by the business remains after both expenses (including interest) and principal repayment on financing are paid. A projected cash flow statement indicates whether the business will have cash to pay its expenses, loans, and make a profit. Cash flows can be calculated for any given period of time, normally done on a monthly basis. Also, one of the Five "Cs" evaluated in determining a loan applicant's credit-worthiness
CERTIFICATE OF DEPOSIT	Short-term instruments issued by commercial banks.
CERTIFICATION(s) or QUALIFICATION(s) REQUIREMEMTS(s)	"Certification" as a small business, as a socially and economically disadvantaged small business, as a woman-owned or veteran-owned business is required to be eligible for some SBA programs.
CERTIFIED 8(a) FIRM	A firm owned and operated by socially and economically disadvantaged individuals and eligible to receive federal contracts under the Small Business Administration's 8(a) Business Development Program.
CERTIFIED DEVELOPMENT COMPANY - CDC	A Certified Development Company is a nonprofit corporation set up to contribute to the economic development of its community. CDCs work with the SBA and private-sector lenders to provide financing to small businesses. There are about 270 CDCs nationwide. Each CDC covers a specific geographic area
CHARACTER	The degree to which a potential borrower feels a moral obligation to repay debts as evidenced by the borower's credit and payment history. One of the "Five Cs" used in a lending officer's determination of a particular loan applicant's credit-worthiness.
CHARGED OFF LOAN	An uncollectible loan for which the principal and accrued interest were removed from the receivable accounts.
CHARGE-OFF	An accounting transaction removing an uncollectible balance from the active receivable accounts.
COLLATERAL	Something of value--securities, evidence of deposit or other property--pledged to support the repayment of an obligation. Also one of the Five "Cs" used in determining a loan applicant's credit worthiness.
COLLATERAL DOCUMENT	A legal document covering the item(s) pledged as collateral

on a loan, i.e., note, mortgages, assignment, etc.

COLLECTION POLICY	Actions a business takes to collect slow-paying accounts.
COMPROMISE	The settlement of a claim resulting from a defaulted loan for less than the full amount due. Compromise settlement is a procedure available for use only in instances where the government cannot collect the full amount due within a reasonable time, by enforced collection proceedings or where the cost of such proceedings would not justify such effort.
CONDITIONS	External factors such as government regulation, competition, industry trends, national economic trends, that can affect the success of a business. One of the "Five Cs" of credit.
CONSORTIUM	A coalition of organizations, such as banks and corporations, set up to fund ventures requiring large capital resources.
CONTINGENCY FUND	Cash held for emergencies or unexpected outflows of funds. Also known as "Precautionary Balances."
CONTINGENT LIABILITY	A potential obligation that may be incurred dependent upon the occurrence of a future event. Two examples are: (1) the liability of an endorser or guarantor of a note if the primary borrower fails to pay as agreed and (2) the liability that would be incurred if a pending lawsuit is resolved in the other party's favor.
CONTRACT	A mutually binding legal relationship obligating the seller to furnish supplies or services (including construction) and the buyer to pay for them.
CONTRACTING	Purchasing, renting, leasing, or otherwise obtaining supplies or services from nonfederal sources. Contracting includes the description of supplies and services required, the selection and solicitation of sources, the preparation and award of contracts, and all phases of contract administration. It does not include grants or cooperative agreements.
CONTRACTING OFFICER	A person with the authority to enter into, administer, and/or terminate contracts and make related determinations and findings.
COPYRIGHT	The legal right granted to authors, composers, artists and publishers to protect their thoughts and ideas
CORPORATION	A group of persons granted a state charter legally recognizing them as a separate entity having its own rights, privileges, and liabilities distinct from those of its members. The process of incorporating should be completed with the state's secretary of state or state corporate counsel and usually requires the services of an attorney.
COSTS	Money obligated for goods and services received during a given period of time, regardless of when ordered or whether paid for.
COVENANT	A prescription for action in a loan document.

COVENANT NOT TO COMPETE	The agreement by the seller of a business, not to enter into competition with the buyer of the business within a specific area for a specific period of time.
CREDIT	Time allowed for the payment of goods or services sold on trust as well as confidence in the buyer's ability and intention to fulfill their financial obligations.
CREDIT PERIOD	Length of time allowed before the credit buyer must pay for credit purchases.
CREDIT POLICY	Actions taken by a business to grant, monitor and collect the cash for outstanding accounts receivable.
CREDIT RATING	A grade assigned to a business concern to denote the net worth and credit standing to which the concern is entitled in the opinion of the rating agency as a result of its investigation.
CURRENT ASSETS	Money, inventory and equipment that will be used up in the short term -- usually within one year.
CURRENT RATIO	The ratio of current assets to liabilities. Also called "quick ratio."
CUSTOMER TARGETING	Identifying and marketing to those groups of customers most likely to buy a particular product or service, e.g., promoting boat products to boat owners.
DATA ELEMENT	The basic unit of identifiable and definable information. A data element occupies the space provided by fields in a record or blocks on a form. It has an identifying name and value or values for expressing a specific fact. For example, a data element named "Color of Eyes" could have recorded values of "Blue (a name)," "Bl (an abbreviation)," "06 (a code)." similarly, a data element named "Age of Employee" could have a recorded value of "28" (a numeric value).
DATA UNIVERSAL NUMBERING SYSTEM (DUNS)	D&B's Data Universal Numbering System, the D&B D-U-N-S Number, has become the standard for keeping track of the world's businesses. The D&B D-U-N-S Number is D&B's distinctive nine-digit identification sequence, which identifies information products and services originating exclusively through D&B. The D&B D-U-N-S Number is an internationally recognized common company identifier in EDI and global electronic commerce transactions.
DEBENTURE	Debt instrument evidencing the holder's right to receive interest and principal installments from the named obligor. Applies to all forms of unsecured, long-term debt evidenced by a certificate of debt.
DEBT CAPITAL	Business financing that normally requires periodic interest payments and repayment of the principal within a specified time.
DEBT FINANCING	The provision of long term loans to small business concerns in exchange for debt securities or a note.

DEBT TO TOTAL ASSETS RATIO	Total debt divided by total assets.
DEED OF TRUST	A document under seal which, when delivered, transfers a present interest in property. May be held as collateral.
DEFAULTS	The nonpayment of principal and/or interest on the due date as provided by the terms and conditions of the note.
DEFERRED LOAN	Loans whose principal and or interest installments are postponed for a specified period of time.
DEPRECIATION SCHEDULE	An accounting procedure for determining the amount of value left in a piece of equipment.
DISBURSEMENT	The actual payout to borrower of loan funds, in whole or part. It may be concurrent with the closing, or follow it.
DISBURSING OFFICER	An employee authorized to pay out cash or issue checks in settlement of vouchers approved by a certifying officer.
DUNS - Data Universal Numbering System	Data Universal Numbering System: the D&B D-U-N-S Number, has become the standard for keeping track of the world's businesses. The D&B D-U-N-S Number is D&B's distinctive nine-digit identification sequence, which identifies information products and services originating exclusively through D&B.
EARNING POWER	The demonstrated ability of a business to earn a profit, over time, while following good accounting practices. When a business shows a reasonable profit on invested capital after fully maintaining the business property, appropriately compensating its owner and employees, servicing its obligations, and fully recognizing its costs, the business may be said to have demonstrated earning power. Demonstrated earning power is the foremost test of the business risk in pressing upon an application for a loan.
EASEMENT	A right or privilege that a person may have on another's land, as the right of a way or ingress or egress.
EEOC - Equal Employment Opportunity Commission	Small Business Information - The U.S. Equal Employment Opportunity Commission (EEOC) enforces the federal laws that prohibit employment discrimination on the basis of an individual's race, color, religion, sex, national origin, age, or disability.
EFTPS	See Electronic Federal Tax Payment System.
EMPLOYEES	Any person on the payroll must be included as one employee regardless of hours worked or temporary status. The number of employees of a firm in business under 12 months is based on the average for each pay period it has been in business
ENTERPRISE	Aggregation of all establishments owned by a parent company. An enterprise can consist of a single, independent establishment or it can include subsidiaries or other branch establishments under the same ownership and control.

ENTREPRENEUR	One who assumes the financial risk of the initiation, operation and management of a given business or undertaking.
EQUITY	An accounting term used to describe the net investment of owners or stockholders in a business. Under the accounting equation, equity also represents the result of assets less liabilities.
EQUITY FINANCING	The provision of funds for capital or operating expenses in exchange for capital stock, stock purchase warrants and options in the business financed, without any guaranteed return, but with the opportunity to share in the company's profits. Equity financing includes long-term subordinated securities containing stock options and/or warrants. Utilized in SBIC financing activities.
EQUITY PARTNERSHIP	A limited partnership arrangement for providing start-up and seed capital to businesses.
ESCROW ACCOUNTS	Funds placed in trust with a third party, by a borrower for a specific purpose and to be delivered to the borrower only upon the fulfillment of certain conditions.
ESTABLISHMENT	A single-location business unit, which may be independent--called a single-establishment enterprise--or owned by a parent enterprise.
FAIR AND REASONABLE PRICE	A price that is fair to both parties, considering the agreed-upon conditions, promised quality, and timeliness of contract performance. "Fair and reasonable" price is subject to statutory and regulatory limitations.
FAIR MARKET VALUE	What a qualified buyer will pay for goods, services, or property.
FINANCIAL FORECAST	Projection of revenues and expenses for the next one to five years.
FINANCIAL PLAN	An outline for how to use the money (capital) you have and how to raise the money you will need.
FINANCIAL RATIOS	Measures of capital, including debt to asset, current, and debt to worth. See individual definitions for "acid," "current," "quick" ratios.
FINANCIAL REPORTS	Reports commonly required from applicants request for financial assistance, e.g.: Balance Sheet -A report of the status of a firm's assets, liabilities and owner's equity at a given time.
FINANCING	New funds provided to a business, by either loans or purchase of debt securities or capital stock.
FIVE "Cs" OF CREDIT	A system used by lending officers to evaluate a loan application: Character, Cash Flow, Collateral, Capitalization and Conditions. See individual definitions.

FIXED ASSETS	Equipment, buildings, etc., which are purchased and used for long-term purposes.
FIXED COSTS	Costs of doing business such as rent, utilities, depreciation, taxes, etc., that remain generally the same regardless of the amount of sales of goods or services.
FLOW CHART	A graphical representation for the definition, analysis, or solution of a problem, in which symbols are used to represent operations, data, flow, equipment, etc.
GEOGRAPHIC TARGETING	Specializing in serving the needs of customers in a particular area, thus restricting advertising and other marketing efforts to that area.
GOODWILL	An intangible asset of a business that relates to a favorable relationship with customers, and excess earning power.
GRANT	Money given to a business that does not need to be repaid.
GUARANTEED LOAN	A loan made and serviced by a lending institution under agreement that a governmental agency will purchase the guaranteed portion if the borrower defaults.
GUARANTY	Promise by an individual or organization to repay a loan in the event of default.
INCOME STATEMENT	Financial statement showing a company's sales, expense and net income or loss for a specific period of time.
INSOLVENCY	The inability of a borrower to meet financial obligations as they mature, or having insufficient assets to pay legal debts.
INSTALLMENT LOAN	One in which the amount of interest is added to the principal and repaid by the borrower in equal periodic payments.
INTEREST	An amount paid a lender for the use of funds.
INVENTORY	Merchandise that is purchased and/or produced and stored for eventual sale.
INVENTORY TURNOVER	How often the inventory is sold and replenished over the course of a year.
INVERSE ORDER OF MATURITY	When payments are received from borrowers that are larger than the authorized repayment schedules the overpayment is credited to the final installments of the principal which reduces the maturity of the loan and does not affect the original repayment schedule.
IRS	Internal Revenue Service - with our link going to their publications and notices
JOINT VENTURE	In a joint venture both firms share, in some proportion, the responsibility and the profits or loss on a contract. They are considered affiliated (see "Affiliates," above) for the purpose of that contract. Normally, the revenues or the employees of both firms are added together to determine the size of a joint venture. However, on certain large Federal procurements, a

joint venture comprised of only small businesses would qualify as a small business joint venture. This is limited to procurements that exceed $10 million in value that are classified with an NAICS industry having an employee-based size standard, or that exceeds one-half of the size standard for procurements classified with an NAICS industry having a revenue-based size standard

JUDGMENT — Judicial determination of the existence of an indebtedness, or other legal liability.

JUDGMENT BY CONFESSION — The act of debtors permitting judgment to be entered against them for a given sum with a statement to that effect, without the institution of legal proceedings.

LEASE — A contract between the owner (lessor) and the tenant (lessee) stating the conditions under which the tenant may occupy or use real estate or equipment. Terms usually include a specific period of time and a predetermined rate.

LEASE RATE — The period rental payment to a lessor for the use of assets. It may also be considered as the implicit interest rate in minimum lease payments.

LEGAL RATE OF INTEREST — The maximum rate of interest fixed by the laws of the various states, which a lender may charge a borrower for the use of money.

LENDING INSTITUTION — Any institution, including a commercial bank, savings and loan association, commercial finance company, or other lender qualified to participate with SBA in the making of loans.

LESSEE — The user of equipment or property being leased.

LESSOR — The party to a lease agreement who has leagl or tax title to equipment or property, who grants the lessee the right to use the equipment or property for the lease term, and who is entitled to the rental fees.

LEVERAGED BUY-OUT — The purchase of a business, with financing provided largely by borrowed money,

LIABILITY — Debt owed by the company such as bank loans or accounts payable.

LICENSE - LICENSES - BUSINESS REGISTRATION — Businesses are licensed and registered at local and state levels of government. Each state has their own mechanism or criteria for obtaining licenses.

LIEN — A charge upon or security interest in real or personal property maintained to ensure the satisfaction of a debt or duty ordinarily arising by operation of law.

LINE OF CREDIT — A short-term loan, usually less than one year.

LIQUID ASSETS — Cash, checks and easily-convertible securities available to meet immediate and emergency needs.

LIQUIDATION	The disposal, at maximum prices, of the collateral securing a loan, and the voluntary and enforced collection of the remaining loan balance from the obligators and/or guarantors.
LIQUIDATION VALUE	The net value realizable in the sale (ordinarily a forced sale) of a business or a particular asset.
LITIGATION	Refers to a loan in "liquidation status" which has been referred attorneys for legal action. Also: The practice of taking legal action through the judicial process.
LOAN AGREEMENT	Agreement to be executed by borrower, containing pertinent terms, conditions, covenants and restrictions.
LOAN PAYOFF AMOUNT	The total amount of money needed to meet a borrower's obligation on a loan. It is arrived at by accruing gross interest for one day and multiplying this figure by the number of days that exist between the date of the last repayment and the date on which the loan is to be completely paid off. This amount, known as accrued interest, is combined with the latest principal and escrow balances that are applicable to what is now referred to as the loan payoff amount. In the case where prepaid interest exceeds the accrued interest the latter is subtracted from the former and the difference is used to reduce the total amount owed.
LONG TERM	Period usually greater than one year.
LOSS RATE	A rate developed by comparing the ratio of total loans charged off to the total loans disbursed from inception of the program to the present date.
MARKET	The existing or potential buyers for specific goods or services.
MARKET VALUE	What a willing buyer will pay for goods, services, a property or a business.
MARKETING	The total of activities involved in the transfer of goods and services from the producer or seller to the consumer or buyer. Marketing activities may include buying, storing selling, advertising, pricing and promoting products.
MARKUP	Markup is the difference between invoice cost and selling price. It may be expressed either as a percentage of the selling price or the cost price and is supposed to cover all the costs of doing business plus a profit. Whether markup is based on the selling price or the cost price, the base is always equal to 100 percent.
MATURITY	The date on which a loan becomes due.
MATURITY EXTENSIONS	Extensions of payment beyond the original period established for repayment of a loan.
MORTGAGE	An instrument giving legal title to secure the repayment of a loan made by the mortgagee (lender). In legal contemplation

there are two types: (1) title theory -operates as a transfer of the legal title of the property to the mortgagee, and (2) lien theory -creates a lien upon the property in favor of the mortgagee.

NEGATIVE NET WORTH A business condition when total liabilities exceed total assets.

NET WORTH Property owned (assets), minus debts and obligations owed (liabilities), is the owner's equity (net worth).

NORTH AMERICAN INDUSTRY CLASSIFICATION SYSTEM (NAICS) The North American Industry Classification System (NAICS) is replacing the U.S. Standard Industrial Classification (SIC) system. NAICS was developed jointly by the U.S., Canada, and Mexico to provide new comparability in statistics about business activity across North America.

NOTES AND ACCOUNTS RECEIVABLE A secured or unsecured receivable evidenced by a note or open account arising from activities involving liquidation and disposal of loan collateral.

OBLIGATIONS Technically defined as "amount of orders placed, contracts awarded, services received, and similar transactions during a given period which will require payments during the same or a future period." Also, another term for debt: money, merchandise or service owed to someone.

ORDERING COSTS Administrative costs of placing, tracking, shipping, receiving and paying for an order.

ORDINARY INTEREST Simple interest based on a year of 360 days, contrasting with exact interest having a base year of 365 days.

OSHA (OCCUPATIONAL SAFETY & HEALTH ACT) To assure safe and healthful working conditions for working men and women; by authorizing enforcement of the standards developed under the Act; by assisting and encouraging the States in their efforts to assure safe and healthful working conditions; by providing for research, information, education, and training in the field of occupational safety and health; and for other purposes.

OUTLAYS Net disbursements (cash payments in excess of cash receipts) for administrative expenses and for loans and related costs and expenses (e.g., gross disbursements for loans and expenses minus loan repayments, interest and fee income collected, and reimbursements received for services performed for other agencies).

PARTNERING A mutually beneficial business-to-business relationship based on trust and commitment and that enhances the capabilities of both parties.

PARTNERSHIP A legal relationship existing between two or more persons contractually associated as joint principals in a business.

PETTY CASH A small fund maintained for incidental expenses.

PROPRIETORSHIP The most common legal form of business ownership; about

	85 percent of all small businesses are proprietorships. The liability of the owner is unlimited in this form of ownership.
QUICK RATIO	Current assets less inventories divided by current liabilities. Also called "acid ratio."
RATIO	Denotes relationships of items within and between financial statements, e.g., current ratio, quick ratio, inventory turnover ratio and debt/net worth ratios.
RECEIVABLE CONVERSION PERIOD - RCP	Time between the sale of the final product on credit and
RETURN ON INVESTMENT	The amount of profit (return) based on the amount of resources (funds) used to produce it. Also, the ability of a given investment to earn a return for its use.
REVOLVING CREDIT ACCOUNT	A formal line of credit offered to larger businesses in exchange for up-front fees and standard interest payments.
SHORT TERM	Period usually one year or less.
SIMPLE INTEREST RATE LOAN	One which provides the borrower the face value of the loan; the borrower repays the principal plus interest at maturity.
SIZE STANDARDS	The term "size standard" describes the numerical definition of a small business. In other words, a business is considered "small" if it meets or is below an established "size standard."
SMALL BUSINESS	A business smaller than a given size as measured by its employment, business receipts, or business assets.
SMALL DISADVANTAGED BUSINESS (SDB)	SDBs are at least 51 percent owned by one or more individuals who are both socially and economically disadvantaged. This can include a publicly owned business that has at least 51 percent of its stock unconditionally owned by one or more socially and economically disadvantaged individuals and whose management and daily business is controlled by one or more such individuals.
SOLVENCY	The financial ability to continue business.
SOPs	Standard Operating Procedures.
SPECULATIVE CASH BALANCES	Cash necessary to take advantage of special opportunities.
STANDARD INDUSTRIAL CLASSIFICATION (SIC) CODE	A code representing a category within the Standard Industrial Classification System administered by the Statistical Policy Division of the U.S. Office of Management and Budget. The system was established to classify all industries in the US economy. A two-digit code designates each major industry group, which is coupled with a second two-digit code representing subcategories. NAICS is replacing this system
TAX or TAXES	The contribution required of persons or businesses for the support of governmental programs.

TRADE NAME — The term used to identify a company. Any type of business may call itself a company.

TRADEMARK — Words, names, symbols or devises, or any combination of these, used to identify the goods of a business and to distinguish these goods from the goods of others.

TRUE LEASE — A type of transaction that qualifies as a lease under the Internal Revenue Code. It allows the lessor to claim ownership and the lessee to claim rental payments as tax deductions.

TURNOVER — Turnover is the number of times that an average inventory of goods is sold during a fiscal year or some designated period. Care must be taken to ensure that the average inventory and net sales are both reduced to the same denominator; that is, divide inventory at cost into sales at cost into sales at cost or divide inventory at selling price into sales at selling price. The turnover when accurately computed, is one measure of the efficiency of a business.

VARIABLE COSTS — Those costs of doing business such as cost of goods, shipping, handling and storage, sales commissions, etc., which are directly related to the sales of goods or services.

WORKERS' COMPENSATION — A state-mandated form of insurance covering workers injured in job-related accidents. In some states the state is the insurer; in other states insurance must be acquired from commercial insurance firms. Insurance rates are based on a number of factors including salaries, firm history and risk of occupation.

WORKING CAPITAL — Cash and short-term assets that can be used for current needs -- bills, etc.

Index

Breinigsville, PA USA
18 August 2009

222538BV00003B/158/A

9 780979 780509